SAVILE ROW

SAVILE ROW
An illustrated history

Richard Walker

RIZZOLI
NEW YORK

First published in the United States of America in 1989 by
RIZZOLI INTERNATIONAL PUBLICATIONS, INC.
597 Fifth Avenue, New York, NY 10017

Copyright © 1988 Multimedia Books Limited, London

Library of Congress Cataloging-in-Publication Data

Walker. Richard (Richard Kennedy)
Savile Row: an illustrated history/
Richard Walker.
       p.   cm.
Includes index.
ISBN 0-8478-1020-8.

1. Tailors – England – London – History –
19th century. 2. Tailors – England – London –
History – 20th century. 3. Costume – England –
London – History – 19th century. 4. Costume –
England – London – History – 20th century.
5. Savile Row (London, England) I. Title.
TT580.W35 1989
846'.32'0942132 – dc19   88-28750
                                   CIP

Printed and bound in Italy

Contents

BESPOKE

A garment cut by an individual, for an individual, by an individual is one definition of the word that is synonymous with Savile Row and which has been purloined by practitioners of less personalized tailoring. A bespoke suit is cut from a pattern made specifically for a particular client (i.e. the material is spoken for), whereas a made-to-measure suit is cut from a standard pattern and amended to suit the contours of the individual. The difference is vast.

The American translation of 'bespoke' is custom tailoring.

MASTER TAILOR

Incapable of precise definition. In the past, a man who had passed his apprenticeship examinations and was accepted into his trade guild. While a master may be thought of as a tailor in charge of other tailors, or a director or owner of a tailoring firm, there are no longer any constraints on the use of the title. The proprietor is commonly referred to by his tailors as the 'governor', always pronounced 'guv'nor'. A few guv'nors like to encourage the genteel first-name-as-surname affectation, as in 'Mr Jim', 'Mr Malcolm', 'Mr Robert', and so on.

CUTTER

The one who measures, cuts and fits the garment: the architect rather than the builder.

TAILOR

The one who actually 'makes' it.

Foreword

Mr Speaker

Savile Row is the heart of bespoke or custom tailoring in Great Britain. It takes the material it receives, enriches it and circulates it back into the body of society.

A living body is not just flesh and blood but spirit and personality too. Craft tailoring is an intensely personal trade and this aspect is clearly brought out in this illuminating book by Richard Walker. Personality consists of three ingredients: hereditary, environment and personal response. It is the slightly differing nature of these aspects that produces individuals that are nevertheless closely bonded and are known as Savile Row tailors.

I was born to the trade and became a Master Tailor in the generic area of Savile Row. I find it remarkable that Richard Walker has in months grasped an in-depth understanding of the life of The Row which most of us took many years to acquire. He has embraced the rich variety of craftsmen with an accuracy of eye that would be the envy of most tailors.

The story starts with a tailor, Robert Baker, who founded Piccadilly, and weaves a rich tapestry of social life and the tailors' responses to its changes from the beginning of the seventeenth century. The social history is presented in a warm and interesting way that makes the reader feel they are actually observing the happenings at Court or smelling the odours of the streets and the sweatshops. It is inevitable that the book has to end and the author has to place parameters to his researching insight. Therefore this book can only show you the heart of the trade rather than the body as a whole.

Tailoring abounded throughout the country and it was from the country that many of the tailoring greats came. My own family business illustrates this, starting out of London and eventually leading the riding trade from the heart of The Row.

There are still good men and women crafting tailoring beyond The Row and it was amongst these large ranks that one hundred years ago they formed the Federation of Merchant Tailors that in 1988 celebrated its centenary. London joined the Federation ten years after its commencement and has gradually taken more of the lead in tailoring affairs. Throughout the years it has encouraged better working conditions and relationships. Its leaders negotiate the annual wage rounds and plan training with Government and its agencies. It also contributes largely to the development of technical education. The FMT, as it is known, is always there to fight for the trade when it is under threat, which it does now over legislation developments on property. This it does quietly on the whole, for it is the craftsman who must be seen and not his problems.

There could be no better time for Richard Walker to write *The Savile Row Story* than to mark one hundred years of these skilled craftsmen helping each other. Whatever or wherever the future of Savile Row is to be will depend on the collective strength of the tailors working through their Federation. They are like a flight of geese gaining uplift from each other and especially from their leaders.

Savile Row should be preserved not just for its historical richness so brilliantly displayed in this book but because of the other reasons so clearly seen in these pages. The clothes we wear undoubtedly reflect our attitude to life. The comparatively small population and the limited area of the British Isles does not matter overwhelmingly so long as there is quality in its people, quality in their standards and quality in all they produce. Did not John Ruskin remind us at the height of Britain's prosperity in the last century that 'there is hardly anything in the world that some men cannot make a little worse and sell a little cheaper and the people who consider price alone are that man's lawful prey'.

Those were the days when it could be truly said – British and Best! Then to buy cloth which was not home produced for to wear clothes which were not made in Britain would have been unthinkable. To appear to be British, to dress like an Englishman and to use English words was the world height of fashion in every civilized country.

Our history of freedom of expression is part of the rich inheritance that in turn is part of the personality of the Savile Row tailor. Who better to continue to lead the world in the correct portrayal of the ever changing world of man.

Speaker's House

Westminster

London SW1A 0AA

Speaker Bernard Weatherill in the Court dress gifted by Savile Row. He carries a thimble in a waistcoat pocket, a present from his mother, to remind him to stay humble.

Bernard Weatherill

1

Pickadils and Lordly Dreams

Above

Richard Boyle, the first Lord Burlington, whose purchase of a half-built mansion with a big back yard was the first step in the development of the tailors' domain. A few steps from the jolly Restoration Court and with open country to the north, it was a choice location.

Lord Burlington sniffed the breeze. He sniffed again. The pungent odour drifting down upon his suburban mansion had clearly issued from something other than apple blossom.

London was bursting at the seams and what had been a semi-rural retreat was now – in 1693 – under sordid siege. Over His Lordship's garden wall, someone was boiling human excrement to extract the potassium nitrate, or saltpetre, to make glass. By joining forces with the local sewage contractor, an enterprising glass-maker had all the raw material he needed.

Lord Burlington fired off a formal protest. Then another. A year later, there was no mincing of words when the vestry of St James's took up the matter of 'the Place behind his Lordship's House and Garden where they shoote the Night Stuffe and Boyle for Salt Peter'. It evidently worked: Lord Burlington signed a new lease in 1695.

Thus was secured for elegant development the area that has come to be known as 'Savile Row': Savile Row itself and a cluster of other small streets centred upon the one-time Burlington Estate. A memento of what might have been survives in a name – Glasshouse Street – now blocked off by Regent Street, but originally extending the length of modern Burlington Gardens, along the line of the Earl's garden wall. Exactly where they shot the Night Stuffe is hard to tell, but romantics might choose to speculate on somewhere between Gieves & Hawkes's sartorial citadel at No. 1 Savile Row and the workrooms of its fabulously expensive neighbour, Huntsman – about the spot where Frederick Scholte, legend of the 1930s, used to flick his cigar butt after attending to the Duke of Windsor or terrorizing some lesser client who had dared question the fit of his suit.

If Night Stuffe posed a threat to the embryonic Savile Row, Fire and Pestilence were its making. Endemic plague and then the Great Fire of 1666 were the major forces that drove the gentry west from the old City of London and sparked a property development boom that reverberates to this day. The attendant crafts and trades followed the gentry and the result was the sublime mix of Mayfair, with the tailoring fraternity wedged into their enclave in Mayfair's south-eastern extremity.

Yet the story goes back far further than that. Not the mere 150 years assumed by most of the tailors themselves, but almost 400 years to Robert Baker, an Elizabethan tailor-turned-property developer whose activities go to the origins of Piccadilly. Baker's is a cautionary tale, of sudden success and of the woes that money can bring. In tracing the rise of a fashionable tailor, the story could serve as a model for today.

Tailoring was a creation of the thirteenth century, when the coat, a walk-in device, supplanted the climb-in tunic. This novel garment with its new-fangled buttons was put together in sections; hence the tailor, from the French '*tailler*', to cut. The existence of the tailor in turn stimulated style and fashion among those able to afford the adroit new artists in cloth.

Robert Baker was the son of a cloth merchant from Staplegrove in Somerset. He was cheated out of his father's estate by a wicked uncle and then served as an apprentice to a Taunton tailor named Tompkins. After that, he set out to seek his fortune in London, a journey of at least a week by waggon or pack-horse. Records exist showing that he found work at the Sign of the Flying Horse in the Strand, where he 'wrought as a journeyman att Mr Brales ye Taylor' alongside 'other journeymen tailors that were Somersettshire men'.

There is some evidence that Baker served in the army when the Spanish Armada threatened invasion in 1588 and that he took part in

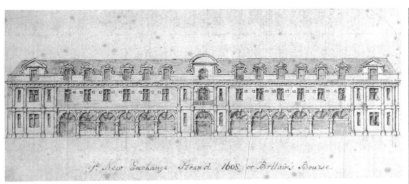

the capture of Cadiz under the Earl of Essex in 1596. It is certain that in 1599 he sold his cottage in Taunton – the deed of surrender still exists, signed with his crudely written initials – and on 16 November 1600 he married Elizabeth Nightingale, a 'flaxwoman', at St Martin's in the Fields. The Bakers opened a 'poore little shoppe in ye Strand', at the Sign of the Seven Stars, among a parade of riverside palaces a little downstream from modern Charing Cross Station. Elizabeth's experience in linen-making would have been an asset as they pitched their trade at the rich.

An early customer was Lady Cope, wife of the builder of Cope Castle (which long afterwards became Holland House, a Regency hotspot in Kensington where early Savile Row clients paraded their finery). It was 'by ye means of ye Ladie Cope, whose Taylor hee was,' that Baker 'fell into a way of makinge Pickadillys . . . for most of the Nobilitie and Gentrie'. The pickadil was a late development of the ruff. From its beginnings as a frilly shirt collar, the ruff grew grander with the introduction of starching techniques and attained such millstone proportions that it needed wire supports — the result being termed pickadillies, from '*pica*', Spanish for spear. Soon Baker had 'three score men att worke'. While building an extension at the back of the shop to ease the overcrowding, he found 'a pott of money' to augment his new wealth. It seemed that nothing could go wrong.

The Bakers got a further boost from the construction of the New Exchange, a shopping arcade for the elite designed by Inigo Jones, right next door to the Seven Stars. King James I personally performed the opening ceremony in April 1609 and his extravagant Court of 'fooles, bawdes, mimmicks and catamites', as one foe saw it, was in a mood to spend .

When James married his sixteen-year-old daughter Elizabeth to Count Frederick of Bohemia, he splashed out £10,000 on the trousseau alone. To general delight, and surprise, the arranged marriage turned out to be a love match and even the death of the King's son and heir,

Below
Tailoring in the mid-seventeenth
century. The scene might equally apply
to the previous two hundred years, or
the next two hundred.

Below
Tailoring in the mid-seventeenth
century. The scene might equally apply
to the previous two hundred years, or
the next two hundred.

Above Right
A late seventeenth-century engraving
of the original Burlington House. The
Museum, of Mankind now occupies the
area of the gardens. The gardens on the
right are now occupied by the Albany.

Right
The parish of St James, about 1720. An
updated version of a seventeenth-
century map, showing the Burlington
Estate in mid-development. Cork and
Old Burlington Streets are complete,
but not Savile Row. Piccadilly at this
stage is still Pickadilly, and the fork
determining the route of the future
Regent Street is shown as Shug Lane, a
name dating from medieval times.

Henry, was not allowed to mar the lengthy preliminaries of fetes,
masques and fireworks. Instructed to achieve 'an even mixture of joy
and mourning', the Princess wore a betrothal dress of black and silver,
with a plume of white feathers on her head – a fashion instantly taken
up by all young gallants who, we are told, 'made white feathers dear on
the sudden'. For the ceremony on 14 February 1613, the bride was
gowned in embroidered silver cloth and her hair tumbled to her waist
from a crown of gold studded with diamonds and pearls.

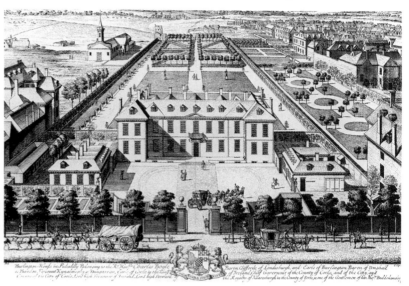

The royal trousseau accounts in the Public Records Office credit
'Robert Baker, Taylor' with payment of £21 12s 'for Twelve collars of
white satten, lyned with taphata, stitched with silke, stiffenynge, and
making six tyssued collors and embroidered Collers'. Just as well for
Baker that the commitment was so modest: he had the benefit of royal
patronage without the burden. The wedding bankrupted the
Exchequer and Lord Harrington, Master of the Princess's Household,
was left to pay off his costs by minting brass farthings; poor Harrington
even had to cover the £20 that the King won off the bride in pre-nuptial
card play. James I was to die leaving debts of £5,891 2s 10d to his
favourite tailor, Robert Erskine.

By 1613, ruffs were going out of fashion and the bloom was off the
pickadil business, but Baker was already one jump ahead. Some time
before the royal wedding and after much anguishing over the risks, he
had invested £50 in buying land in open country, about a ten-minute
walk from his shop. His 1⅜ acres lay alongside a lane leading to a
windmill – marked today by Great Windmill Street. Here Baker built
his comfortable new home, complete with garden and cowshed, at
about the present site of the Lyric Theatre.

Baker's rise from 'poore Countrey Taylor' on a quirk of fashion
caught the imagination of the wits, for very soon his house was being
dubbed 'Pickadilly Hall'. Some said that it was the Queen herself who
coined the name, though Paul Bettering, one of the 'Somersettshire
men' who had worked with Baker in the old days, claimed that it was
his idea. Baker himself seems to have felt slighted, for he avoids any
reference to it in his will, in which he refers merely to 'the howse or
messuage wherein I now dwell'. But the matter was out of his hands.
When he built other houses on the property, the entire isolated
development came to be known as Pickadilly Hall. From this, it was a
short step to the nearest roadway also acquiring the name.

The origin of London's most famous place-name was quickly lost and energetic enquiries by nineteenth-century etymologists only served to obscure things further. Archdeacon Bickersteth's notion that Piccadilly was a corruption of 'peaked hill' had many adherents, while other experts believed that it had something to do with daffodils (pick-a-dilly). It took a sustained effort beginning in the 1940s to uncover the truth.

Baker's wife Elizabeth died not long after the move to Pickadilly

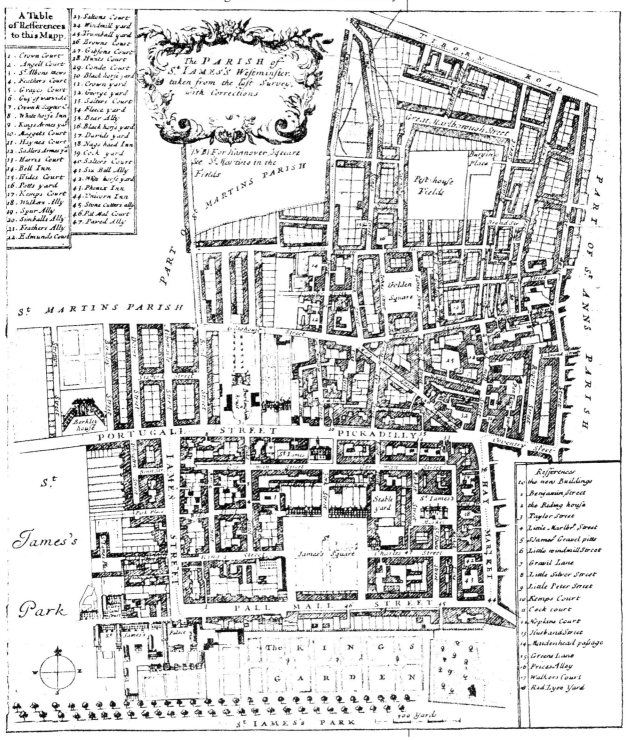

Hall; he waited a year and then married the widowed daughter of an apothecary named Stephen Higgins, a meddlesome man with a reputation for dubious property deals. Mary Baker – he called her Moll – was evidently wealthy in her own right and the property development proceeded apace, with more houses going up at Pickadilly and leasehold investments near the business in the Strand. Then, in 1619, Baker made his boldest move when he bought a twenty-two-acre patchwork of plots radiating from his original purchase. Baker territory now reached from modern Pall Mall to Oxford Street. Included, in present-day terms, was much of the north side of Piccadilly Circus, half of the Haymarket, all of the Golden Square area that is home to Savile Row's cloth merchants and several of the Soho streets where the Row's subcontracting 'outworker' tailors are traditionally based.

Now Baker could style himself 'gentleman' and cut a dash on visits home to Somerset, where he was welcomed by Taunton's mayor and struck awe among his relatives, who in turn sometimes ventured up to London. One time, hoping to 'gett some preferrment or advantage', his nephews equipped themselves with new clothes and 'sent up their Cloakes by the carryer, that they might come the more handsomer unto their uncle's presence'.

There is a description of Baker at the height of his success: he was 'of a middle stature, a good complexion and of a browne hayre mixed with some gray hayres'. He was building busily, had just staked £500 on a dowry for his eldest daughter to marry into the gentry and seemed destined to found one of the great landowning dynasties when, quite unexpectedly, he died. He was buried in St Martin's in the Fields on 15 April 1623. His funeral cost £3 10s 3d, which made it the most lavish in the parish for that year.

Though Baker wrote a will a few hours before his death, all that he bequeathed was anguish and bitterness. The struggle over his inheritance was to last a hundred years and left his descendants with nothing. Four trials failed to resolve the issue, which grew increasingly complex as claimants died at a pace brisk even for those times; the fourth trial was delayed by the Great Plague and a fifth trial forestalled by the Great Fire. All of Robert's many children were dead by 1652 (he had eight children by his first wife alone, of which only two survived infancy). Mary Baker lived on until 1668, still resident at Pickadilly Hall. By then, rival clans of Somerset Bakers had sprouted rival family trees that put the very identity of Robert Baker into dispute. Bit by bit, in murky deals and enormous legal fees, the estate was chopped up and bartered away.

Looking for a last time from Pickadilly Hall, Robert Baker would have viewed field and meadow hardly changed in the century since their seizure by Henry VIII in his dissolution of the monasteries. The land rolled away in gently rising folds contained between the rutted road heading west and a lesser track forking off to the right. In springtime, the air was sweet with blossom, and Gerarde mentions in his *Herbale* how throughout summer the little wild bugloss grew in profusion 'upon the drie ditch bankes about Pickadilla'. Idyllic, if you allowed for the lurking highwayman and a glimpse of the Tyburn gibbet a mile off through the fields.

Within eighty years of Baker's death, much of this would be built over, as Mayfair and the West End sprouted from the isolated road fork, which today forms the western bracket of Piccadilly Circus; Piccadilly itself traces the line of the rutted road and Regent Street the track to the right. And tucked within the fork lies the domain of the Savile Row tailor, whose signature product, the three-piece suit, also dates from this time. Partly to placate the Puritans, who saw the Great

Plague and Fire as God's vengeance upon a sinful Court, King Charles II on 7 October 1666 declared his intention to set a permanent male fashion based upon a modest, knee-length vest of Persian origin; the royal tailors fell to work and eight days later Charles appeared in the prototype, in black and white to signify national mourning and virtuous intent. Sobriety lasted less than a month and soon the Court was aglow with fancy vests, or waistcoats as they became (except in America, where the name did not change), to complete the most enduring and universal of all clothing ensembles.*

The enterprise of Baker and its aftermath of feverish courtroom campaigning helped to energize others, so that by the time of Plague and Fire the developers were jumping like fleas in a pesthouse; haphazard and often crude construction pockmarked the landscape as opportunists dodged the law to meet the needs of expanding London. It was left to the noble favourites of Charles II to clean up, in every sense.

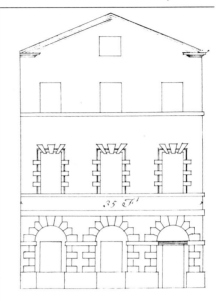

Lord Berkeley of Stratton, also a Somerset man, made a bid for the Baker estate, but then had second thoughts and settled for doing what all the big winners of the Restoration were doing in the 1660s – building noble piles on the advancing line of Piccadilly. When he died in 1678, the gardens of his mansion were built over to create Stratton and Berkeley Streets; these joined Albemarle, Dover and Bond Streets, built by speculators on the site of the short-lived mansion of a hapless Lord Chancellor who had to flee charges of taking bribes from the French. In this way, aristocratic Mayfair quickly began to rise out of a countryside which still endures as an echo in such other street names as Farm, Hay, Mill, Brook . . . and in Mayfair itself.

For Savile Row, the key date is 1667, when Richard 'Richard the Rich' Boyle, first Earl of Burlington, Earl of Cork and Lord Treasurer of Ireland, joined the Piccadilly mansion set; he bought the half-built home of lovelorn, demented Sir John Denham, whose wife had just died, possibly from drinking a cup of poisoned chocolate. Times were hard. The Dutch were raiding up the Thames and reconstruction of the City meant that materials were in short supply: there was a black market in stone and the price of floorboards had gone through the roof. 'Doe all we can to quicken ye workmen, whoe in these unsettled times are generally very backward to worke,' the Earl instructed his son, who managed to have the red-brick building finished in 1668 at a cost of £5,000. The inquisitive Samuel Pepys was an early visitor; he was to remember the occasion well, since his wig caught fire.

Lord Burlington had unwelcome neighbours to deal with. Ever since early peasant revolts against the enclosure of public pasture, the development of London's outskirts had proceeded with messy abandon, despite a series of stern government edicts. Lord Burlington's back garden looked across an expanse of orchard and pasture known as Ten Acre Close, but activities crowding in upon him included a foundry for gun metal and the already mentioned glassworks.

With the Great Fire making refugees of much of the city population, the pressure was bound to intensify and so, in 1670, Lord Burlington acquired the leasehold to 'six acres, one rood and sixteen perches' of Ten Acre Close. Building restrictions were severe and the agricultural intent clear in a regulation that the lessee 'bestow at least three loads of muck or compost for every load of hay there should be moved off the premises'.

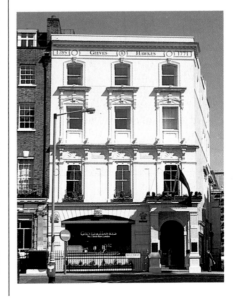

*The jacket, from the French 'jacques', was introduced in the late fifteenth century, when it was at first known as the 'little jack'. The tie can be traced to the neck cloth introduced in the decade following Baker's death, though the term 'neck tie' dates from the 1830s, when cravats began to be worn with big bows, variously knotted. The modern tie evolved from the 'four-in-hand' knot, whose long ends were likened to the reins of a stage-coach.

Above

Henrietta, Countess of Suffolk, astute royal mistress who retired into matrimony and a home in newly built Savile Row. Her home later housed the Savile Club, whose members were described by Oscar Wilde as 'true democrats . . . because they cannot muster a sovereign between them', and subsequently was the first to be rebuilt with tailoring specifically in mind.

To guard this leafy retreat, Lord Burlington built a brick wall and did what he could to limit development on the other side. He was not very successful, for among those paying rates for part of the close beyond the wall was one Windsor Sandys, who had the street-cleaning contract for the parishes of St Martin's and St Giles. It is known that Sandys was in partnership with a potter and that in 1676 they signed a contract with the Glass Sellers' Company. It seems obvious that here was the source of his Lordship's deepest distress. In 1682, Lord Burlington managed to acquire the lease to all of Ten Acre Close, but that did not end his problems. Sandys had died, but the business apparently persisted, for ten years later a fresh complaint was lodged about a 'place erecting behind the said Earles house and Garden for the making of Salt Peter'. It took further campaigning to drive away finally all noxious trade. Lord Burlington celebrated by buying a new lease on the Ten Acre estate and, with this accomplished, he died. His son soon followed him.

Richard Boyle, third Earl of Burlington, was an exuberant young aesthete who returned from the Grand Tour with his head filled with the delights of Italian architecture. He surrounded himself with architects of like mind – William Kent, Colin Campbell and Giacomo Leoni – and began rebuilding Burlington House in neo-Palladian splendour. He was the ultimate enthusiastic amateur (he was also patron to the composer Handel) and it cost him plenty.

Though he had inherited a fortune and added another when he married an heiress, Lady Dorothy Savile, his estimated income of £24,000 was never enough. Shortly after returning from Italy, he determined to raise money by building on most of the area walled in by his grandfather. There he laid out Old Burlington Street, Cork Street, Clifford Street and Boyle Street, using family names in each case. By the summer of 1718, house construction had started and the young Lord went back to Italy for further inspiration.

However, Lord Burlington's financial woes worsened. He took out mortgages and, in 1730, he began to develop what remained of the Ten Acres. Structures dating back to the days of Sandys were pulled down and in their place Savile Row and New Burlington Street were built. He moved with such haste that Savile Row was already half finished before he brought a bill into the House of Lords to legalize his action.

On 12 March 1733, the *Daily Post* reported that 'a new pile of buildings is going to be carry'd on near Swallow Street by a Plan drawn up by the Right Hon. the Earl of Burlington, and which is to be called Savile Street.' This is the first published reference to Savile Row. Like all the other streets in the estate, it was given a Burlington family name, in this case that of the Earl's wife.

Lord Burlington never escaped his financial straits and, by the late 1730s, he was selling off estates in Ireland to meet debts of around £200,000. He died in 1753, aged fifty-nine, weary and distrustful of those around him. When the Countess died six years later, the Burlington Estate passed to their grandson.

Despite his scramble for money, which resulted in erratic, piecemeal design by umpteen architects, notable and obscure, the enthusiastic amateur produced something unique – a little neighbourhood tucked away from the rest of Mayfair in spirit as well in fact. Seemingly inspired by Italian notions of small-town planning, each street was closed by a cross street dominated by some interesting architectural feature ('Make the passenger at every step discover a new structure,' Leoni instructed in 1727) and yet the whole was kept spacious. Cork Street and Savile Row flanked Old Burlington Street and were both left open with no houses on their Old Burlington side; to prevent the empty frontages from becoming an ugly clutter of stables and outhouses, strict provisions were inserted in the Old Burlington leases. It was these peculiar circumstances that were to prove ideal for Henry Poole to establish the Parthenon of tailoring here a century later.

Tailors continued to tramp to town throughout the century, their mode of travel and their hopes no different from long before. Typical was James Creed, who hitched a lift with a carrier leading a span of six horses and arrived in London from Leicestershire in 1710. He was penniless, but 'gifted and ambitious', according to his great-great-great-grandson Charles, last head of the House of Creed. He worked around inns and taverns, 'and as long as he had twopence a day to spend on ale, he didn't at all mind sleeping in the stables'. His strategy was to seek out the inns frequented by valets to the rich and to offer a slightly higher bribe than they normally received for farming out repair and alteration work. Soon his rented room was piled with velvet coats, waistcoats and satin breeches, in one of which he found a guinea. On the strength of this windfall he married a lady's maid named Lucy, and the Creed family saga had begun.

The Creeds took several generations to achieve grandeur, but fortunes could be made faster than that. Sometime in the 1760s, Thomas Hawkes walked from Stourbridge with £5 in his pocket, cast a baleful glance up at the Tyburn gallows as he trudged into town and eventually arrived at the shop of Mr Moy, a velvet cap-maker in Swallow Street, where he was taken on as a journeyman. Swallow Street was the narrow, cobbled thoroughfare that the smaller track leading from the Piccadilly fork had by then become. Mr Moy was 'on the cod' – tailoring slang for drinking heavily – which left Hawkes plenty of scope to cultivate the aristocratic customers. Soon Hawkes had his own shop and a clientele that included King George III and his son, the clothes-horse Prince of Wales. He left £20,000 when he died in 1809. Like Robert Baker two centuries earlier, Hawkes achieved this through royal recognition and a gimmick – in this case a technique for hardening leather to withstand sabre strokes.

On Savile Row and the rest of the Burlington Estate, the gentry settled into a life of eighteenth-century ease, the residents ranging from the Dukes of Queensberry, in their Leoni-designed mansion, to the somewhat more humble in homes farther away from the anchoring mass of Burlington House. Most of the houses were built by individual tradesmen-contractors, who were then expected to find a tenant. Here and there the Earl's celebrated architect friends tried their hand, as did the Earl himself. The leases were for sixty years and the purchase price ranged from around £800 for a small frontage to £1,900 or more for a larger one. A visitor in 1723, when Phase One was nearly completed, noted 'noble Streets finely pav'd; the Houses balustraded with Iron, and few of them under a hundred Pounds a Year Rent, most of them more. . . .'

Each street had its quota of nobility; mixed in with these were a few famous military men like General Wade, whose roads opened up the Scottish highlands, but who subsequently had a great deal of trouble with Bonnie Prince Charlie. There was also an unusually high proportion of 'gentlewomen', a number of them military widows. William Pitt was in Savile Row for a time as his letters show, though where is uncertain. Alexander Pope thought about taking a house, but did not, though several of his friends did, including Dr John Arbuthnot and his physician Dr Simon Burton, who set a trend for the top medical men to base themselves here.

Many were drawn by the 'Burlingtonian' atmosphere of the little neighbourhood, since about a third of all the original occupants can be found on the subscription lists of the architectural publications of the day. Many of these original residents were, like General Wade in Old

Burlington Street, to live out their lives there. Other than a couple of wine merchants, there was little encroachment by 'trade' and change was gradual. The mood of this early Savile Row might best be evoked by a series of images:

There is 'Old Q', most Rabelaisian of the Queensberrys, dispatching his footman in pursuit of some delectable wench he has spied from his carriage, the scene lost in the night except for what little is caught in the flickering glow of the linkman's taper. There is John Gay, composing *The Beggar's Opera* while a guest in Queensberry House and finding his ideal Polly Peachum in the actress Lavinia Fenton – who moves in round the corner at 8 Cork Street just as her performance makes her the rage of London; as the mistress and eventual wife of the third Duke of Bolton, she never looks back.

There is a frightened dinner party at 1 Savile Row during Bonnie Prince Charlie's advance south (which Wade failed to stop). The architect Kent would recall how he and Fernando Fairfax 'was bravo'd down by Brian as two cowards that we at this time ought to have courrage and resolution and not be lamenting about the times'. Brian was Bryan Fairfax, grandson of General Fairfax, Commissioner of Customs, art collector and friend of Lord Burlington.

And there is Henrietta, Countess of Suffolk and mistress to George II, living the last thirty-two years of her life between 15 Savile Row and Marble Hall, her country seat on the Thames at Twickenham – a Burlingtonian building bought for her by her royal lover. Discreet and adroit enough to become a trusted confidante of Queen Caroline, she inspired Pope, who found her 'most uncommon . . . a reasonable Woman, Handsome and Witty, yet a Friend,' and stirred one of the most diligent of lifelong passions in the quixotic Lord Peterborough, who, upon nearing his end, resolved to show how 'a soldier, a philosopher, how a friend of Lady Suffolk's ought to die'.

Right
A chunk of drainpipe from sixteenth-century Swallow Street shares a tailor's window with old irons and military hardware. Heritage, in any guise, is fondly cherished.

2

The Prince and the Beau

Savile Row was maturing nicely, but it was to take revolution, war and a remarkable, if unlikely, individual to make tailoring a match for its future home.

The Americans and French provided the turmoil; the individual was home-grown: George Bryan Brummell, nicknamed Buck Brummell in his youth and, ever after, The Beau.

People had been getting out and about, discovering what they called 'the truth of nature' and digging to discover the past. Powder and wigs were being discarded and Ancient Greek torsos admired. The body was back in fashion and coats were cut back, waistcoats shortened and breeches tightened to reveal thigh and masculine bulge. In France, the aristocracy was confined to Court and had little room to breathe the new air, but in England the gentry spent most of the time on their country estates and, consequently, on their horses. The consuming passion was fox-hunting, which called for simple, comfortable clothes – a plain coat cut away at the front, linen and stout boots.

It happened quickly in mid-century: one moment the average aristocrat was wrapped in velvet and lace and the next he was stepping out in rustic simplicity. Around 1770, even the three-cornered hat got the treatment: hopeless in a wind, it had its brim shrunk and crown raised to create a sort of primitive crash helmet. In town to present the King with a petition on land reform, a Norfolk landowner named Coke stopped by a hatter named Lock to have one of these new creations made up; at Lock's, which still thrives on the same spot, a bowler hat is to this day called a Coke.*

William Coke, 1st Earl of Leicester of Holkham (whose father and brother happened to live on the Burlington Estate), gave impetus to sartorial revolution by retaining his country clothes on that London visit. Others plucked up courage to do likewise and the formal clothes of today began their upward advance from field and farmyard. George III may have been called other things in his American colonies, but at home he was 'Farmer George', in this, at least, he was in tune with the times. When the royal periwig-makers petitioned him to try to stop the trend among young men to wear their own hair, George said no.

The rest of the Western world was of a mind to take notice. The ideas of liberalism and republicanism were on the march and the English country look seemed the perfect complement to an age in defiance of the old rules. Even in France, a crumbling kingdom jealous of its fashion supremacy, the democratic look crept in, with the frock coat franglaised into the '*fraque*' and the riding coat the '*redingote*'. 'The well-dressed men wear a new coat every time, but a plain coat of cloth with nothing sumptuous about it,' the future Duke de la Rochfoucauld reported back from a London visit in 1784. When the *ancien régime* fell in 1789, just a dozen years after helping the Americans to liberty, the velvets and satins went to the guillotine and

George Brummell, Esq.: studied
languidity, refined to exquisite excess.
When Mr Brummell, at his mirror,
conceived the notion of trousers and
simple coats, the chaotic history of male
costume came to a close – as seen by
Max Beerbohm.

Above Right
The Dandy, as Brummell made him,
'stands on an isolated pedestal of self',
wrote Ellen Moers. No occupation, no
visible means of support, no
attachments – 'a wife or child would be
unthinkable'.

post-Terror Paris adopted the English look with gusto. Trousers, plebeian and long-despised, were especially an emblem of revolution and were soon on the way to ousting knee-breeches everywhere.

At this point, enter Brummell. Born on 7 June 1778, the son of Lord North's private secretary (and grandson of a valet who might have been an army tailor), 'Buck' Brummell was able early on to sharpen his wit on the likes of Charles James Fox and the playwright Richard Brinsley Sheridan, who visited his father's country retreat in Berkshire. Once at Eton, he perfected an elegantly languid manner and a tart tongue. He fascinated the Prince of Wales, who arranged a commission for him in the 10th Hussars, a pet regiment that followed the Prince on his round of dissolute pleasure-seeking. The confident teenager and the clownish voluptuary almost twice his age made a curious pair.

Brummell was in personal attendance at the Prince's wedding and is even said to have joined the royal couple on honeymoon at Windsor. He rose to captain, but heroics were not his line and he quit the army when menaced with a posting to the industrial north. ('Think, your Royal Highness, Manchester!' he is said to have exclaimed, before coyly adding: 'Besides, you would not be there.') In 1797, when still just nineteen, the Buck turned Beau and set himself up as a man of fashion on £2,000 a year bequeathed by his father. Faced with choosing between the horsey look of the Tories and the casual sleaziness of Fox's Whigs, he created a style of his own, of stunning simplicity.

Efforts to convey precisely the Brummell look, or better the Brummell image, have continued from that day to this. It remains the central theme of the sales patter of any Savile Row tailor. Brummell began by stressing cleanliness, a novel idea at the time. He is said to have spent at least two hours a day scrubbing himself, bathing in milk and scouring his body with a pigskin bristle brush. Then he would dress – a mesmerizing performance of several hours that drew the Prince to the Beau's home in Chesterfield Street. The Prince was now the pupil and Brummell the arbiter of taste.

Thomas Carlyle once dismissed Brummell as a Thing made by a tailor. It might be more appropriate to turn that thought around. Under Brummell, the country garb was cleansed of its horse-dung and transformed into the smart, all-purpose uniform of the gentleman.

*When the first top hat appeared in 1797, several women fainted, dogs howled, children screamed and the younger son of a cordwainer broke his arm, according to the St James's *Gazette*. The wearer was charged with inciting a riot. Eighteen years later, General Picton wore one at the Battle of Waterloo.

There is a description of him in blue coat of perfect fit, snowy-white cravat and buff buckskin pantaloons tucked into shiny black boots, of which even the soles were polished, the whole set off by simple brass buttons and gold watch-chain with just two links visible.* For evening, he put the Prince into dark blue or black coats and, since knee-breeches tended to be dark too, here was the genesis of the dark evening suit.

Shorn of fashionable artifice, the Brummell Look depended upon perfection of line – sharp, precise, deceptively simple and devilishly daunting to all but the most disciplined. It was rumoured that ears were lost and throats cut in the desperate attempts of rivals to emulate Brummell's arrangement of stiffly starched cravat and high collar.

From the late 1790s, no social event was complete without the presence of the Beau. His was the sort of legend that feeds upon itself, so that the stories of his exquisite refinement grew ever more exquisite with the re-telling. Excusing a cold caught on his way home from Brighton, he is said to have explained that he had been put in a room 'with a damp stranger'. When a hostess enquired whether he ever ate vegetables, he conceded that he 'once ate a pea'.

The Prince is said to have burst into tears when told by Brummell that his breeches did not fit, and the sixth Duke of Bedford rued the day he sought Brummell's opinion of his new coat. Brummell had the Duke stand to attention and then turn around; after due deliberation, the Beau stepped forward, delicately felt the Duke's lapel with thumb and finger, and asked earnestly: 'Bedford, do you call this thing a coat?'

He had a wit of timing and occasion. 'A sort of quaint, dry humour,' the courtesan Harriette Wilson called it, and she reflected that 'indeed he said nothing which could bear repeating' even while exerting his magnetic hold.

'All feared, many admired, none hated him. He was too powerful not to dread, too dextrous not to admire, too superior to hate,' Disraeli suggests in a novel on the Brummell theme.

The costume historian James Laver even sees in Brummell a fifth-columnist engaged in a 'conspiracy against the aristocracy' and contributing to their overthrow; Laver reasons that wider issues of social conduct became encapsulated in a choice between two Georges, Brummell and the Prince . . . and the commoner had the neater fit.

Brummell was all the more a marvel when set against the gross, gluttonous, licentious society in which he circulated, in a mind-numbing round of 'deep potations, blade-bones of mutton and the music of the dice box'. Compared with the Beau, the rest of the dandies were a sorry lot, cluttering the bay window at White's club, vapid even in their excess.

The Beau's strategy was to ration his appearances, for maximum impact. 'Stay until you have produced your effect, and then go,' he once advised. Sadly, he failed to heed his own advice. The Prince was a fickle friend and with his accession as Regent he found the Beau's impertinence difficult to take. Brummell may have tolled his own knell by ordering His Highness in public to 'Ring the bell, George,' to fetch his carriage. Brummell always denied this popular tale. More likely, it was the too visible disgust he showed towards the Prince's growing corpulence and gross mistress Mrs Fitzherbert (he dubbed them Big Ben and Benita) that led to his dismissal from the Prince's Carlton House set.

Being disowned did not lessen the Beau's sway over Society. He found sanctuary in the 'Little Court' of the Prince's brother, the Duke

Above

The Prince of Wales as Brummell found him. The taste of the self-proclaimed 'first gentleman of Europe' was for anything glittery and gaudy. He loved tight-fitting attire, particularly uniforms, which was unfortunate for his troops and for his tailor, who never could contain so abundant a figure. When he abandoned the Beau, he abandoned all discretion in a relentless quest for more and more clothes.

* Blue and buff, the colours of the American revolutionaries, were earlier adopted by Fox as a means of goading the Tories, but there is no evidence of Brummell ever being influenced by a political consideration.

of York, and saw his fame reach new heights when he was credited with 'cutting' the Prince Regent while out walking in Bond Street. 'Who's your fat friend?' he is said to have asked his companion, well within earshot of the royal personage.

Yet the strain was beginning to tell. Gambling became a compulsion and eventually Brummell was forced to flee into permanent exile. Mouldering in France, he found his Boswell in Captain Jesse, whose Life, published shortly after Brummell's death, might be regarded as the Old Testament of the Savile Row bible. We read how 'the just proportions of his form were remarkable' and how Brummell 'was a Beau in the literal sense of the word – fine, handsome . . . always carefully dressed, but never the slave of fashion.' Captain Jesse proceeds:

> In the commencement of his career, he perhaps varied his dress too frequently. The whim, however, was of short duration, and scorning to share his fame with his tailor, he soon shunned all external peculiarity, and trusted alone to that ease and grace of manner which he possessed in a remarkable degree.
>
> His chief aim was to avoid anything marked; one of his aphorisms being that the severest mortification that a gentleman could incur was to attract observation in the street by his outward appearance. He exercised the most correct taste in the selection of each article of apparel, of a form and colour harmonious with all the rest, for the purpose of producing a perfect elegant general effect. . . . There was, in fact, nothing extreme about Brummell's personal appearance but his extreme cleanliness and neatness, and whatever time and attention he devoted to his dress the result was perfection; no perfumes, he used to say, but very fine linen, plenty of it, and country washing.

Present-day spokesmen for Savile Row religiously stick to this prescription for sartorial sublimity and, consciously or not, invariably end up paraphrasing these teachings of the Beau.

Below

Brummell in action at an Almack's ball. The Duchess of Rutland is receiving the word. The Comte de St Antonio, a noted ladykiller, prances with Princess Esterhazy, the Austrian ambassadress, while Sir George Warrander and the handsome Count St Aldigonde watch. Brummell prized this sketch, which was among the effects auctioned following his flight to France. This was said to be a very accurate depiction of the Beau at his peak, making Stewart Granger an appropriate choice to play him in a 1954 film.

The tailors with whom Brummell scorned to share his fame rightly qualify as the first generation to rate as 'Savile Row'. Advancing gradually, by the late eighteenth century the fashionable tailors had come to form a tight circle centred upon the Burlington Estate. Thomas Hawkes was established at 14 Piccadilly by the 1790s, by which time Sackville Street, another of present-day Savile Row's outer marches, was beginning to harbour workrooms filled with hissing goose irons and cross-legged stitchers. One firm still in Sackville Street, Adeney & Boutroy, has a direct link with these days. Sackville Street was built in 1730 and has a history of high and low enterprise similar to the Burlington experience.

On the other side of Burlington territory, tailors had begun to set up shop on Bond, Conduit, Princes, Hanover and Maddox Streets (the last being named after a merchant tailor who held the original freehold to Ten Acre Close). These streets still today define the northern and western ranges of 'Savile Row'.

Within the Burlington property, the tailors began their colonizing with Cork Street; one of the first there was John Levick, at No. 9 from about 1790. Clifford and Old Burlington Streets soon followed. The first tailor to establish himself in Savile Row itself did so in 1806.

Stuffed away in Sackville Street premises that are encrusted in ancient royal warrants, there is a huge, frayed, metal-bound ledger that is the last surviving link between the present Savile Row, Brummell and the Prince. The firm of Meyer & Mortimer exists today as the military wing of Jones, Chalk & Dawson, which is itself a mere 100 years old. John Meyer was a German military tailor who would have felt at home with the heavy German presence in the Hanovarian Courts of the Georges. Mortimer was a sword-maker and gunsmith from Edinburgh, who was doing very nicely when they set up in partnership: in 1801 Mortimer had received a 5,000-guinea order from the United States Government to supply the Bey of Tunis with a pair

Above
A St James's macaroni. Some young beaux led by Charles James Fox tried to fight the new 'country look'. They liked the tight style, but piled on old-fashioned decoration and mountainous wigs. The Prince of Wales was mostly macaroni when Brummel went to work on him.

Left
Like riding to hounds . . . the Battle of Waterloo provided the St James's tailors with a fine showcase and plenty of orders afterwards. The Prince Regent, when deep into the iced punch and sherry, used to irritate Wellington by talking as though he had personally led the charge on the French.

of diamond-studded 'fusées' – pistols.

Meyer was also prospering, as would be expected of a tailor serving both the Prince of Elegance and the Prince of Wales. How Brummell chose his tailors is not known, but the Prince followed a similar selection. Brummell's tailors were Schweitzer and Davidson in Cork Street, Weston in Old Bond Street and Meyer, who was in Conduit Street. Meyer and Schweitzer worked also for the Prince.

Only one of the old ledgers survived a World War II bombing. It shows the range of demands made upon Meyer by his royal customer; apart from his substantial personal needs, the Prince was forever ordering fresh outfits for his beloved 10th Hussars and its band. The Prince's orders range from the glitzy to the surprisingly mundane – a silver Garter star, £1 15s; 102 gold embroidered holes at 4s 6d a hole; smoothing and repairing a brown coat, 2s 6d. We are told that 'on great occasions', Meyer was summoned to attend the Prince at Carlton House and 'superintended the adornment of His Royal Highness's person' – and that he wore a page's uniform in the royal presence.

The ledger provides a novel slant on Regency high-life. The ornately scripted accounts of military officer, noble, prince and servant follow in no apparent order – General Keilmansegge, Watier the royal cook and club-owner, Lieutenant Gooch of the Coldstream Guards, Lord George Lennox, the Carlton House coachman, Lord John Somerset, Lord William Somerset and Lord Fitzroy Somerset, who fought by Wellington's side at Waterloo: an eyewitness account exists, describing how they 'seemed so gay and unconcerned, as if they were riding to meet the hounds in some quiet English county'.

Far Right
Sheridan. A hell-raising spendthrift awash with charm until 'in consequence of continued excesses, nothing remained of his once expressive face but the remarkable brilliance of his eyes'. Until the bills ceased to be paid, tailors clamoured to dress his actors.

Below
Lord Barrymore playing the part of Scrub in *The Beaux' Stratagem*.

Above Right
Savile Row Passage and a print-seller's shop in the 1770s. The building in the rear housed the bad Lord Barrymore's theatre. The scene had changed little, and the shop still sold prints and stationery, when the passage was demolished just before World War II.

The present guardians of the book are tailors John Peacock and Alan Kruger. Scanning the ledger and alighting on another Somerset, Peacock mutters an involuntary 'Good customer, Lord Somerset.' Since the ledger entry is dated 1811, it has to be taken that the Somersets have stayed loyal to the firm, unless Mr Peacock, with that legendary patience of the Savile Row tailor, is still waiting in hope of Lord Fitzroy's return to settle his bill for £61 6s 6d.

Tantalizingly little is known of Brummell's relationship with his tailor; Meyer's military background possibly appealed to the man intent on tidying up the unkempt look of the day. They were conveniently close. It is a five-minute walk from the Beau's home at 4 Chesterfield Street to the Westbury Hotel, which now occupies the site of Meyer's shop (from whence it took a German bomb in 1942 to force a move). Presumably it was Meyer who did the walking. At Chesterfield Street, he would have been greeted by Brummell's man Robinson, a Jeeves-like character who ran the household in a manner as immaculate as its master: the place was a bower of boulle furniture and rare Sèvres porcelain, carefully assembled as a setting for Brummell's noted dinner parties.

Brummell was a perfecter rather than an innovator, but he did introduce a system to keep the tight trousers of the day from creasing: a set of ankle buttons and foot loops. Brummell's biographer states that these 'were invented either by Meyer or Brummell: the Beau at any rate was the first who wore them, and they immediately became quite the fashion'.

Brummell ruled fashion as by divine right; nobody before or since has enjoyed such dictatorial powers. Jesse writes of some baronet seeking advice on cloth from his tailor, in this case Schweitzer: "'Why, sir," said the artiste, "the Prince wears superfine, and Mr Brummell the Bath coating. . . . Suppose, sir, we say the Bath coating – I think Mr Brummell has a trifle the preference."'

Once abandoned by the Prince and consorting with the Duchess of York's circle, Brummell circulated among a wider crowd and Savile Row certainly saw him often. This period, which marked the arrival of the first tailors, was probably the liveliest in the Burlington Estate's history and some of its residents knew the Beau well.

Lord Barrymore was the oldest and most notorious of these acquaintances and it was possibly he who first introduced Brummell to the Prince; if so, the youth had a lucky escape. Lord Barrymore was dissolute, even by the standards of his day. Club-footed like Byron, a veteran of unmentionable Carlton House orgies and celebrated for the foulness of the oaths he hurled at his servants, he loved cockfighting and bare-knuckle fighting and – most of all – driving his coach-and-four with utmost fury up the north road. He was a founder of the Four-in-Hand Club, whose departures from George Street, Hanover Square, were a focus for the Bon Ton, the fashionable elite. He also took to driving around town in a smart Stanhope carriage 'with a little boy', whose role and origins are obscure.

Lord Barrymore fancied himself as an amateur actor and spent £1,500 to set up a little theatre in Savile Row, where one summer night in 1790 he and his sister Lady Caroline performed *The Beaux' Stratagem*. *The Times* praised their 'Theatre of Varieties Amusantes' as 'one of the prettiest theatres we ever saw'. Seats cost 3s and boxes 5s, but the venture eventually failed as Barrymore became stricken by that plague of the age, overwhelming debt. The site of the theatre, at Nos 22-23 Savile Row, long afterwards became a home for the YMCA and the Alpine Club. In 1939, the building was pulled down to open the northern end of Savile Row to through traffic.

Barrymore was a close friend of such great actors of the day as Kean and the Kembles, who in turn were close to the Sheridans, who were very close to Brummell. Charles Kemble, father of the famous family, lived for a time at 6 Sackville Street, where Meyer & Mortimer is to be found today. Such coincidences abound.

Sir Robert Mackreth, bookmaker and userer, who rose from billiard marker and waiter to owner of White's – and thence into Parliament on the basis of the hold he had over his aristocratic victims – lived at No. 1 Cork Street through most of Brummell's reign. Mackreth had convictions for taking advantage of a minor and assaulting a lord, yet still contrived to receive a knighthood for 'services to Parliament'.

Then there was Lord Blayney at 23 Old Burlington Street; a hard-drinking habitué of the clubs, it was said of him and the Lords Panmure and Dufferin that 'wonderful to relate [they] were six-bottle men'. One wonders whether he ever staggered round the corner to pay his respects to Lady Hunloke at 13 Savile Row.

A sister of Coke the bowler-hat inventor, Lady Hunloke was the central figure in a minor episode that wonderfully captures the witty, bored indolence of Brummell's world. Lady Hunloke had stirred some interest at a Chatsworth party by ogling Sir Robin Adair, another of the guests. Georgiana, Duchess of Devonshire ('the best-bred woman

Above
Hardy Amies under the casement supposedly used by Sheridan to spy on his waiting creditors.

Above
John Peacock and Alan Kruger with an 1801 sword, in safe keeping for the Royal Hussars, and a ledger filled with orders from the Prince Regent and his set. Their Sackville Street premises is the repository of the few items that survive from Savile Row's Regency days.

in England', according to the Prince Regent), and Lord John Townsend thereupon amused themselves by trading verses, as if between the two lovers. Brummell preserved the results in a collection of *vers de société* that he took with him into exile, presumably for nostalgic recall. First the Duchess, taking the role of Lady Hunloke, fired her poetic dart 'To Robin Adair':

> Undone, plunder'd, waddling, sad, and slow,
> From Chatsworth to my dingy home I go . . .
> For soon as poor Sir Harry breathes no more
> I'll fly to meet the lover I adore!
> Bucks and archbishops I'll alike discard
> And thou of all mankind alone regard . . .

The poem is lengthy, clever and full of scatological reference, as is the reply. Sir Harry was Lady Hunloke's husband:

> Soon as Sir Harry's fatal knell shall toll,
> Oh, that 'twere mine his widow to console!
> But, ah! some youth more delicate than I
> Shall hush thy murmurs, and thy tears shall dry.
> Some sturdier swain more suited to thy taste,
> With keener stomach for the rich repast . . .

The hungry Lady Hunloke was fifty-one at the time, 'a merry, talkative and coquettish lady, and like her friend the Duchess, very fond of play'. Sir Harry died in 1804, but there was no lovers' rapture. Sir Robin married a countess in 1805 and Lady Hunloke died a dowager in Savile Row on 22 January 1820.

Another redoubtable widow was the Countess of Cork, the hub of heavy social traffic throughout her forty-six-years' residence in New

Burlington Street. There 'she gave many parties to persons of all nations and contrived to bring together foreigners from the wilds of America, the Cape of Good Hope, and even savages from the isles of the Pacific; in fact, she was the notorious lion-hunter of her age'. Lady Cork's speciality, as noted here by the memoirist Captain Gronow, was to lionize the social lions of each succeeding season. It was said of Brummell that he was the dandy-lion: being, like the weed, alone in flourishing year after year.

Living opposite the boozy Lord Blayney in Old Burlington Street was the honourable exception – a leading figure of the clubs who was renowned for his self-discipline. This was Colonel James Armstrong, an old soldier remarkable for his many splendid qualities. Like Brummell, a frequent guest at Oatlands, the Duke of York's country estate, he features in another of the Brummell poems, this one a sort of versified guest list for an Oaklands dinner party on New Year's Eve 1812. The author was Lord Erskine, a Scottish soldier and lawyer who was Lord Chancellor in 1808. After some pretty compliments to the hostess ('The fair princess sat first, far the highest in place/But her rank in eclipse by good nature and grace . . .') he got down to the guests:

> Next, Armstrong was seated; on Armstrong depend,
> For wit as a companion, for truth as a friend;
> As a man of the world he's completely at ease,
> No effort he makes to amuse or to please;
> Yet is sure to do both, with his manner so quiet,
> Sliding in better things than many who try it.

Brummell had an on-off relationship with Byron, but spoke of their being 'very intimate . . . in our familiar days'. Byron's unstarched look offered the poetic counterpoint to the dandies. He contributed some trite love poetry to the Brummell verses ('Ashamed of my weakness, however beguiled/I shall bear like a man what I feel like a child') and was forgiven his vanities, including the revelation that those famous curls were artificially induced. He was a true fan of the Beau and raved over that 'certain exquisite propriety' that was Brummell's essence. They had something curious in common when it came to women. It was said of Brummell that he suffered from a 'deficiency in warmth and perseverence' – and once when he did get warm, he confessed to having 'cut the connexion' when he discovered that the lady ate cabbage. Byron, the great lover, is said to have disliked seeing women eat, because it disturbed his ethereal image of them. They did not share the same tailor. Byron evidently felt obligated to James Milne of Grosvenor Street, who had bailed his father out of a debtors' prison. He also used Thomas Edwards at 52 Conduit Street. When last heard of, Mr Edwards was awaiting payment of £173 19s 6d.

Brummell had known Sheridan since a child and took pride in being permitted to see the playwright's work in its manuscript stage. Sheridan may have lived at 17 Savile Row and he certainly lived at No. 14, for that is where he died. It was a dreadful end, as drink, debt, disease and defeat closed in. He is said to have had a closet over the staircase enclosed in glass, so that he could spy on arriving creditors. The rate book traces the final days. He is £16 15s in arrears and there is a hasty note from the rent collector: 'Why not get this?' Then a scribbled reply: 'Watson has tried but not yet settled.' Later: 'Goods distrained by Sheriff.' Then: 'Distraint resisted.' And finally: 'Dead and insolvent.'

Sheridan died on 7 July 1816, seven weeks after Brummell's flight into exile. It was on 16 May that the Beau suddenly took his leave. For several years, he had been gambling heavily; he won £26,000 one night

Below
Brummell in exile. He eked out an existence for almost a quarter of a century, sustained by his memories but the end was grotesque. Rescued from a debtor's prison by London friends, he then suffered a stroke and ended his days in a Sisters of Mercy asylum.

and lost it all a few nights later. The 1814 season saw 'a most relentless run of bad luck', which was followed by the loss of 'an unfortunate ten thousand pounds'.

On an otherwise unremarkable Thursday, he dined off a cold fowl and a bottle of claret sent from Watier's and wrote a note to a club crony, Scrope Davies: 'My Dear Scrope – Lend me two hundred pounds; the banks are shut, and all my money is in the three per cents. It will be repaid tomorrow morning. Yours, George Brummell.' The reply was swift: 'My dear George – 'Tis very unfortunate; but all my money is in the three per cents. Yours, S Davies.' Byron, who was dining with Davies at the time, complimented him on his wit.

Brummell was later seen at the opera. He left early, stepped into a borrowed chaise and changed to his own carriage on the Dover road. He charged through the night and reached the coast by dawn; he hired a boat, had his carriage put aboard and within a few hours was ashore at Calais, by which time, his biographer recounts, 'the West End had awoke and missed him; particularly his tradesmen and his enemies, both of whom had long scores against him'.

Five days later, Society turned out in force to witness Christie the auctioneer dispose of 'The Genuine Property of A MAN OF FASHION, Gone to the Continent.' The Sevres porcelain, the boulle, his snuff boxes and wine cellar went under the hammer and that was the last they saw of Beau Brummell.

He lingered on in northern France for a quarter of a century, a sightseeing curiosity for passing travellers and an object of charity for his old friends. From the Princess of York to the Duke of Wellington, they all came visiting or sent something. Yet he died wretchedly in an asylum, his finery reduced to tatters, his mind failing. 'Loose me, scoundrels! I owe nothing!' were his last words. He was sixty-two.

3

The Artistes of St James's

Lord Byron let it be known that the three great men of his age were himself, Napoleon and Beau Brummell. Napoleon and Brummell fell within months of each other, a fact of utmost significance for the future of Savile Row and British dominance in determining the male ideal.

Brummell had laid out the rules and an imperial Britain was suddenly on hand to champion them. Fashion follows power and Britain in 1816 emerged from the Napoleonic Wars as leader of the allied European nations, master of the seas and crucible of the industrial revolution that was about to transform the Western world; the loss of the American colonies could now be viewed as a minor setback.

Triumphal peace drew energies from war to domestic pursuits and for a time the dandies continued their sublime saunter. White's club moved into Burlington House for a grand victory ball, and the scenes in Hyde Park and behind the sooty walls of Carlton House were as exclusive and dazzling as ever. The elite arrived for a royal fete at 3 o'clock, the ladies in diamonds and pearls, the gentlemen in full Court dress; the Guards' bands played and the glittering company danced on the lawns. The appointed hour for the Hyde Park parade was 5 o'clock. 'By a tacit understanding none of the lower or middle classes intruded,' Gronow noted in a vivid description of the gorgeous equipages bearing the ladies, the powdered footmen and coachman 'with all the gaiety and appearance of a wigged archbishop', and the gentlemen 'mounted on such horses as only England could then produce'.

Lord Alvanley assumed Brummell's throne; 'the wittiest man of his day and the most good-natured,' he fought the French for a while, then took to leisure in a serious way. He lived in Park Street, near Brummell's old home, and adopted the Brummell routine of small dinner parties, at which he was noted for his apricot tart. Unfortunately, he grew corpulent and had too small a nose for the quantities of snuff he tried to stuff up it. Hosts fretted over his habit of extinguishing candles by flinging them on the floor or smothering them with the bedsheets.

Then came the Count d'Orsay, a 6-foot 3-inch vision who was to prove the last of the dandies as Victorian values snuffed the species out. With enormous lapels and towering top hat over tight waist and skin-tight trousers, he provided a very flashy finale. When driving his tilbury he looked to Gronow 'like some gorgeous dragon-fly skimming through the air'. The son of one of Napoleon's generals and an illegitimate beauty, he so enjoyed being conquered by the British that he came to England, where he charmed Lady Blessington, a spirited Irishwoman with a raunchy past who competed with Lady Holland and Lady Cork for the title of top Regency hostess. Despite the presence of a husband and her twelve-year age disadvantage, they set up a

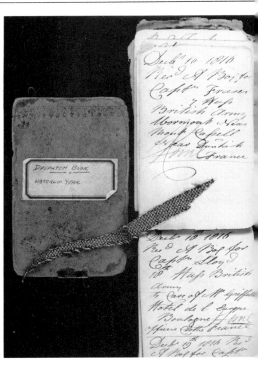

Above
Meyer's Waterloo year despatch book. The mail-coach system was extensive and remarkably efficient, enabling clothes 'boxes' to be despatched virtually anywhere — including the various units of Wellington's victorious army, wherever they were bivouacked

ménage together that drew the great and the curious to Gore House, the Blessingtons' Kensington mansion.

D'Orsay's tailor was Henry Creed, great-grandson of the James Creed who hitched a lift from Leicestershire in 1710. James's eldest son, also James, had served his seven-year apprenticeship under his father and in due course took over the business, then in the City. The process repeated itself with James's son Henry, who married a prosperous banker's daughter and moved west to set up shop in the Strand. Henry's son was the Henry Creed who tailored for d'Orsay and thereby assured fame and fortune for the family business. This Henry also went through the apprenticeship mill, but had the advantage of having been sent around the Continent to gain polish. D'Orsay 'wore clothes splendidly, he knew everybody who was anybody, and whither he went the beau-monde followed,' grandson Charles Creed wrote in 1961. 'They followed him to Henry Creed.'

Above

D'Orsay, Alvanley and other dandies at Crockford's in 1843, with Brummell's influence still evident in the stiff white neckcloths, blue coats and white waistcoats. Old Crockey, a retired fishmonger, beggared the entire aristocracy in 'that dangerous little room' where the suave croupiers swept up the money 'with almost miraculous quickness and dexterity', according to Gronow.

Henry Creed was by then established at 33 Conduit Street, two doors away from Meyer & Mortimer. Savile Row was consolidating within its present boundaries, even if the Row itself had yet to be attained and the locale of the tailors was usually identified as St James's, that being the parish in which they operated.

War had been good for the tailoring trade: uniforms galore, an undisturbed aristocracy and an excess of demand that kept income and wages rising.

The industrial revolution's start in the textile mills had inspired much invention, resulting in more varied and cheaper fabric. A German visitor had noted in 1791:

> In former times, people of some consequence and fortune thought themselves to appear very decently, if they had every year a new suit of clothes. But at present three or more are annually required by a man in the middling station of life, who wishes to make what is called only a decent appearance. Besides the fashions alter in these days so much, that a man can hardly wear a coat before it is out of fashion. No wonder,

therefore, that the clothiers find that the demand for their manufactures has increased, and they can even increase the price of them without exacting a murmur.

The widening choice made greater demands on the tailor, as well as widening his opportunities, while from 1784 onwards the advance of the mail coach as a highly efficient service made mail-ordering practical. Several Piccadilly inns – the Bull & Mouth, the Three Kings, the Lemon Tree, the White Bear, the White Horse, the Spread Eagle – were starting-points for various routes and were only a short walk away for the tailors' 'trotters'.

Meyer & Mortimer still has a mail coach dispatch book for 1815 that lists numerous clothes 'boxes' bound for Wellington's troops as they rested after Waterloo. One for Lord Percy, the Duke's aide-de-camp, is addressed simply 'headquarters of the British Army, France'. Another for a Lieutenant Earl of the Second Light Infantry merely identifies him as 'with the Duke of Wellington's Army'. Some heroes had it easier than others. The box for Baron Tripp, Colonel of the 60th Regiment of Foot, was addressed to the Hôtel Cardinal Fasche, Rue Mont Blanc, Paris. There was also a box for the Prince Regent at Hampton Court and another for 'His Serene Highness the Prince of Saxe Cobourg, Pavillion, Brighton' – Queen Victoria's future father-in-law.

. Home-grown styles had led to home-grown wool becoming the material of choice and this was helped by the high cost of wartime silk (it was the block on silk imports caused by Napoleon's 1806 Berlin Decree that led to the Clark brothers of Paisley developing a cotton thread); here greater experience with wool gave the English tailors an advantage over their Continental colleagues. The squire-inspired, Brummell-disciplined British look soon held sway over all of Europe, so that by 1824 Beethoven in Vienna was lamenting his lack of a black coat to wear for the first performance of his Ninth Symphony.

This all led to a great deal of business and any Savile Row firm with pretensions to history has one going back at least this far. Gieves owes its existence and enduring image to the fact that its founding father, 'Old Mel' Meredith, picked 1785 to set up shop in Portsmouth's High Street. This was three years after Admiral Rodney had secured the West Indies for Britain at the Battle of the Saints and nine years before the Glorious First of June, the first naval encounter of the French Revolutionary War.

As the wartime navy swelled to ninety-eight Sail of the Line and 130,000 officers and men – and as the Royal Navy for the first time standardized uniforms – Old Mel had plenty of work to cut out. Nelson was a customer, so Gieves can bear some of the blame for creating the brightly braided target that spelt his doom at Trafalgar in 1805. Nelson's Flag Captain Hardy was also a customer and actually stayed in the room above the shop in 1827. Captain Bligh of the *Bounty* was another, and actor Charles Laughton achieved a new high in authenticity when he was able to inspect the specifications for that respected customer before playing him in the 1936 Hollywood version of *Mutiny on the Bounty*.

Thomas Davies was principal clerk at Greenwood's, the army agents, while his brother was one of the first tailors to move into Cork Street; the brother died suddenly and Thomas inherited the business. His connections were evidently sufficient to outweigh his lack of experience and Davies & Son thrives still. Thomas moved into 19 Hanover Street in 1804, only to be driven from there by escalating rents and a declining supply of gentry in 1979. Between times, Davies ministered to a client list that progressed from Sir Robert Peel to

Above
Nelson's dazzle proved fatal when a French sharpshooter picked him out in the midst of the Battle of Trafalgar. His gold lace was woven by Gieves on looms in Peckham that have long been retired, but a firm in Preston still has a pair of looms dedicated to making lace to the old specifications.

Benny Goodman, by way of King George V and President Truman. Now in Old Burlington Street, the firm is back to within a few yards of its eighteenth-century birthplace.

None of the St James's tailors were more directly involved in the conflict than Thomas and William Adeney, whose call-up papers for the Battle of Waterloo still exist; they consist of an old milk bill from Wells of Old Bond Street ('Purveyors of Milk & Cream to Their Royal Highnesses The Prince of Wales and Duke of York'), on the back of which a Constable Pearce Hall has attested that both were under orders to rejoin their regiment 'whenever Government may require their services'. Family legend has it that the milk bill was the first thing that came to hand when they were confronted in the street.

The Adeneys kept a careful record of their military career: careful enough to suggest that they were taking every precaution to avoid a roving press gang hauling them off to some wilder shore of warfare. The Adeneys had ensign commissions in the St James's Westminster Loyal Volunteer Regiment, the local element of a substantial part-time army that paraded on state occasions and could be quickly mobilized. (Brummell was a major in the Belvoir Volunteers, on the Duke of Rutland's estate, and was as dubious in this role as he had been as a regular. When a general was sent from London to inspect the corps, Brummell went missing; he managed to placate the general by wangling him a dinner invitation from the Duke.) The Adeneys carefully preserved their regimental orders for musket practice, parades at Hyde Park and Wimbledon Common, and stand-by service during periods of social unrest. During an invasion scare in 1804, they were issued with knapsacks and ordered to prepare to head for the coast 'at a moment's notice'. The following is the marching equipment of a soldier-tailor of the Napoleonic era:

> Two Flannel under Waistcoats, made to come down well over the Loins.
> Two pair of Flannel drawers
> Two pair of worsted stockings, or half stockings
> Two pair of strong Shoes, made to come above the ankle
> Two pair of Half gaiters, according to the pattern at the guard room
> Two shirts
> Of all the foregoing articles, one on and one off
> Comb, brush and implements for shaving, as few as possible
> A piece of pipe clay, blacking ball, sponge, tow with a piece of grease wrapped in it, and such other articles as may be used for cleaning arms
> One small tin bottle of sweat-oil, picker, turn screw and brush, two spare flints, and lead to fix them
> The foraging cap rolled in the pouch
> Three days' provisions in the haversack
> Whatever spare room may remain in the knapsack will be filled by each member as best suits his own convenience
> It is to be understood that the shoes and gaiters are to be worn only when the regiment is in marching order
> The half-boots to be retained for parades and all town duty.

The Adeneys proved adept at combining their professional and patriotic duties. The business at 16 Sackville Street prospered, with high church officials a lucrative source of income. The Archbishop of Canterbury might have been the one Gronow had in mind, for he ran up page after page of orders. In 1817, he paid a bill for £1,499 12s – at a time when the best breeches cost £2 8s and a fine kersey waistcoat £1 16s. Sackville Street still sports the Adeney sign.

About the time that Brummell was alienating himself with the Prince and the Adeney volunteers were exercising themselves into a state of preparedness, a Shropshire draper named James Poole used the assets he had accrued from marrying a moneyed widow to open a

Far Right
When Charles Laughton was cast to play the lead in the film *Mutiny on the Bounty*, he called at Gieves, where a search in the basement produced a leather-bound ledger containing the specifications and measurements for their late customer, Captain William Bligh. Gieves was subsequently gratified to note that Laughton 'was correctly dressed in every respect'.

Above
Thomas Davies's military connections helped boost business. His firm was to stay in the same spot for 175 years.

small shop in London. When Napoleon escaped from Elba in 1815 and struck panic throughout Britain, Poole was swept up in the general mobilization and found himself in a volunteer corps that had to provide its own uniforms. He and his wife Mary cut and stitched a tunic that caught his officer's eye at the first parade. 'You a tailor?' the officer wanted to know. 'Er, yessir,' came the reply. So the officer placed an order with the amateur tailor.

Few benefited as much from Napoleon's Hundred Days as James Poole. Besieged by further orders, he expanded his business into tailoring and, by 1822, he had an emporium in Regent Street, the new and supremely fashionable shopping mall. The following year, he set up a home and headquarters nearby at 4 Old Burlington Street, following a trail of titled tenants into the patrician dwelling. It was from here that his son Henry was to dominate elite tailoring through the rest of the century and – by extending his operations into the street behind – to effectively put the Savile Row into Savile Row.

Regent Street cut a sabre stroke through the West End, dividing privileged from proletarian to such an extent that today, 175 years after its creation, a suit from an establishment on the eastern – Soho –

side of the great divide will cost half the price of a suit from an establishment on the western – Savile Row – side: even if both suits are made by the same craftsmen. The slash was conceived in princely egotism – the Prince wanted a royal route from Carlton House to a villa he fancied having built for himself in what was to become Regent's Park. What transpired was Britain's answer to Napoleon's 'nation of shopkeepers' sneer. General von Blücher, doing the town after Waterloo, contemplated its beginnings and raved: 'What a place to loot!'

Regent Street was completed by 1820 and was largely a re-bore of Swallow Street, by then, according to Augustus Sala, a 'long, devious, dirty thoroughfare, which three generations since was full of pawnbrokers' dram-shops, and more than equivocal livery stables, which were said to be extensively patronized by professional highwaymen'. As designed by Nash, the elegant arc from the road fork of Robert Baker's day was colonaded with shops on the ground floor, the shopkeepers' residences on the mezzanine and costly accommodation for visitors or rich bachelors on top. Aspiring to create 'fashionable lounging places for the great and titled ones', the rules were strict: no butchers, greengrocers or other domestic trades and certainly no pubs were allowed; indeed, the standards were so limiting that there were some early bankruptcies. 'The buildings of this noble street chiefly consist of palace-like shops, in whose broad shewy windows are displayed articles of the most splendid description, such as the neighbouring world of wealth and fashion are daily in want of,' a survey of Regent Street at its zenith reported.

The creation of Regent Street not only defined the eastern limits of 'Savile Row'; the zone beyond, into which the pawnbrokers, etc., were thrust, soon declined into a cheap and handy warren in which the master tailors could locate their burgeoning numbers of outworkers, conveniently close and yet out of sight of their noble clientele.

Below
The Burlington Arcade in its early days. Lord's at No. 69 is still there today . . . modernizing sedately until recently it even extended into mail order.

To the south, Savile Row's approaches gained equally from the construction in 1818 of the Burlington Arcade, a glassed-over esplanade of tiny shops ushering the genteel from Piccadilly to Burlington Gardens (ex-Glasshouse Street) along the side of Burlington House. A Regency gem, it remains today much the same as when it opened as 'A Piazza for all Hardware, Wearing Apparel and Articles not offensive in appearance nor smell'. Now as then, liveried beadles are on hand to point wayfarers to a stringent set of rules that include a ban on whistling, singing, running, playing a musical instrument, carrying a bulky package, opening an umbrella or pushing a pram. Now as then, a bell is rung and the gates locked at night.

Sala in 1859 rhapsodized over the Arcade's wares:

> Paintings and lithographs for gilded boudoirs, collars for puppy dogs, and silver-mounted whips for spaniels, pocket handkerchiefs, in which an islet of cambric is surrounded by an ocean of lace, embroidered garters and braces, filigree flounces, firework-looking bonnets; scent bottles, sword-knots, brocaded sashes, worked dressing-gowns, inlaid snuff-boxes and falbalas of all descriptions; these form the stock-in-trade of the merchants who have here their tiny boutiques.

George Eliot met the man in her life in the Burlington Arcade in 1851 and the future Duke of Windsor used to buy toys there for his nieces, the Princesses Elizabeth and Margaret Rose, in the 1930s. One firm, Lord's, a 214-year-old gentlemen's outfitters, has inhabited the Arcade since the beginning.

Lord George Cavendish, great-grandson of the first Lord Burlington, let it about that he had the Arcade built 'for the gratification of the publick, and to give employment to industrious females'. However, he had other more pressing reasons. The family lease on the Burlington Estate expired in 1809, with a loss of £10,400 a year in rents. All sorts of plans were considered and it is possible that if Lord George had not inherited a fortune from his scientist relative Henry Cavendish, Burlington House might have been pulled down and replaced by shops and houses.

Lord George was living at No. 1 Savile Row and Burlington House lay in limbo when, from 1811 to 1816, Lord Elgin was able to leave his looted Greek marbles in the garden, but by the time the British Museum could take its bulkiest treasure the fate of the big house was determined. It was to be remodelled yet again. In the course of this, Lord George had his architect, Samuel Ware, design the Arcade on a strip of vacant land along the Old Bond Street margins of the property; it was probably built as much as a screen from prying eyes – and from oyster shells that kept being thrown over the wall – as the imaginative business speculation it surely was.

Within these increasingly elegant confines, the conditions were perfect for the evolution of the genus Savile Row tailor. The range of customer was growing as more sought to aspire to the best, and latest, cut. Cravat and neckerchiefs went through such dizzying changes that the poet Robert Southey noted one 'professor' who was doing a brisk business giving lessons in the art of tying them at half-a-guinea a time.

Southey asked his tailor – 'a sensible man in his way' – who had invented the fashions. "'Why, sir!" said he, "I believe it is the young gentlemen who walk in Bond-Street. They come to me, and give me orders for a new cut, and perhaps it takes, and perhaps it does not. It is all fancy, you know, sir."' Southey left it clear who was his mentor: 'It is of much importance to man as to woman, that he should appear in the prevailing colour. My tailor tells me I must have pantaloons of a reddish cast, "All in the reds, now, sir" . . . and reddish accordingly they are, in due conformity to his prescription.' Southey's tailor might well have been Henry Creed, since Creed married his sister Eleanor.

Probably the most successful of this first 'Savile Row' generation was George Stulz (later spelt Stultz), another with German military origins, who moved into No. 10 Clifford Street in 1809. The firm he founded was to remain in the same spot until World War I.

References to Stultz keep cropping up. Harriette Wilson, who was fascinated by Brummell but irritated by the way he remained 'indifferent' to her charms, mentions in her memoirs visiting 'Mr

Stultz, the German regimental tailor and money-lender in Clifford Street'. She and a friend wanted 'a modest disguise' for a masque at Watier's club to mark the peace with France. 'Stultz brought home our dresses himself in his tilbury, on the morning of the masquerade, being anxious that we should do him credit,' she wrote. 'Everything fitted us to a hair.' The money-lender reference was presumably a snide allusion to the extended credit terms the fashionable tailor was obliged to endure, or perhaps rather encouraged, in his competitive quest for top customers.

Stultz had a country trade too – and at least one eager cash customer. Shopping historian Alison Adburgham found an 1829 letter giving instructions for the purchase of a riding habit from Stultz. 'Chuse the cloth, good, stout, and dark blue, pay for it and send me the amount of the damage and I will return the money by post,' Sara Hutchinson, Stultz's customer, instructed a London friend. She sent the note with a parcel containing her measurements; Stultz was to enclose the finished garment and send it by mail coach 'to be left at the Greyhound for Mr H., Brinsop Court'. She wanted it 'as soon as possible' and added, 'I wish to pay for it immediately that I may have a discount.'

Above
Count d'Orsay strikes a pose in Hyde Park. The others are Wellington with Mrs Arbuthnot on his arm and Prince Talleyrand, a Wellington admirer. The park then was more rustic, with cows and deer grazing under the trees.

Thackeray picked Stultz as tailor to his fictional beau, the 'neat and radiant' Major Pendennis. The dandy hero of Bulwer Lytton's *Pelham*, who set a precedent for the real-life adoption of black evening dress, was another fictional character sent to Stultz, who was required to make his clothes without padding – another style point that was taken up in real life.

Public appetite for the fashionable novel was a further symptom of a mood that meant business for tailors, and fashion plates and magazines appeared to fan the interest. *The Gentleman's Magazine of Fashions, Fancy Costume and the Regimentals of the Army** made its debut on 1 May 1828, with a picture of the Prince – by now 'His Most Gracious Majesty George IV' – as a frontispiece and the brave boast that it 'may be had of all booksellers in any part of the world'. It introduced itself thus:

As a passport to good society, dress is equally necessary with address; for although, in some respect, manners make the man, still do we not also appreciate his taste, and fix his standard in genteel life by his good habits? Consequently, his tailor is quite as necessary and influential an ally as even the schoolmaster 'armed with his primer'.

We are not like Frankenstein about to make a man; but we do intend to show the great world how a person of *ton* ought to be dressed; and which is pretty much the same thing, inasmuch as he who is not from 'head to foot, from top to toe' apparelled à la mode, is to all intents and purposes nobody! This is our paramount intention – now to fulfil it!

The magazine carried excellent colour prints of sumptuously uniformed gents and detailed descriptions of the seasonably appropriate styles, well spiced with Society chit-chat. It also featured theatre reviews, poetry and worldly advice in the form of a series of 'maxims for married people'. For example, 'The smiles of a woman are the tears of your purse.'

'Pupil of fashion stand up! – and that you may speedily be turned out a finished scholar, we will thus apparel you,' the unidentified author of 'Critical Observations on Gentlemen's Fashion' enthused:

First your COAT! Go not then to breakfast, at the Clarendon; saunter not of a morning into Crockford's, unless your 'builder' has fitted you, sans wrinkle, with a coat fumée de Navarin (smoky brown), setting tight round the waist, and (that it may give a resemblance in the male form to that of the female) being very full in the skirts. It should be left (as if carelessly) open in the front, so as to discover a pale silk under-waistcoat with gold buttons, which en passant should be buttoned up to the coloured cravat, which may be so disposed, or arranged, as to clasp about the throat like the cordon of Field Marshal Wellington on a Court day . . . .

Courtesan Harriette Wilson. Brummell declined to tweak her lovelock, but he did impress her with his advocacy of 'no perfume, but very fine linen, plenty of it, and country washing'.

Such advice was written at the height of d'Orsay's reign, when the firm lines of Brummell were being softened with curves and his brass accessories cast aside for glint and gold. But any retreat to pretty decadence was blocked once and for all by the death of George IV in 1830. This was a watershed and everybody knew it. It was said that even the dandies did not stay to mourn, but seemed to age overnight into Old Bucks.

The ageing degenerate – the Prince of Whales, Charles Lamb dubbed him – had finally gained the throne in 1820, when George III died after many years of madness. His reign was as miserable as it was short, and he was unpopular enough to place the future of the monarchy in doubt. Queen Caroline so grew to loathe him that she had taken to sticking pins into wax images of him that she then placed by the fire. His clothes' auction was his epitaph. It realized £15,000, although it was reckoned that the original cost of the garments must have been nearer £100,000. A list of the sale items was published with the comment: 'Wealth had done wonders, taste not much.' Eighteen years without Brummell had not done him much good.

Meyer and Stultz might revel in the extra business that the mail coach brought, but Mrs Fitzherbert was on to something when she wrote from Brighton in 1818: 'When I tell you that 52 public coaches go from hence to London every day and bring people down for six shillings, you will not be surprised at the sort of company we have.' Rising expectations were on a collision course with privilege and the

---

The Gentleman's Magazine of Fashions was part of a husband-and-wife publishing empire in which the creative genius appears to have been a Mrs Bell, who, apart from her literary endeavours, was an inventive corset-maker with a royal warrant from the Duchess of Kent; in this role, she would have provided embryonic support for the future Queen Victoria. Of one of her products, it was claimed that it 'prevents flatulency, reduces protuberance, supports the stomach and bowels, relieves dropsical symptoms'.

MORNING   NOON   NIGHT

high taxes, costly bread and oppressive laws that kept it in place. The revolutionary spirit had fired Britons too, and the kind of unrest that brought out the Adeney volunteers in 1810 was to repeat itself with increasing intensity.

The social gap was tremendous. For example, it is interesting to compare Lady Cork with the men who stole cloth from the tailor Poole. Lady Cork had one little foible: she was a thief. 'It was supposed that she had a peculiar ignorance of the laws of meum and teum, and that her monomania was such that she would try to get possession of whatever she could place her hands upon; so that it was dangerous to leave in an ante-room anything of value,' Gronow relates in one of his droll anecdotes. There was less understanding for the lesser orders. In the case of the cloth theft – six yards of brown broadcloth valued at £5, later reduced to 40s – at least three death sentences were passed.

The case provides a fascinating glimpse into the world of James Poole, at the point when he had begun tailoring his way towards the Savile Row summit. At 5 o'clock on 15 December 1815, he left his shop to visit a customer, but did not stay away long, having noticed three men 'lurking about the street'. He arrived back in time to see one of the men carrying away some cloth. He shouted 'stop thief', the cloth was dropped and the men scattered, but he caught them with the help of two Bow Street runners who had appeared on the scene. A month later *The Star* reported that an Old Bailey jury had 'convicted capitally' Thomas 'Long Tom' Batts, Robert Rowley and Jack Farthing for theft.

The case created a stir when it was reopened before the Attorney-General nine months later. It turned out that only one of the Bow Street officers was genuine and that he was in cahoots with an informer named John 'Jack-a-Dandy' Donelly, who was an instigator of the crime. The idea was to profit from the robbery and then to collect rewards for the subsequent arrests.

Poole had been set up by the crooked constable, who came to warn him that robbers were on the way and that his family ran the risk of being murdered in their beds if he did not cooperate by laying out rolls of cloth on the counter as a trap for their conviction. He left the house as instructed, leaving only a candle lit in the back-parlour and a boy stationed out of sight on the stairs. In a confused hue-and-cry, the plot backfired when Poole managed to grab one of the 'sneak party', a young sailor named Bob Rowley, after they had doubled back to grab a second load of the conveniently placed cloth. In investigations following the first trial, a tall, thin man in a long, brown greatcoat seen with the robbers was identified as a man seen earlier with the Bow Street officer in a nearby pub. This was Jack-a-Dandy Donelly. The trial ended with both Jack-a-Dandy and the officer, George Vaughan, convicted. 'Damn his eyes,' Donelly swore when arrested. 'I never knew a bigger rogue than Vaughan is.' The fate of all those convicted is not certain, though it is a Poole family tradition that three were hanged. Any clemency would have meant transportation and so some modern Australians might owe their origin to the events at Poole's shop on 15 December 1815.

By the time of the second Poole trial, mass discontent in London was at a height, and there was talk of insurrection among the riotous crowd of 70,000 who turned out to listen to Henry Hunt, a maker of blacking which kept the dandies' boots so shiny. The 'notorious' Hunt was described as a large man who 'might have been taken for a butcher'. Hunt narrowly escaped being shot by troops that day, yet within a dozen years he was to win a seat in Parliament – and defeat an aristocrat in the process.

The new era ushered in by the death of George IV was given an extra sense of urgency by an outbreak of cholera, which caused the rich to become, in the words of the day, 'suddenly solicitous at the state of the poor'. The Reform Bill was passed in 1832 and two years later Bulwyer Lytton had a best-seller with the allegorical *Last Days of Pompeii*. By 1840, poor Brummell was finally dead. Lady Blessington's Gore House was auctioned off in 1849 and became a restaurant at the time of the 1851 Great Exhibition; it was eventually torn down to make room for that ultimate symbol of the new age, the Royal Albert Hall.

Above

Lone black pointer under portico of St George's Church was one of a pair that did similar duty for a Conduit Street tailor until the shop was destroyed in the blitz. St George's congregation once included nine dukes, two marquesses, twenty-two earls, six viscounts and twelve barons. The vault contains no bodies, but it used to hold wine. People married here ranged from Lola Montez to Teddy Roosevelt, who wore bright orange gloves for the ceremony and registered his occupation as 'ranchman'.

4

Craft Wars

London in the early nineteenth century has been called the Athens of the artisan. It certainly held true for tailoring's journeymen. They had been organized for years around the most militant and effective union of the eighteenth century, they had defeated all government attempts to curb their wages and they had escaped unscathed a post-war depression that had impoverished the less fortunate.

Now they found themselves with craft supremacy, dictating to Europe in the new disciplines of the new clothes. The adoption of pliable cloth and improving techniques had made it possible to give much more attention to fit, and so the subtle skills of moulding by stretching and shrinking under the iron came more into play.

The coat of the mid-1700s had been a quite simple, loose affair; more sophisticated garments called for more sophisticated methods of cutting. In the nick of time, somebody – nobody knows exactly who – invented the tape measure. This little item, to the tailor what the stethoscope is to the doctor, drew tailoring into the third dimension. A wholly new approach to cutting based on a geometric appreciation of anatomy sprang from the realization that the various body measurements were in a constant ratio to one another.

The 1804 *Dictionary of English Trades* conveyed the new exuberance:

> A master tailor ought to have a quick eye, to steal the cut of a sleeve, or the pattern of a flap, or the shape of good trimming at a glance . . . . Any bungler may cut a shape when he has the pattern before him; but a good workman takes it by his eye in the passing of a chariot, or in the space between a door and a coach; he must be able not only to cut for the handsome and well-shaped, but bestow a good shape where nature has not granted it; he must make the clothes sit easy in spite of a stiff gaint or awkward air; his hand and head must go together; he must be a nimble cutter, and finish his work with elegance.

Imbued with a new sense of the scientific, tailors rushed into print to promote their latest drafting system, however harebrained. *The Taylor's Complete Guide, or a Comprehensive Analysis of Beauty and Elegance in Dress, Containing Rules for Cutting Out Garments of Every Kind, and Fitting Any Person with the Greatest Accuracy and Precision, Pointing Out in the Clearest Manner the Former Errors of the Profession, and the Method of Rectifying What May Have Been Done Amiss, Rendered Plain and Easy to the Meanest Capacity* had benefit of a title that said it all. Published in 1796, it was first to address such conundrums as 'How to Measure a Thin Gentleman for a Single-Breasted Coat'. Then came the German mathematician Dr Henry Wampen, who was deep into a study of the proportions of Greek statues when his tailor suggested that his findings might have a practical use. In 1834 he published *The Mathematical Art of Cutting*

Left
Somebody invented the tape measure and tailoring entered the third dimension . . .

Left
Extract from a wages book of 1827 in which ten journeymen shared a total of £14 5s 11d for their week's efforts on behalf of a West End tailor. The journeyman's lot was to worsen through the century.

Garments According to the Different Formation of Men's Bodies, the first serious study of the problem. It was to take the doctor a further thirty years to produce his masterwork, *Mathematical Instructions in Constructing Models for Draping the Human Figure*.

Where the dress coat had just three body seams at the turn of the century, by 1840 it had attained its full development, with five seams and a construction involving six separate pieces. The same period saw an extreme diversity of styles coalesce into a few standard designs that were to endure.

Alas for the journeymen, by 1840 it was they who had come apart at the seams. The collapse of their fortunes – it took about twenty years for the masters to break completely worker power – needs to be explained with a brief backward glance at what had been happening in the workrooms.

In theory, very little had happened. Old Elizabethan laws applied in 1800 just as they had in 1600 and made it illegal for a master to hire non-apprenticed artisans; the regulations attending the seven-year apprenticeship were rigorous and patriarchal in the extreme. Take the 1808 indentures of George Adeney, a son of William. For seven years,

The said Apprentice his Master faithfully shall serve, his Secrets keep, his lawful Commands every where gladly do. He shall do no Damage to his said Master nor see to be done of others, but that he to his Power shall let or forthwith give warning to his said Master of the same. He shall not waste the Goods of his said Master nor lend then unlawfully to any. He shall not commit Fornication, nor contract Matrimony within the said Term. He shall not play at Cards, Dice, Tables, or any other unlawful Games, whereby his said Master may have any Loss. With his own Goods or others, during the said Term, without License of his said Master, he shall neither buy nor sell. He shall not haunt Taverns or Play-houses, nor absent himself from his said Master's Service Day nor Night unlawfully, But in all Things as a faithful Apprentice he shall behave himself towards his said Master and all his during the said Term.

The Master, in turn, undertook to provide young Adeney with 'sufficient Meat, Drink, Lodging and all other Necessaries during the said Term'. It was probably a fine arrangement for the traditional craftsman, whose home was his workplace and his apprentice a natural extension of his family, but it had been breaking down since the days of Robert Baker.

Attempts by London tailoring's 'journeymen and serving men' to unionize go back to 1417, when there was an edict to stop them organizing; thereafter, journeymen's clubs began to appear, much in the manner of the 'clubb' mentioned in connection with Baker's Somerset group in the 1590s. By the late seventeenth century, the 'Master Working Taylers, Freemen of the City' were protesting the 'great number of foreign and other unlawful workers of divers kinds who . . . have for many years eaten out the bowels of our trade'. A few years later, Queen Anne was petitioned to do something about 'the vast swarms of unlawful workers and other unqualify'd persons who never served apprenticeships and . . . have been of late years clandestinely broken in upon the taylory trade'.

In 1721, a surprise strike was met by drastic legislation to curb the clubs, and minimum work-hours and a maximum wage rate were made law. The hours were 6 a.m. to 8 p.m., with one hour off for meals. The wage limit was set at 1s 8d a day, rising to 2s for the seasonal peak of April to June. The master was also required to contribute one halfpenny a day for the journeyman's breakfast. It was, of course, a six-day week, since Sunday was for prayer. Even a royal summons could be spurned on a Sunday, as Thomas Hawkes proved. 'Tell his Royal Highness that on six days I serve my King. On the seventh day I serve God,' he told the King's messenger.

Through the rest of the eighteenth century, the rate was grudgingly eased up as the journeymen gradually gained strength to become the most organized of any trade group. In 1744, the men were out in militant force, defying jail sentences and with a new ally, the pub landlords. A report states that the strikers were 'supported by the keepers of the ale-houses where they resort, that they threatened to fire the masters' houses and abused those who in obedience of the law continued to work'. A year later, some publicans lost their licences for harbouring strikers and some constables were fined for lack of zeal in obeying orders to impress malingering tailors into the army and navy.

Thirty years of effort were rewarded in 1751 by a fourpenny rise in the rate. This was 'heartily acknowledged' by the men, who soon resumed their demands, as always electing to make their push at the start of the busy season in April. Counter-efforts failed to break the men's organization, the London Society of Journeymen Tailors, and there were further increases. By 1765, the struggle had become such a part of London life that it inspired a play presented at the Theatre Royal. *The Tailors: A Tragedy for Warm Weather in 3 Acts* was sufficiently memorable to be revived forty years later in the same theatre. A farce written in tragic style, it concerned rival gangs of journeymen, the Flints and the Dungs, who marched from their pub headquarters to a pitched battle in the Strand. The militant Flints landed in jail and the masters were victorious.

In fact, many masters were by now defying the law and paying over the odds, often adding a daily pint of beer as a bonus. The tailors' pubs had become an integral part of an employment system geared to the seasonal fluctuations of the trade. With twice as much work available from April to June than from August to October, even the best firms tended not to have a permanent labour force. As a consequence, certain pubs became designated as 'houses of call', where tailors seeking work registered their names and waited, and where masters applied when they needed men. A typical house of call might have three 'books', based on a seniority system in which those registered in the third book did not get work until the first two were filled.

Even in a good year, a tailor could be out of work for five months, yet the demands of the busy times sustained earnings. To gain some security the men formed benefit clubs, again based on the houses of call, and these developed into union branches. Helping this process was the emergence of the high quality West End firms, who vied for the competitive edge that the best craftsmen provided and who therefore tended to grant wage demands.

Above
Military tailor and family toil in a Bethnal Green slum. Sweating had its origins in the large clothing contracts of the Napoleonic Wars.

The labour shortage created by the Napoleonic Wars boosted tailors' wages to a peak in 1813 of 6s a day, or 36s for a twelve-hour, six-day week. By the time peace came, about two dozen houses of call had a monopoly of the best workers; in overall control of the tailors' organization was a secret and powerful five-man executive.

The 1812 rules of the tailors' club based at the Scotch Arms near St Martin's Lane still survive. They form an elaborate code for meetings, contributions and pay-outs: sick pay, superannuation of 2s 6d a week for life and a funeral benefit of £13, of which £4 could be withdrawn in the event of the wife dying first. The club's funds were not to fall below £500, kept in the 3 per cents. Rule 12 stipulates that any member 'impressed into His Majesty's sea or land forces' may retain membership and claim benefits upon their return to the trade, but any who joined the army or navy by choice faced immediate exclusion. The Adeneys' precaution of carrying a personal note from their colonel, Lord Amherst, becomes understandable.

The journeymen's position appeared very strong, but the masters – particularly the smaller and less affluent – had grown resentful as wages rose. There was also a fatal crack within the men's ranks: a rigorous self-imposed system of standards, under which three complaints from the masters meant a man's expulsion from his house of call, had encouraged a schism between the in-house 'flints' and the excluded 'dungs', who were ready to work for less and accept piecework which they took home, instead of the traditional day rate of the man working in his master's shop. This dung underclass, coupled with female and child labour that had been mobilized for army contract work during the war, was to power a downward spiral that proved unstoppable.

The undercut flints, who also went by the title of 'honourable men', maintained the 1813 day rate, but their actual earnings began to decline from reduced work. A depression in 1826 drained their unemployment funds and then they lost two strikes – one against female labour, their first defeat in sixty years, and another in 1830.

They decided that their only hope was to regroup and they saw their opportunity in the economic recovery of 1833. That September, the London Operative Tailors was launched. It was to be a non-exclusive union with no privileged groups and no seniority systems. From the masters, it sought an end to piecework and outwork: all work must be done on the employers' premises.

With no action contemplated until the following April, the Operative Tailors in the meantime took the lead in founding the Consolidated Trades' Union with other trade groups; there was dreamy talk of opening a bank for the working classes, abolishing money, replacing employers by Boards of Trade and Committees of Industry, and eventually negotiating with American and European governments for the creation of a new world order.

In March, the conviction and deportation of the six Dorchester farm labourers – the Tolpuddle Martyrs – for union organizing brought everybody back to reality, but strike plans went ahead and a set of demands was presented to all the masters on 25 April. The union had an estimated strength of 9-13,000 tailors, organized into thirty-one lodges, most of them among the bespoke shops of the West End. Perhaps 1,000 were able to return to work when their employers agreed to settle, but on 28 April the masters met at the Thatched Cottage in St James's Street and voted to reject the demands and to recruit strike-breakers. The old statute requiring them to hire only fully apprenticed artisans had been repealed in 1814, which gave them an added weapon.

The union organized a cooperative workshop to help eek out its funds, but within a fortnight it had to cut strike pay from 10s to 7s 6d. City tailors began to drift back to work, though the West End remained solid for a little longer. By 14 May, the strikers had offered to negotiate and, on 20 May, they found their funds had been embezzled and their workshop robbed. The crushed union offered to return to work on the old terms, but the masters refused to take men back until they had signed a pledge renouncing trade unionism forever. On 4 June, 5,000 men were still out, but they had begun to drift back under whatever conditions the masters set. The strike not only broke the tailors, but was a fatal blow to the Consolidated Trades' Union; when in September the builders met the same fate as the tailors, trade unionism in London was for a time wiped out.

A few houses of call survived in the West End with some masters prepared to pay able 'honourable men' twice as much as the cheap new labour source, but a failed attempt in 1843 to reverse the defeat of 1834 marked the start of a long decline in the position of the elite workers in the best shops.

The Blue Posts, just off Golden Square, was one of the houses of call infiltrated by Abel Hall, a police spy who gave excellent value for his

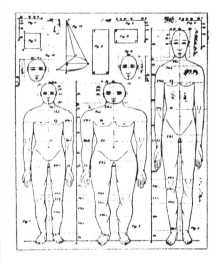

Above
Anthropometry, or 'the measurement of man', became the rage, with many suggested solutions to the problem of systemizing human proportions. This one was published in the *Tailor and Cutter* in 1883.

£1 a week. Some of Hall's secret reports have survived. They include an account of the bizarre initiation ceremony he was put through upon joining the striking union. Blindfolded and with his hat hanging from the top button of his coat by a piece of string – and having paid a toll of 7d – he was led into the meeting room to the accompaniment of three loud knocks.

Still blindfolded, Hall listened while several biblical extracts were recited, all 'selected as bearing on the Equality of Man and his right to oppose tyranny'. A hearty rendering of the 'Union Song' followed, then a long address on the iniquities of governments through the ages, and finally he was ordered to kneel with his right hand on his exposed left breast and his left hand on a leaf from a Bible. To loud hand-clapping and foot-stamping, the blindfold was removed and Hall found himself peering into dim gaslight in a packed chamber. His report continued:

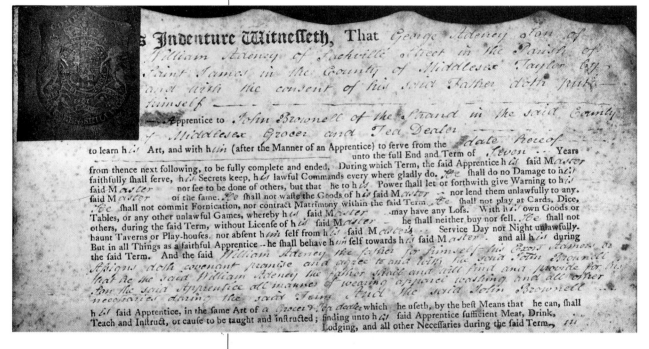

Above
Apprentice George Adeney's 1808 indenture committed him to seven years' servitude, with gambling, fornication and even marriage among proscribed activities.

The President and Vicepresident behind him standing on a table with White Surplices on and Red Sashes round them and each has a Bible in his hand. Just before them is a Black Ground Transparency well light and on which is painted the perfect Skeleton of a Man. The President then takes a Sword in his hand the point of which he directs your attention first to the Skull and then to the Heart, the Arms, Legs and Body and in a short address goes to prove that when a Man is in work and in full vigour he soon becomes a skeleton by being tyrannized over by his Governors and Masters who employ him and who rob him of substance – themselves to live in luxury on his Vitals. Over the head or Skull is inscribed Beware of your latter end, to which he directs your attention by stating that such an end will soon be yours if you do not by Uniting prevent it and that if you after you are sworn do anything to injure the Union or be a Traitor to it Death will surely be your reward. There are also 8 Brothers who have naked Swords in their hands and wear red Sashes and several others who carry large Wooden Axes and Battle Axes and who surround this Skeleton and the President with his Sword and Vice with his go round to each person saying and at the same time putting the edge to your neck and taking your left hand in his what are you, the answer is a Taylor, he then says you are willing to protect the Unions to the risk of your life to which you answer I will.

With hand still on naked breast, he was required to swear an oath

> that I will never reveal their Laws or secrets to any one . . . so help my God.
>
> This being done we rise and we are told we are now Brothers, that our Monthly Subscriptions would be One Shilling and that as the Union at Derby had been requested by the Masters to sign a Paper to return to work on grounds derogatory to their principles and had nobly refused it was intended to further assist them by each member giving S1/- as well as getting what they could from non Members.

Finally, they were given the secret sign:

> We were then told that to know any Member of the Universal Sign was by placing the Right hand thumb and finger to the top on the left side of your waistcoat and carry it from thence across the body to the right thigh and if it was not answered by the same signal on the reverse side the Party so asked was no member.

Left
Lunchtime at the Blue Posts in Soho. A hundred and fifty years ago, police spies infiltrated the journeymen organizations which operated from such pubs.

All too soon, there were to be no members. For the next thirty years the masters had a free hand. In 1849, average weekly earnings of journeymen in the West End shops was estimated at 18s 9½d, little more than half the rate of 1813; the shops' outworkers were getting about half that again.

In Charles Kingsley's novel of the same name, Alton Locke's employer was respectable – 'one of the old sort of fashionable West End tailors in the fast-decreasing honourable trades, keeping an honest shop . . . he paid good wages for work, though not as good, of course, as he had given 20 years before'. When this old master died, he was succeeded by his son, who 'resolved to make haste to be rich' through subcontracting and piecework.

The effect of all this was important in the shaping of Savile Row. A gulf was growing between the West End's best and a new breed of Slop and Show shops – 'plate-glass palaces where gents buy their cheap and nasty clothes' was how one critic saw them. Between 1844 and 1849, the number of West End 'traditional' shops declined from 72 to 60, while Slop and Shows doubled from 172 to 344.

5

Henry Poole, Savile Row

As a money-maker, 'compare it to witchcraft', advised a magazine in its review of the best bespoke tailoring, four years after the strike that broke the journeymen. 'The march of refinement has made rapid strides in this particular walk of scientific improvement,' *The Town* continued. 'There is now no longer a tailor to be found in the classic region of St James's. No! they are one and all professors of the art of cutting.'

Right at the top of these 'colleges of fashion', it placed Stultz:

> This establishment has no rival; it stands so far above all competition, that comparison would be idle; it is the first of its kind, we may say, without exaggeration, in the world. It is conducted upon the most extensive scale, there being not less than three hundred persons employed in its various departments; and so numerous are its patrons, that the profits arising from the professorship are estimated at, at least, £40,000 per annum.

Below
The sporting set in Tattersall's Yard was a magnet for the young Henry Poole.

The profit estimate may be hard to accept, but, even allowing for hyperbole, the rest can be taken as accurate.

Ranked second was Burghart, situated opposite Stultz in Clifford Street. Burghart also had a military background and was credited with being 'an artiste of infinite taste and ability'. Third came Meyer, 'professors to majesty during three reigns', and by this point judged 'very old-fashioned, but very respectable'. The Meyer recommendation came with a caution – 'These artistes are not famed, like those of the two preceding establishments, for the elegance and originality of their "style"' – and a reprimand: 'Bill discounting, we should imagine, has not added to the wealth or respectability of this firm.'

A dozen other firms got honourable mentions. They included Davidson, of Brummell memory and still in Cork Street; the steadily progressing Poole, now in Burlington Street; Willis & Co., who had been tailors to the briefly reigning William IV; Hudson, Storey, Nugee, Buckmaster, Cooke, Sparding, Hummell & Sporer, Curlewis ('an artiste of exquisite taste'), Inkson, Anderson and Pike. The last three were especially celebrated for their trousers, ever a cause for customer concern. The late Duke of Windsor used to go to America for his trousers, for which Savile Row never forgave him.

This 1838 review shows how little the internal processes of Savile Row have changed. The atmosphere of tailoring's 'classic region of St James's' is likened by *The Town* to that of 'a delightful little village', in which individual firms evolve and devolve in a lifespan, yet the community hardly changes. Thus, Meyer by now has '& Sons' tacked on to it, while the old man himself is acknowledged to be 'the very patriarch of his profession'. Stultz is still Stultz, but direction has passed on to Housley, who is identified as a staff member elevated through 'his own superlative abilities'. Housley is credited with transforming styles in frock coats.

It is further explained that Burghart had trained under Meyer and that Sparding, Hummell and Sporer all began with Burghart – Sparding and Sporer as cutters and Hummell as a book-keeper. This is precisely the manner of growth and change in Savile Row today.

Burghart's rise in the world found expression in his cultural pursuits, and we learn how in aspiring to be acknowledged as a connoisseur, he had become 'the possessor of quantity, if not quality, his house being literally crowded, from the attic to the shop, with paintings of every kind, class, character, and subject'. Burghart's art collecting had a touch of the desperate about it and the reasons are easy to understand. As Southey saw it, 'a transit from the City to the West End of Town is the last step of the successful tailor, when he throws off his exuvia and emerges from his chrysalis state into the butterfly life of high life'. It was more complicated than that. Going west offered the opportunity of getting rich, but at a cost in social status. The City of London respected trade and commerce (a pastry cook was Lord Mayor in 1815 and a linen draper in 1821), but the West End was the preserve of inherited privilege and of attitudes enshrined in the likes of Colonel Sebright of the Guards, stomping past the lair of the dandies at White's and cursing: 'Damn these fellows – they are upstarts and fit only for the society of tailors!'

French observer Francis Wey found a 'degree of hierarchy between the social classes' in 1850s London 'so rigid and intolerable as to be inconceivable'. It was a hierarchy in which the tradesman came last. As the new breed of industrialist and businessman gained acceptance at Court, even the most patrician of shopmen stayed strictly the servants of Society. Acceptance of a sort could be bought, but the price was as steep as the bad debts that were too often part of the reward. The attraction of the very high born lay in the status his custom conferred, yet such custom could be a burden, as the sneering references to money-lenders and bill discounting suggest. It was, rather, the tailors who needed the great money-lenders like Solomon – a difficult man, according to Gronow, but 'of inestimable use' to the jewellers, coach-makers and tailors 'who were obliged to give exorbitant accommodation to their aristocratic customers, and were eventually paid on bills of an incredibly long date'. Byron once hinted that it was 'Solomon's judgement' that forced the departure of Brummell. Nazi bombs obliterated any record of whatever Brummell owed Meyer, but maybe Meyer was able to lay off some of the debt with Solomon.

Long and diligent service could purchase a degree of respect. Hoby, greatest of the boot-makers, became 'something of a privileged person and his impertinence was not only overlooked, but was considered as rather a good joke', according to Gronow. Hoby looked any man in the eye and attributed the Duke of Wellington's victories to 'my boots and my prayers'. He was the first man to drive a tilbury in London (it was black and drawn by a beautiful black cob) and he is said to have left £120,000 when he died. Then there was James Lock the hatter, a neighbour of the tailors Nugee and Willis, who was honoured with occasional invitations to visit a noble client's home. When it came to matrimony, of course, Lock stayed within his class, though the circumstances were unusual. He waited until he was seventy and then married the twenty-eight-year-old daughter of a Fortnum & Mason's partner.

If they could not join Society, they could at least shadow it. The season being over, 'the tradesmen of St James's were abroad taking their pleasure,' wrote Thackeray in *Pendennis*. 'The tailors had grown mustachios and were gone up the Rhine; the bootmakers were at Ems or Baden, blushing when they met their customers at these places of recreation, or punting beside their creditors at the gaming tables.'

Below
This 1820 Cruickshank print captures the mood of the sporting gentry who patronized Poole.

48

One man determined that he could join. It took him all his life to achieve it – or just about achieve it – and in the process he turned the artiste of St James's into the Savile Row tailor, with an image as immutable as his product. Henry George Poole was born on 8 November 1814, the second son of the draper who discovered a talent for making army tunics. He was an infant upstairs with his mother when Jack-a-Dandy Donelly and the sneak party made their cloth raid; he was eight when his father opened in Regent Street and nine when the family moved into Old Burlington Street.

Heightening fortunes enabled Henry to receive some schooling at the Academy for Noblemen's and Gentlemen's Sons. When a stockbroker found a position for his older brother Jim, Henry at fifteen was consigned to the back shop to learn the trade, step by step, starting with the sewing room. Henry's entry into the business coincided with the exit of a partner, William Cooling, who moved to Maddox Street and founded a firm that exists there to this day, now under the name of Wells of Mayfair. The reasons for the split are not known, but there still exists a copy of the letter, carefully crafted with professional help, by which Cooling attempted to lure away Poole's customers, within a week of his own departure. Nothing is more sacred to Savile Row than the client list, and the subtle art of pillaging within the bounds of propriety has exercised minds from that day to this. The Cooling letter remains a classic of its kind:

> Sir, I beg to inform you that the partnership hitherto existing under the firm of Poole & Cooling Tailors, No. 4, Old Burlington Street, was dissolved on Tuesday the 8th Inst. by mutual consent. Allow me to return my most sincere and greatful acknowledgements for that kind preference so liberally given as to enable me during the period of my management and cutting to encrease nearly double the Business of the late Firm. I now beg to solicit a continuance of the same encouragement

Below
Poole's showroom today features trappings fondly preserved from Henry's day. The old weighing chair was intended to quiet customers who disputed a change in girth between fittings. The idea may have come from wine merchant Berry Bros & Rudd, whose weighing scales bore many a noble bottom – Brummell was a regular, as the ledger shows.

to my new establishment trusting to my assiduity and unremitting attention to afford that entire satisfaction which I should hope that a long and active experience in Business will enable me to give. I have the honor to be, Sir, Your most obedt. and humble Servant.

PS – As Mr Poole continues in the premises where the Business has hitherto been conducted, for the convenience of all parties, it is mutually agreed, that he shall receive and pay all debts outstanding.

In the event, young Henry proved more of a problem than loss of trade to the disaffected Cooling. By the time he had graduated to holding chalk and notebook for the head cutter, it was clear that padding a lapel or cording an edge was never going to be the consuming interest of a young man too much taken by the life of the noblemen's and gentlemen's sons he had met. He was especially fascinated by the sporting set who hung about Tattersall's Yard and he became fast friends with Jem Mason, the 'handsome, larkish' rough-rider son of a Huntingdonshire horse dealer who made racing history by winning the first Grand National on a horse called Lottery.

Poole Senior decided to make the best of the situation by kitting out Henry to perfection and giving him a roving commission to drum up business with his charm and fast-developing social flair. Before he was twenty-one, Henry was riding his own phaeton in Hyde Park, scouting the fringes of Society. While the drawing rooms of the nobility were as much off-limit as the ladies they contained, bachelor circles were more liberated; in this way the ever-affable Henry made progress. The next step was a welcome from the Stamfords. The rich young Earl of Stamford had disgusted everybody by marrying a circus rider and only the more raffish sporting bloods would visit him and his déclassé countess. The Earl was master of fox hounds of the Albrighton Hunt and, as Henry could stay on a horse with the best of them and was helpful in sorting out the lads in the Earl's great ancestral stable, the friendship grew. When the Earl took over the Quorn Hunt, he introduced Henry there too.

It was apparently at the Stamfords, during an after-dinner game of billiards, that a fellow guest occasioned one of the great Poole anecdotes by complaining to Henry about the fit of his coat. Henry slashed and stabbed at the offending garment with a piece of billiard chalk, then told its startled occupant to take it to his shop for alteration when he got back to London. 'The puppy must either have had the mortification of going up to change, or remaining a sight for the remainder of the evening,' wrote Percy Armytage in one of many re-tellings of the tale. Tailors' tales, like those of fishermen, tend to grow, so that it has come to be related as an episode between the audacious Henry and the Prince of Wales himself.

Jem Mason retired from racing in 1844 to keep a stud of hunters with Henry at the Bell Inn, Winslow, where they supplied remounts to followers of the Queen's Buckhounds. Jem was by now Poole's fashion plate: the greatest cross-country rider of all time was a living advert for Poole's elegantly cut coats and petershams. Henry had his passport to adventures with the Buckhounds, but by this time all of the hunting world had opened to him – which was most profitable for the sporting department that his father had opened to cope with the referrals.

Poole Senior was doing very well in his own right and, in 1839, he initiated a new style of Court dress, offered in mauve or bottle green. Yet to outward appearances, No. 4 Old Burlington Street remained the same unremarkable, if superior, residence it was when the widow of General Lumley first took occupation in 1723. Trade was not something to shout about. The gap was virtually complete between Henry's high life and the rest of the family's sustaining routine of six days' hard work, church three times on Sunday, roast mutton and early to bed. Two of Henry's step-sisters had left to marry tailors, but elder brother Jim was now permanently at home and dying slowly of consumption in this little world of domesticity amid dusty workrooms.

The year 1846 was portentous, for James Poole died and left the business to Henry, who literally turned it around. His father already had a counting-house and workshop at the rear – Savile Row – end of the property; Henry made Savile Row his main entrance.

One of the enduring myths of Savile Row holds that Poole was the first tailor to reach the Row itself and that this intrusion of 'trade' so distressed the many surgeons then practising there that they took flight and resettled in Harley Street. In fact, as far back as 1828, when Poole had not long moved into Old Burlington Street (by no means a meaner address), there were already two or three other tailors in that street, nine in Cork Street, four in Clifford Street and three or four in Savile Row. By the time that Henry Poole succeeded his father and reversed the polarity of their premises, about a fifth of the Burlington Estate residents were tailors, which was not far short of the number of doctors and dentists then in residence.

It was Henry Poole's achievement to concentrate attention so thoroughly upon himself that his rivals ceased to exist, at least in the popular mind.

To convert the old rear workshop into the new front showroom, he had a gallery built in 1851. Then he expanded his Savile Row frontage with more land acquisitions and, in the late 1850s, he had the fashionable architect-builder Cubitt design and erect a low, flat-roofed, Belgravian-style structure that exuded dignity and quiet grandeur. By 1869, Poole's stretched from 36 to 38 Savile Row on one side and from 3 to 5 Old Burlington Street on the other. It also had a satellite building for its livery trade on the corner of Savile Row and Clifford Street, where the ostentatiously secretive Anderson & Sheppard is today located. Livery was a Poole speciality, and the firm came to dictate the attire of superior servants everywhere – 'footmen tricked out by Poole in brimstone and ruby loafed like great golden carp in half the palace entrance halls of Europe, and made the Hyde Park drive from mid-May to July blaze like a bed of Dutch tulips,' wrote Donald Macandrew in his study, *The Prince of Tailors*.

Poole's showroom was weighted with much ornate bronze – mirrors, sculptures and vases, all from the 1851 Great Exhibition, populated its niched and columned depths; above loomed the Peers' Gallery, a showplace of the accoutrements of nobility as well as their storage place between ceremonial engagements. Since Henry was in pursuit of the sporting set, the front of the showroom displayed such items as stalking capes. Military uniforms were kept at the back, while the middle distance was filled with dress coats, morning coats and every variety of greatcoat. The stockrooms and pattern rooms were in the basement.

Hunting attracted the very rich, and in hunting the hunters Henry showed a keen eye for those of greatest influence and promise. The rising Jewish bankers and merchant princes were excluded from upper-crust Society of the 1840s, but they could hardly be kept out for long. In Baron Meyer de Rothschild, Poole secured one of his first superstar clients. Another follower of the hounds was a political chancer with an interesting name: Prince Louis Napoleon was a low-rated pretender to the throne of France and something of a joke around town, but Rothschild reckoned him worth a gamble. The Prince was dressed by Poole and Henry participated with the Baron and others in giving the Prince's campaign funds a £10,000 boost. No horse ran at longer odds, but lucky Louis cantered in as the Emperor Napoleon III. Poole to this day carries the late Emperor's arms on its

Below
Lily Langtry, most famous of Bertie's mistresses, took his advice and went on the stage. They also shared a tailor.

MRS. LANGTRY.

letter-head, as much a lucky mascot as its first royal warrant.

By 1858, Poole was supplying 'more men and masters of hounds than any tailor in London, but his customers must be prepared to pay for perfection,' J. S. Rarey wrote in his *Art of Training Horses*. Two years later that perfection won Poole its most important customer, though in unusual circumstances. The Prince of Wales was at the theatre when he noticed that the actor Fechter, although playing a ragged, penniless adventurer, had on a jacket of impeccable cut. 'Who's your tailor?' the Prince wanted to know, and Fechter told him.

This Prince of Wales was Bertie, prodigal son of Victoria and Albert, and a clothes freak. As a sanitized version of that previous prince of identical title, Bertie loved both women and dressing up, and it happened that Henry Poole was in a position to serve both these interests. The Prince 'paid many visits to his tailor, Poole in Savile Row, who served as a kind of post office in helping him keep in touch with friends,' Philip Magnus explained politely in *King Edward the Seventh*.

Right
Poole's ledgers: stacked in the basement, the vital statistics – and ancient debts – of departed dynasties.

Poole was by then actively courting female custom. As an offshoot to the sporting department, he had installed six tiny satin-lined cubicles and a dummy horse, Bucephalus, with which to meet the needs of a tremendous vogue for female horsemanship. The proprieties were strictly observed, of course, with the appointment of a dozen young ladies to attend to the Amazone à la Mode, and Henry himself capped it all by marrying the senior lady, a draper's daughter named Emma Walker. Yet he also had the entrepreneur's eye for publicity and had no qualms about dressing for free Catherine 'Skittles' Walters, the Liverpool sea captain's daughter who was the Harriette Wilson of the day. Lily Langtry, most famous of Bertie's mistresses, was to stay a Poole's customer until the word 'Dead' was scrawled across her name in the ledger (that being the effective, if unsentimental, method by which many celebrity accounts were terminated . . . in some cases, like that of the Grand Duke Serge of Russia, the word 'Assassinated' was substituted).

'There is only one Poole – all the rest are puddles,' was the happy slogan of an era before Savile Row thought to abjure advertising. The orders came flooding in, until it seemed as though two-thirds of the beau monde was being clothed by Henry Poole. Emma, who had been head saleswoman at Holbrook's, the royal glove shop, was packed off to Dorset Cottage, a riverside retreat up the Thames, and each day of the season found Henry in Rotten Row at the fashionable hour, now from noon to one. From the Achilles Statue to Kensington Gardens, Hyde Park was 'a choppy, glinting sea of thoroughbred horses and well-bred riders, well-cut habits and well-blocked tall hats,' which the rest of humanity would gawk at through the railings. Accompanied by Jem Mason (now the owner of a Mayfair riding stable and 'Poole'd up to the eyes in black coat and doe-skin breeches, soft and supple as a lady's glove'), Henry was the artist-general taking the salute at a parade of his own creations.

Armed with Poole ledgers from the period, it is easy to recreate a typical scene. There is Lord Cardigan, who led the charge at Balaclava, riding a grey charger and still wearing a heavily padded Master of Cavalry uniform, while Lady Cardigan in 'sapphire velveteen Hussar's pelisse with 14 gilt buttons' and enormous 'astrakhan busby with plume' ogles all the good-looking young men. There is Kitty Stamford, stagily perfect in 'hortensia blue twilled Elysian beaver habit, amethyst velvet facings . . . gauntlets . . . a Francois 1st hat . . .', Lady Jocelyn's 'Ophelia dingle cloth habit, dragonet braids' and Princess Czartoryska's 'black vicuna, embossed, crowsfeet olivettes'.

His tour of inspection complete, Poole would return to Savile Row, where from 3.30 to 5 he played the genial and generous host to sundry sporting nobility in a candelabra-lit parlour behind the showroom, where cigars, hock and claret were in liberal supply. 'A great rendezvous for gilded and sporting youth . . . more like a club than a shop,' is the description of one memoirist, who adds that 'the firm's well-known trio of high priests, Mr Cundey (General Supervisor), Mr Dent (Coats) and Mr Allen (Trousers) frequently joined the convivial gathering'.

The rickety but rapturous Second Empire of Louis and his Empress Eugénie opened up a second front for the tailors. Henry Creed in Conduit Street had a head start through his d'Orsay connection which, though costly in itself (d'Orsay went bankrupt in 1849 and was 'not a man to worry over bills'), gave Creed access to London's lively French aristocratic set and to Louis and Eugénie themselves. From 1850, he had a Paris branch in the Place de l'Opéra, where he spent more and more time. The credit rating of the customers remained a worry and the Creed family long cherished an 1856 letter from the Prince de la Moskova, Marechal Ney's son, beginning: 'Being at this moment rather short of money . . .'; but the firm persevered to become, like Worth the dressmaker, a part of Parisian culture. Henry Creed was wounded by a shell fragment during the siege of 1871 and was near death for several months, but he recovered to live well into his nineties.

The other Henry limited his French travels to an annual pilgrimage to the Court of Napoleon, usually in late autumn, when their imperial majesties were at Compiègne and indulging in all sorts of elaborate fun and games, including bi-weekly stag hunts in the forest. This was Rotten Row with a French accent – costumed, again, by Poole. From the Chief Ranger, the Baron de Wimpferen, in 'rifle green jacket with gold lace, laced tricorne hat, cockfeathers', to the little Emperor himself and his accompanying trail of chausseurs in their four-horse carriages with periwigged postilions, all were kitted out in green and gold uniforms by Poole.

It was in 1866, at one of these great processionals, that Savile Row was elevated to a higher plain. The event is described by Donald Macandrew: 'While they were drinking stirrup cup, a fat, pale, young man with blue bubbly eyes and a blase look rode up to Henry and conversed with him languidly. Henry was in transports.' Small

Above
The young Bertie, about the time he was first Poole'd. His first adventure with an actress also occurred about this time.

wonder: Bertie was befriending his tailor – in public!

> The Prince's pink cut-away coat and white leathers made a pretext for mutual congratulation and, presently, laying a genial hand on Henry's shoulder, the royal patron led his tailor to where a group of horsemen surrounded a tiny basket chaise with Shetland ponies. In it, holding the ribbons, sat the Empress Eugénie, now in the later afternoon of her beauty, and beside her, as fair as May blossom, the young Princess of Wales . . . .

Never mind that Henry was about to be rudely dragged back to London by the threat of a strike; he had the accolade of royal acknowledgement in the highest social sphere, whereas intimacy of a business nature and only in strictest privacy had always been the rule. Never mind, either, that it was no more than part of a trend, for the genial hand of the Prince had begun to flick down the Victorian social barriers at a rate that alarmed his relatives. He startled the Kaiser by going 'yachting with his grocer' – Glasgow slum-born Thomas Lipton – and inviting upholsterer John Maple to dine. Actors, Americans, Jews and self-made men were invited into his Marlborough House set. He went to synagogue for a Rothschild wedding and he sat down to supper with the likes of the actress Ellen Terry. The lovely and the rich were Bertie's meat and it did not bother him where he found them. Bored with waiting so long to become King, and with a highly developed sense of Divine Right, he did not give a damn so long as his guests were dressed right (and there the Americans did tend to distress him).

Henry set about satisfying a royal craving for clothes that put even the Prince Regent in the shade. Bertie had the largest wardrobe in the world – the robes of nine British and fifty foreign orders of chivalry, a complete set of uniforms of every British regiment and plenty of foreign ones besides, plus enough civilian wear to satisfy a man who was pleased to change his dress five or six times a day.

Bertie was hardly twenty when he made his first purchase at Poole's, a youth fretting to be free of the 'schoolboy discipline' imposed by his father. He was off to Canada and the United States aboard HMS *Hero* and it seems likely that among the first to see him 'all Poole'd out' was the crowd that crammed into the Academy of Music on Manhattan's East Side for what had been billed as a ball. Five thousand turned up and part of the floor gave way; after repairs during supper it was discovered that a carpenter had been nailed under the boards. There were two suicides among the uninvited. It is recorded that Bertie remained calm.

The Prince's purchases are preserved in page after page of meticulous script in Poole ledgers, now stacked high in a basement at 15 Savile Row. So are the purchases of the extended family that followed the Prince to Poole's. By the end of the 1860s, Henry could shuffle his regal warrants like a pack of playing cards. It went something like this:

1860 — Prince of Wales, Prince of Liechtenstein, Prince Nicholas Troubitzkoy, Grand Duke Michel of Russia.
1861 — Grand Duke Constantine of Russia, Archduke Maximilian of Austria (and later Emperor of Mexico), Crown Prince of Germany.
1862 — Grand Duke Frederic of Baden, King Leopold of the Belgians, Prince Mustapha Pasha of Egypt.
1863 — Prince of Orange, Prince Metternich, Duke of Edinburgh, Prince Humbert (later King of Italy).
1864 — The Emperor of Russia.

1865 — King of Portugal, Prince Christian of Holstein, Queen Victoria, Crown Prince Frederick of Prussia, Prince Armadeus (Duke of Aosta), Grand Duc of Saxe Weimar.

1866 — Prince Herman of Hohenlohe Langenburg.

1868 — Duke of Genoa, Sidtan Ali Khan.

1869 — Prince Louis of Battenberg, Duke of Connaught (Prince Arthur), Khedive Ismael Pasha of Egypt.

Below
Hyde Park's 'choppy, glinting sea'. Gronow relates that, by a tacit understanding, none of the lower classes intruded 'in regions which were then given up exclusively to persons of rank and fashion'.

Limitless other luminaries, from Lord Randolph Churchill and Disraeli to the Claridge of Claridge's Hotel, also went on the books in that decade. The Morgans, Poole's first American dynasty, had been acquired back in the 1850s. The crop of the 1870s included Bismarck, further European royals, and such exotics as the Emperor of Brazil and a couple of Japanese princes.

Poole's ministrations played a visible part in some of these august lives. Prince Christian was the 'miserable starveling German princeling' marked down by Victoria for Helena, the ungainly but useful daughter she wished to keep by her side. She called in the doctor, who had diagnosed Albert's fatal typhoid, to see what could be done to put the Prince into better shape. 'It is such a pity . . . if only he looked a little younger,' she mused. Part of the solution was to have Poole kit him out. Others, like Frederick of Prussia, who married Victoria's daughter Vicky, was an enthusiastic recommendation of Bertie's. 'Never forget Uncle Fritz,' he lamented after Frederick's death in 1888, after only ninety-nine days as German Emperor. 'If he had a fault, he was too good for this world.'

As customers, they must have been a rum lot to deal with, and it was as well that Henry Poole was by now master of a manner described by his biographer as 'easy without being familiar, ingratiating but not obsequious'. Bertie's brother, the Duke of Edinburgh ('Alfie'), has been described as rude, touchy, wilful, unscrupulous, untrustworthy, improvident and unfaithful; surely he must have been one of Poole's more difficult customers. Even his mother called him 'a slippery youth'. When she married him off to the daughter of Alexander II of Russia, the event was as unpopular with the public as the bridegroom, but this did not deter Henry and his fellow tailors from marking the occasion with a banquet in St James's Hall. At Meyer & Mortimer in Sackville Street they still have the engraved invitation.

By this time Louis and Eugénie's Second Empire had come to grief

Above
Even a difficult customer like the awkward Alfie merited a tailors' banquet on the occasion of his marriage.

Below
Poole leased its Regent Street premises to Farmer & Rogers, whose shawl emporium gave the founder of Liberty's his start.

and the pair were back in English exile, but Bertie had become imbued with the easy cosmopolitan atmosphere of their Paris and was injecting what he could of it into London Society.

Henry, turning sixty, was at last accepted into some of the best drawing rooms: for by now he was 'Old Pooley', an institution. Disraeli fictionalized him as Mr Vigo in *Endymion* – 'the most fashionable tailor in London . . . consummate in his art . . . neither pretentious nor servile, but simple, and with becoming respect for others and for himself'. The phaeton of his youth had become the enduring symbol of his success. Lord Lonsdale would recall accompanying Henry in this phaeton 'drawn by two of the best horses in London – each had a white sock – a celebrated pair'. 'The most beautiful horses I remember were Lord Calthorpe's and those of Mr Poole, the Savile Row tailor,' wrote the Duke of Portland in his memoirs. Percy Armytage wrote of Henry being 'unusually conspicuous' on Derby Days, when he would drive the phaeton up and down Grosvenor Place, whose residents draped their balconies with red clothes and served 'Derby teas' as they watched the coaches returning from the races.

Henry Poole had special reason to attend the 1867 Derby, with its showdown between the Marquis of Hastings and Henry Chaplin. It had been Poole's brougham that Chaplin borrowed to take his fiancée, Lady Paget, shopping one fateful morning two years earlier. Chaplin, nicknamed 'Magnifico', was a vastly wealthy royal crony from their student days, when he had impressed the Prince of Wales by having his private chef at Oxford. Lady Paget, known as 'the Pocket Venus', was a renowned beauty. While Chaplin dutifully waited with the brougham, she slipped out a side door of Marshall & Snellgrove's store and into the arms of the rakish Lord Hastings, who was waiting with a cab and a marriage licence. Chaplin had not time to return the carriage and down a stiff drink in Poole's parlour before he had lost his Pocket Venus forever and London had one of its juiciest scandals. Queen Victoria was outraged.

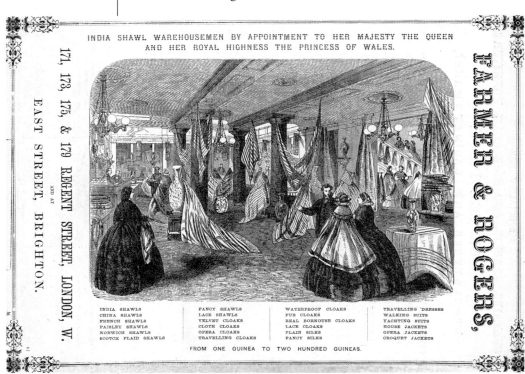

The aftermath proved to be pure Victorian melodrama. Chaplin entered a horse named Hermit in the Derby. When Hermit burst a blood vessel, the odds lengthened, but instead of scratching the horse, he backed it heavily, while Hastings just as heavily wagered against it. With the Prince and Chaplin watching from the Royal Box, and at starting odds of 66-1, Hermit won by a neck. Chaplin won £140,000 and Hastings lost about as much. Within a year, the ruined rake was dead. 'Hermit's Derby broke my heart, but I didn't show it, did I?' were reputedly his last words. Years later, Chaplin would still occasionally borrow Poole's brougham.

The smart carriages were useful for Poole's image, but status-acquisition was also proceeding on many other fronts. There was Henry's hunting stud at Greenford, his collections of water-colours, French furniture, old violins . . . and finally his homes. As well as the Old Burlington base and Dorset Cottage, Henry acquired a large house on the Marine Parade at Brighton. It was to Brighton that his wife Emma, his unmarried sister Mary Ann and other females of the household now repaired, seemingly always in retreat before Henry's social advance. Emma has been described as handsome in a strong-featured way, a less equine George Eliot, but she remains an obscure figure and seems to have played no part in her husband's social life; she is said to have distrusted his friends.

That social life was to find its greatest expression in Dorset Cottage, set amidst beautiful grounds on the banks of the Thames near Fulham, and served by a steam launch. It added up to the perfect way to watch the annual Oxford-Cambridge boat race and thus to the Prince of Wales becoming a guest of Poole the tailor. Henry would pack his launch with as splendid a company as could be mustered and follow the race from Putney to Mortlake, then set course for the cottage and 'a sumptuous lunch', as Percy Armytage described it.

Henry died in early May 1876, under suitably theatrical circumstances. He had suffered an apoplectic fit some months earlier, but appeared to be on the mend after months of being nursed

Thought to be Henry Poole and Sam Cundey, the cousin and faithful shop-minder whose great-grandson now heads the firm.

Left
Tailors' valhalla: seven Pooles and one Cundey occupy this forgotten vault in Old Highgate Cemetery. Records indicate room for one more.

'indefatigably, jealously' by Emma. On a bleak, gusty day, he took his phaeton for a spin along the Brighton sea front, got caught in an unseasonal snowstorm and suffered a relapse; a second violent attack killed him. His body was borne back to Savile Row and from thence to the family vault in that Victorian Valhalla, Highgate Cemetery. His passing was mourned 'in all circles where wealth is paramount', the *Tailor and Cutter* eulogized.

They almost had to bury the business with him. Those elegantly scripted ledgers gave up a sad secret: the outstretched hand of the Prince of Wales had sought more than friendship. It transpired that Henry, possibly fired by the success of his loan to Louis Napoleon, had been extending indefinite credit on loads of goods sent to the Prince and his circle. Emma and Sam Cundey, the cousin who had charge of the shop throughout Henry's reign, were overloaded with liabilities and had to write off £10,000 in bad debts. In the twelve months that she survived her husband, Emma had to sell off the fine horses, the paintings and the French furniture, but it was not enough and Sam spoke of selling out. Persistent efforts to induce the Marlborough House set to pay up proved disastrous when the Prince, in a fit of pique, withdrew his patronage: the privilege of lordly custom should be payment enough, it was intimated.

What saved Poole's was the determination of Mary Ann, who had doted on her brother and did not want to see all memory of him obliterated. To avert a forced sale, Mary Ann is said to have offered all her assets, including a half-share in the lease on the Regent Street shop that Henry's father had taken almost fifty years before. A few difficult years followed, during which Sam's young son Howard took over as principal under the financial scrutiny of trustee Sir Reginald Hanson, a former Lord Mayor of London.

The Regent Street property is a story in itself. From 1848, it was leased by the Pooles to Farmer & Rogers, whose Great Shawl and Cloak Emporium gave Arthur Lasenby Liberty his start. When only nineteen, Liberty pursuaded his employers to buy up all the Japanese exhibits at the International Exhibition of 1862 (which had been held on the site of Lady Blessington's Gore House). Japan was new to the West and the venture was a dazzling success. Liberty acquired a reputation in the best artistic circles and, when Farmer & Rogers refused to make him a director, he opened in opposition and soon eclipsed them with the firm that bears his name to this day.

6

Hustle, Bustle and Suicide

Evander Berry Wall was King of the Dudes, a title accorded in perpetuity following his achievement in parading in forty changes of attire in a single afternoon at the United States Hotel in Saratoga Springs. Every outfit was by Poole, a fact borne next day by newspapers from Maine to California.

Imagine, then, the impact of the news that broke on 1 September 1888: Poole had pursued the great swell to New York and was suing him for $250 in unpaid bills.

'The blow has fallen. Poole has struck!' *Society Times* gasped as it became clear that this was no isolated gesture, but part of a new policy instituted by 'Hanson the Merciless' – the trustee Sir Reginald Hanson:

> From London to Lucknow a cloud of gloom and terror spreads like a vast black, broadcloth suit of woe. At the announcement that Poole & Co. expect their bills to be paid, the cheeks of strong men blanch, and the knees of weak men wobble. We already hear of brazen dunes invading the sacred fastnesses of Mayfair and Belgravia . . . and little Bertie, with a whole invoice of fall splendour due by the next express at his Continental retreat, writhes on the verge of insanity at the prospect of having to leave his shape to the tender but mysterious ministrations of 'anybody' after all.

Poole pulled through without seriously inconveniencing the gentry, though the Prince of Wales maintained his boycott for many years, whatever the personal agony. Nevertheless, just as the fate of the British Empire might have been discerned to be at its zenith, there was an inkling of Savile Row's future problems in these memorial verses to Henry Poole that appeared in a New York paper:

> Yes, Poole's my tailor. Poole! You know!
> Who makes the Prince of Wales's things,
> He's tailor (as his billheads show)
> To half the emperors and kings.
> An introduction is required
> At Poole's, before they'll take your trade.
> No common people are desired,
> However promptly bills are paid.
> Yet my bill shows, 'mong other things,
> 'Discount (for cash) fifteen per cent.'
> Oh, can it be that, sometimes, kings
> Are – shall we call it 'negligent'?
> Some several things about this bill
> Lend me to ponder and to muse;
> Such names – the Emperor of Brazil,
> 'The Emperor of the French' – they use.

Above
Howard Cundey, autocrat of Edwardian Savile Row. The limitations of the era's tailoring show in the clumsy cut of his coat.

Though once those names great lustre shed,
Deposed, deceased, forgot are they;
And Poole, himself, I'm told, is dead.

The loss of the Prince was hardly missed in the continuing crush of potentates of every stripe. Indian princes like the Maharajas of Mysore and Cooch Behar were a feature of the 1880s and so was an increasing accumulation of moneyed Americans, like L. L. Lorillard, William Randolph Hearst and Cornelius Vanderbilt. Under Howard Cundey, the business went into a period of futher expansion, with branches opening in Vienna and Berlin. The sporting image fell away as the sober uniforms of commerce took precedence and widening fame inspired imitation; firms as far afield as New South Wales were claiming some sort of affiliation, and some even used the name of Poole.

It has been said that Henry Poole's legacy was to halt the march of men's fashion, that he drained the colour from the styles that d'Orsay's clique had made fashionable, but left styles untouched (one consequence being modern formal wear, which was correct only for funerals in the pre-Poole age). Henry Poole 'petrified and embalmed the mode which he found,' wrote Macandrew in *The Prince of Tailors*:

> After which, he locked Tailordom itself in a Sleeping Beauty spell. The exterior of each tailoring house, said Henry Poole, should proclaim the good manners within. A man's tailor should be to him as his family solicitor, or his doctor; he should drop in casually as into his club. Eschew, therefore, all advertisement, gold letters, window displays. For a bespoke tailor the correct form is opaque glass windows, dimness.

Below
The Map Room at No. 1 Savile Row, where the great journeys of Victorian exploration were planned and Livingstone's body lay in state.

The mode was an expression of the mood of the time - part reaction to years of licence and extravagance, mostly the puritanical reflection of a new world where success was associated with the sombre shades of smoke and grime. Besides, dry cleaning was still being invented; as the soot settled thicker by the year, who wanted cream trousers? From the 1850s onwards, well-tailored quality cloth in sober colours became the ideal and flashy dressing was increasingly suspect. Disraeli and Dickens cut a dash for a while, but by the 1870s they, too, were conforming. By then black had seeped down to the working classes, who adopted it for their Sunday best. The Hyde Park parade continued, but to veterans like Gronow it was, by the late 1860s, a 'hazy, grey, coal-darkened' backdrop for the 'shabby-genteel' display of a sadly reduced Society.

It irritated some that 'the vulgar' could dress like the nobility and a flood of dress regulations and complicated rituals of etiquette were introduced to deter social climbers. There were also rebels like Oscar Wilde who fought almost from the outset against the funereal look. Wilde appeared at the Royal Academy private view – a fashion frolic on Savile Row's doorstep - in proper black frock coat and silk top hat, but with hair down to his neck and a lily in his buttonhole. By the 1880s, he was campaigning to no avail for a return to the cavalier look: wide hat, cloak and knee-breeches. He, too, submitted to Savile Row orthodoxy in the end. One who did not was George Bernard Shaw, who became a disciple of Dr Gustav Jaeger, the German zoologist who thought trousers and socks were bad for the circulation and preached the health benefits of perspiring under thick wool. Dr Jaeger's 'Sanitary Woollen System' had a fad following in the 1880s and a small shop was opened in Princes Street – Savile Row territory – to sell his curious all-wool garments, but Shaw was among the very few to persist in wearing them.

Savile Row itself was steadily evolving, with clubs springing up in some of the gentry's old homes. No. 17 housed the Ethnological Society for twenty years, then was briefly the offices of London University and then the Burlington Fine Arts Club. No. 15 was the first home of the Savile Club, whose members were described by Oscar Wilde as 'true democrats . . . because they cannot muster a sovereign between them'. Robert Louis Stevenson was a prominent member and was the inadvertent cause of the ruin of Sidney Colvin, Keeper of Prints and Drawings at the British Museum. Colvin was passing in a

Above
Oscar Wilde backed the dress reformers as he sought 'a notable and joyous dress for men', but he submitted to Savile Row orthodoxy in the end.

Above Left
Stanley meeting Livingstone. Savile Row, I presume?

Below
The Maharajah of Cooch Behar, a splendid clothes-horse who favoured Poole and Davies with his trade.

Above
Poole's at its Augustan peak – but the Row was rarely as sedate as this.

hansom cab when he remembered that Stevenson was due back from abroad. He stepped inside after telling the cab to wait, but got caught up in the occasion; by the time he remembered the cab, it had gone, and with it a priceless collection of Italian drawings that had been in his safe-keeping. Restitution had to be made and Colvin was in debt for the rest of his life.

The New University Club was quartered at No. 1 Savile Row and was succeeded by the Royal Geographical Society, which stayed there through much of exploration's heroic period. The courtyard was glassed over to create a map room and it was here, in April 1874, that the body of David Livingstone lay in state before burial in Westminster Abbey. The map room has been lovingly restored by Gieves & Hawkes, who now use it as their ready-to-wear department: if modern economics force occasional compromise with bespoke ideals, then here it is done with commendable swagger.

The explorers made full use of their tailor neighbours when readying for the great expeditions. History suggests otherwise, but Dr Livingstone's response to Henry Stanley's celebrated salutation might well have been 'Savile Row, I presume?' Stanley's preparations for his rescue mission included visits to at least two tailors and legend has it that when he finally caught up with Livingstone, he was wearing a belted poncho – forerunner of the raincoat – by Poole. The doctor would have recognized good tailoring – his uniform came from Gieves.

In his book, *How I Found Livingstone*, Stanley puts in a plug for another celebrated Savile Row name. He writes: 'The first words I heard in Ugogo were from a Wogogo, who in an indolent way tended the flocks, but showed a marked interest in the stranger clad in white flannels, with a Hawkes patent cork solar topee on his head, a most unusual thing in Ugogo.'

This was the civilian version of the Hawkes Wolseley Helmet, first used by a British army under Lord Napier in the Abyssinian campaign of 1867, when it proved an immensely versatile sunshade. 'The troops found it most useful for watering their horses when their buckets were

Above
Regent Street at the start of the season:
crowds outside the shawl emporium.

lost or unobtainable,' the manufacturer noted with satisfaction. Hawkes was then run by Henry Thomas White, a nephew of old Thomas Hawkes. White was handed the prototype topee (a helmet of cork held together by a rubber solution) by a stranger who walked into the Piccadilly shop. Details of the inventor and his reward, if any, have been lost, but the Hawkes white hat (or solar topee) soon became a must for the colonial adventurer and the firm was able to boast how 'all the leading stores of India, Ceylon and the Straits Settlements stock them, not forgetting that emporium which every traveller to the East has visited, Simon Artz in Port Said'.

The pace of exploration eventually obliged the Geographical Society to find larger premises and, in 1912, Hawkes bought No. 1 Savile Row for £38,000. That was £23,500 more than the Society had paid for it in 1868, the seller then being another tailor, H. J. and B. Nicholl.

Why Nicholl chose to own No. 1 for five years in the 1860s without using it is a mystery, though it may have been intended by Henry John Nicholl as a private residence. In contrast to the largely traditional grandeur of Poole, Nicholl was the most innovative in marketing terms. From 1846 it operated in splendid, high-vaulted premises at 114-20 Regent Street, with an exterior festooned with royal coats of arms. Chandeliers were suspended over the large open showroom and spiral stairways led up to twin galleries. Nicholl could lay claim to being the first multiple tailor, since it had two London shops and branches in Liverpool and Manchester. Although basically a men's bespoke shop, it had a ladies department that did far more than hoist Society Dianas aboard a Bucephalus; riding habits were only part of a range that extended from the 'charming and coquettish Zouave Morning Jacket' to the first fitted fur garment, a sealskin cloak 'so very rich and costly that the price, which is of necessity high, cannot be regretted'. In its advertising copy, Nicholl was also much ahead of its time. Nicholl stayed in Regent Street until bought out by Burton after World War II.

The first of the old Savile Row houses to be reconstructed with tailoring in mind was No. 15, which by 1882 was too small for the Savile Club. The ghosts of Lady Suffolk, Lord Northwick, the Dowager Countess of Clare, the Hon. William Gordon and other former residents had to move their haunts as the building came down and a new one erected with ground floor and basement specifically designed for use by the tailor, Strickland & Sons, which still has a corner of 15 Savile Row today.

Before such drastic alteration became possible, a tailor taking a lease in the neighbourhood was not allowed even to put in a shop window, but had to maintain the existing private house frontage – and Strickland's lease contained clauses against such social outrages as tradesmen using the front entrance. With the 1880s, partial or complete reconstructions at odds with the Burlingtonian style began to occur, while solicitors offices, hotels and lodging houses joined the clubs, surgeries and tailor shops.

Life among the tailors through the second half of the nineteenth century comes vividly to life in the private diaries of Jeannette Marshall, daughter of an eminent anatomist, who was born at No.10 Savile Row in 1855 and grew up with a front parlour view of Poole's progress directly across the street. Dr John Marshall was a friend of the painter Ford Madox Brown (he let Brown into University College Hospital to draw corpses) and the Pre-Raphaelites. Dr Marshall was a Poole customer, not quite of celebrity rank. There is a fascinating description of his purchase from Poole of a 'Court dress of great gorgeousness' and his subsequent preparations for a royal reception: he lunched and dressed in front of a specially lit bedroom fire, then came downstairs, 'rather nervous and amused and yet rather gratified too', in full rig, including black silk stockings, shining shoes and cocked hat under his arm. The servants, Jeannette noted, were 'vastly amused'.

Jeannette was the eldest of four Marshall children. Nicknamed 'Sunshine' as a child, she grew up tall, slim and strong-willed; her diarized thoughts and observations as she followed a ritualistic round of visiting, shopping, church-going and Continental travel – and husband-hunting – are the subject of a book by Zuzanna Shonfield.

Daily walks were an important part of life for the Marshall ladies, mother and daughters, and involved a complicated hopscotch around forbidden zones that varied according to the time of day. The 'heavenly' Burlington Arcade was a favourite morning short-cut to Piccadilly, but forbidden from lunch on, since loose women might be about and it was possible for a lady to be molested. Jeannette wrote of a trip to a bootman in St Martin's Lane taking them 'into the unhallowed region of the Clubs' and the region to the south of Piccadilly Circus was best traversed at a brisker pace. Regent Street was the focus of shopping, but the warren of streets beyond, and the lanes and courts that separated it from Savile Row, were out of bounds. North of Savile Row, the terrain was deemed safe and an expedition would usually return through Savile Place, the tunnelled way with tiny shops that led from Mill, Maddox and Conduit Streets until demolished in the 1930s.

Men were the main hazard – not errand boys or tradesmen, who could be ignored, but 'gentlemen' who filled the West End in the afternoons. As recently as the 1950s, prostitutes thronged the Piccadilly Circus area and something similar seems to have prevailed a century earlier. Even the genteel Burlington Arcade was not free from sin, for the upper chambers of the little shops offered opportunities for assignation and at least one bonnet shop served as a front for a brothel. It was stated by the social investigator Henry Mayhew that 'men of position who wished to avoid publicity in their amours dreaded being

Above
The Marshalls' neighbours at No. 12 were the Grotes: he was an eminent historian and she an eminent hostess whose guests included Chopin and singer Jenny Lind. George Grote died from a chill caught while sitting for a portrait by Millais – he was too polite to ask whether he could put on an overcoat.

seen in the vicinity of the Arcade at certain hours'. Girls from Kate Hamilton's night-house near the Haymarket used to haunt the Arcade at certain times, according to Mayhew, 'ready at a given signal to dart into a nearby shop whose upper floors had rooms furnished to their taste and for their purpose'. The Marshall ladies timed their Arcade rambling for the mornings only.

Questions in this regard even have to be asked of certain of the tailors. They did not come more distinguished than Davies, a choice of prime ministers since Sir Robert Peel took his custom to Hanover Street in the 1820s; the shop was expanded in 1830 and became as popular a VIP rendezvous as any club or coffee house. By 1850, a policy of providing every possible facility led to the provision on the top floor of guest bedrooms for customers, with, it was said, 'a discreet eye turned to the ladies who accompanied them'.

The tailor-designer Tom Gilbey has a theory which he believes explains the multiplicity of fittings and general client fastidiousness that distinguished the classic era of Savile Row tailoring. The fitting, he maintains, was used as a cover for activities of a still more personal nature. 'It was a gentleman's world, a gentleman's club,' says Gilbey with a shrug. 'So they had twenty fittings with their tailor . . . and in the back, or round the corner, would be something else – in lots of cases that's where all these dozens of fittings came from.' Gilbey is based in New Burlington Street, but used to have his shop in Sackville Street, at an address that was once the headquarters of the Masini Brothers, who controlled the seedier West End clubs of forty years ago. It was thinking about the Masinis that led to his radical theory of a Savile Row underside. Gilbey, the iconoclast, sees something in tailoring that appeals to the underworld; to the Mafia, for instance, and he cites 'those Chicago gangsters like Al Capone in the tailor's shop, with all the action out at the back'.

Below
Poole illuminations to mark a visit of Louis Napoleon and Eugénie. The great gas shows marked all royal occasions and drew immense crowds.

Whatever the circumstances of the 1870s, the Marshall ladies were taking no chances with their reputation. However short the distance, it was improper for social calls to be undertaken on foot, so these were timed for days when Dr Marshall could spare the coach and horses. Traffic jams were far worse and accidents more common than anything experienced today: with no traffic laws and no one to regulate the surge of carriages, it could take the Marshalls an hour to return home from Bond Street, two blocks away, or three-quarters of an hour to drive to the Piccadilly entrance of the Royal Academy, a one-minute walk away. The diaries record scores of accidents, including one in which the Marshall coach ran over an elderly pedestrian, and another when their coachman got drunk and drove into a post in Bond Street. Winter compounded the dangers; thick smoke-charged fogs could last for months – one extended from October 1873 to February 1874 – and snow or frost brought havoc. Only main arteries like Regent Street were cleared and all the Burlington streets could become impassable, even when long-headed nails were driven into the horses' shoes.

Noise and smell assailed the senses with equal ferocity. The accepted image of Savile Row in its Victorian heyday – 'quiet, respectable, ordered . . . the dearth of traffic, the lack of bustle, the gentle acknowledgement of manners and leisured culture,' is how the *Tailor and Cutter* saw it – is how it never was. Smell was not a subject for polite discussion, though Jeannette regularly alludes to green water aromas. Shonfield sums up: 'The ubiquitous horse dung, effluents from drains during excavations and from open hallways and areas, the reek of cabbage and mutton from kitchens ventilating into front areas, all added up to a curious offensive urban stench, from which there was no escape even at home, for it floated through open windows and every crack in the woodwork.' Deoderants were unknown and body (and clothes) cleaning more perfunctory, so that the pretty phials of smelling salts carried by ladies become understandable. Some, like Jeannette's music teacher, wore gauze-masked respirators to filter out the worst of the sooty, sulphuric stench.

As for noise, Sundays were a blessed relief from the drumming of hooves on the granite road pavings, the cries of street vendors and the constant rap of the telegraph boys who substituted for the telephone. The arrival of electricity brought a generating plant to the rear of Savile Row that thudded and belched smoke and fumes night and day, until Dr Marshall and other residents managed in 1882 to force a shutdown at 2 a.m.

At regular intervals, blazing gaslight would draw a surging throng into Savile Row. These were the nights of the Illuminations, occasions like royal birthdays and weddings, when businesses and clubs throughout the West End 'prepared demonstrations of satisfaction by illuminating their premises' and Prince of Wales's feathers and similar devices glowed all over the place. When Princess Louise married the Duke of Fife, for example, Meyer & Mortimer was aglow with the Garter star and the words 'long may they live', while Scott Adie on the corner of Vigo Street boasted a giant thistle, with a gas jet spurting from every spine. Poole's displays were considered the best in London and the crush of spectators was so great that the firm had to pay for extra police, who were entertained to rollicking cheese-and-pickle supper parties in the cutting room after the lights were doused. On such occasions, £300 worth of gaslight 'streamed and transformed the shop into a genie's palace, while the exterior glowed with a quasi-Renaissance opulence'. Poole's device was said to have cost £2,000, with effects which varied according to the occasion. For Princess Louise's wedding, 'at each side was a transparency of a crystal shield, bearing the royal arms, with crown surrounded by large wreaths of

thistles; in the centre an oval, backed by trophies of banners, and bearing the initials, doubled and reversed'. The night was calm, 'so there was no disagreeable flaring or blowing out of gas'.

Up to the 1880s, the houses of the Burlington streets were uniformly Georgian and, like the Marshalls' 1720s home, three or four storeys high, with the kitchen in the basement. A fashion for bright colours enlivened many of the house-fronts. The Marshalls' colour scheme, selected by Ford Madox Brown, was of grey-green stucco, set off by white and brown window-frames and ironwork, with gilt-lined balcony railings. Blue-and-white-tiled window-boxes were stuffed full of geraniums, fuchsias, lobelias, calceolaris and trailing ivy.

Jeannette was playing the piano early in 1877 when she became aware of 'a strange phenomenon' emanating from across the street in Poole's counting-house. 'The clerks etc. are visible fr. the drawing room, so I suppose we are ditto ditto to them,' she related in her diary. 'As soon as ever I sit down to play, some man over there gets up, comes to the window and gazes for a quarter of an hour together. Sometimes he varies the entertainment by waving about a sheet of paper. What he means I don't know. Possibly he is demented. Of course I appear totally unaware of his manoeuvres.'

However, she obviously studied him closely: 'He is tall, rather thin, dark, with brown hair cut short, and reddish whiskers and moustache. Neither ugly nor handsome.' She put him at around thirty-five to forty years old and concluded that he was a senior clerk. The admiring stares and signals continued through the spring and summer, until the show was interrupted when the Marshalls' venetian blinds were lowered in the hot weather. Jeannette told her diary that it was a great relief: 'It is wretchede not to be able to look at a passing vehicle without finding a pr. of admiring optics fixed on one.'

In late August, a fat letter arrived at No. 10: 'What should it be, by all that's horrible, but an offer fr. that wretch over the way!' An 'astonished' Jeannette looked at the signature – 'Edward Saltwell' – and handed it to her mother, 'who read it out loud among the horror stricken exclamations of the victim, and the roars of the whole family'. The letter was then shown to Dr Marshall, who put it in a fresh envelope with a note to Saltwell saying, 'Sir, I have read, and return you the enclosed communication, and beg that you will send no other.'

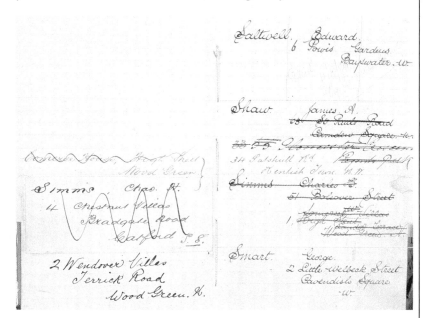

Left
Staff ledger records the lovelorn Saltwell's death. Customers received the same unsentimental treatment.

Saltwell contined to gaze adoringly across the mighty social divide of doctor's daughter and tailor's clerk. Once she saw 'the Horror' at the corner of Regent and New Burlington Street – 'He evidently saw me as he was crimson . . . . I crossed the road with one bound, narrowly escaping being run over by a passing hansom.' Two years later, Saltwell tried again, this time enclosing his letter to Jeannette in another to her mother, asking that she read and destroy Jeannette's letter if she felt that anything in it would cause her daughter to 'grieve'. Dr Marshall responded with a 'perfectly plain and dignified threat of legal proceedings should Jeannette be molested any more. This brought an apology from Saltwell, who promised to do his best, but occasional lovelorn glances from the counting-house feature in the diaries for four more years.

Jeannette Marshall eventually married the Medical Officer of Health for Surrey. Poole's records show that Edward Saltwell committed suicide on 11 August 1883. It is unlikely that Jeannette was ever aware of this fact.

7

Swank and Sweat:
The Duke of York's Trousers

The headline in *Lloyd's Weekly London Newspaper* of 11 September 1892 was modest in size, but not in impact: 'THE DUKE OF YORK'S TROWSERS MADE IN A FEVER ROOM.' Next day *The Star* felt it had the whole story: 'GARMENTS FOR PRINCES AND PEERS MADE AT SWEATING RATES IN CROWDED TENEMENTS WHERE FEVER LURKS.' It was Savile Row's most embarrassing moment.

There was no stopping the tumbling headlines. The Prince of Wales himself was said to be alarmed and to have summoned his tailors to Marlborough House. Soon there were follow-up horrors: a riding habit made in a fever den had allegedly killed a daughter of Sir Robert Peel and the late Duke of Clarence was, the press hinted, the victim of a diseased double-breasted jacket.

Opponents of sweating, the treadmill production system that had enslaved thousands of tailors and their families, had found the perfect means of shock attack. Miss Fanny Hicks, a tailoress, dropped her bombshell at the Trades Congress in Glasgow. She had been working for a Savile Row subcontractor making trousers for the Duke of York when two children living in the building caught a fever and one died. Subsequently she let it be known that waistcoats for the Prince of Wales and a further consignment of eighteen pairs of trousers destined for the Duke of Connaught and the aforementioned unfortunate Duke of Clarence had been made in the same place. It had the makings of a gorgeous scandal and the papers played it for all it was worth.

Sweating – 'as Victorian as railroads and the music hall' – can be traced back to home workshops set up to meet the huge demand for uniforms during the Napoleonic Wars, but it was after the collapse of the tailors' unions in 1834 that sweating (the polite euphemism was 'outworking') began to spread as a malignancy. Though allied in theory to the old cottage industry, in which a family would apply their labour on a piecework basis, sweating was employment at second, or sometimes third hand, with subcontracting middlemen squeezing the life out of their worker-victims. The elite employers around Savile Row did not set out to exploit, but the temptation of cheap services was hard to resist. 'Do you think I should be such a fool as to send my trade out if I could get it made as cheap indoors?' a Conduit Street tailor expostulated in 1866. That was the year that Henry Poole was startled to find that he had a strike on his hands. It was also the year that the *Tailor and Cutter* was founded.

Poole, by virtue of its size and status, became a forcing ground for issues. Henry at first tried bullying tactics, but then settled upon a compromise formula that combined the piecework principal with a guaranteed minimum rate of 6d an hour. He also threw in the sweetener of two sewing machines – new-fangled contraptions that he had vowed never to accept. The other masters grouped around him

Above
The Duke of Clarence with his fiancée, later Queen Mary. Did a diseased double-breasted jacket spell his doom?

69

and the workers regrouped under a national movement for another test of strength within the year, with Poole again a focus of the struggle. This round went to the masters, as a prolonged lock-out culminated in the conviction of three workers on conspiracy charges.

Above
Contemporary depiction of a sweating den, by H. H. Flere.

Poole by that time was employing 500 people at the height of the season, according to union reckoning, but the actual staff was only a fraction of this. Wage books going back to 1857 indicate a three-tier system of employment: a core of salaried workers based at Savile Row, backed up by a large number of sewing tailors paid by the piece and mostly located in the firm's workshops at Savile Row, Clifford Street and Kingly Street in Soho; these, in turn, were augmented by a shifting force of outworkers based in their own homes or in the workshops of subcontractors. The wage books indicate a constant salaried complement of around eighty-five throughout the latter part of the nineteenth century. At the apex was the cutting-room staff, a third of the total and many of them earning more than £5 a week. The counting-house employed about a dozen, the showroom ten, packing and portering another twenty. The top cutters and salesmen received a 5/8 per cent commission, which elevated senior cutter Garwood Dent to a lordly £948 and senior salesman David Belinfante to £748 in 1890. The porters were lowest paid at an average of 30s a week. As a clerk, the hapless Saltwell would have been making maybe £3 10s. With a holiday bonus and a pension for long-service, a permanent post at Poole's must have been the envy of the ordinary sewing tailor, for whom there seems to have been no place.

'The treasures of the British Museum, the Art Collection at the National Gallery, and even the Natural History specimens at South Kensington have less attraction for the young man of sartorial

aspirations than this home of the highest class tailoring in the West-End' – such was the sort of write-up Poole was getting by the 1890s. It had twelve cutters, each with his own customers and his own journeymen to make up his garments. The sculptured image of the Prince of Wales's feather emblem and other coats of arms stood guard over the Italianate exterior and similar emblems woven into the carpeting carried the imperial theme within. It was a place 'where even princes might be seen without loss of dignity in a forward baist [half-finished garment],' the *Tailor and Cutter* marvelled. A few doors away, the livery department had a high-tech allure, with customers able to see the men at work – without themselves being seen – through an arrangement of mirrors, while speaking tubes kept the cutters in touch with their men. The counting-house offered another sort of grandeur. It was arranged like a bank, with thirty 1,000-page ledgers arrayed around the wall in alphabetical order, and an impressive counter.

Tours stopped there. Visits to Kingly Street, the Poole workshop in nearby Soho, were actively discouraged. It was no sweatshop, but neither was it a feature of the atelier of princes that the princes needed to know about. Kingly Street housed about seventy journeymen on four floors. Trouser-makers on the bottom, above them coat and vest hands, then coat hands and, on the top, breeches and more trouser hands. The iron-heating stoves burned coke and the rooms were a fair size so that the place was considered healthier than other workshops, especially in the top room, which had roof ventilators.

The men squatted cross-legged on the floor, twenty or more to a room. The workshop opened at 6 a.m. and closed at 7 p.m., except in summer, when the men worked until it was dark. There were two 'trotters' to fetch and carry work and a timekeeper, who registered the work and kept out strangers. A freelance messenger, living on tips, cleaned the men's boots and fetched the beer, usually bringing in fresh supplies at 10 in the morning, 1 p.m. and 5 p.m. Some of the men used the stoves to cook on. Drinking water came from a tap where they cooled their irons. The sanitary arrangements were primitive, just some urinal troughs and three seats open to view.

Sometimes there would be spontaneous singing, and an evangelist might come by to read from the Bible and preach temperance. The only organized entertainment was a midsummer 'bean-feast', when the firm donated money for the men to hold a dinner among themselves. Each man gave a penny every Saturday to a hospital fund, but there was no organized sickness or other benefit scheme. Pay day was Saturday, with the men usually finishing in the early afternoon. 'I must say it's a splendid shop for money, if you can turn out the work,' one worker told an investigator of the time. In the busy season, a trouser hand could average 42s a week and a coat hand about 63s. Two-thirds of the hands were let go in the off-season and only the best retained.

To provide succour and wholesome encouragement, there was the *Tailor and Cutter* and the quaint little Scots gentlewoman who financed its launch, Angelica Patience Fraser. With the first issue it proclaimed itself 'a powerful auxiliary to the many noble efforts which are being made towards the amelioration of our trade from the degraded position it has hitherto occupied'. It was priced at tuppence and reduced to a penny from the second issue.

The *Tailor and Cutter* evolved out of the protest tracts of a Scottish do-gooder and tailoring technician named John Williamson; by the time it died in the 1970s, it had become the most-quoted trade paper in the world and Savile Row's unquestioned voice and arbiter. It started in a Drury Lane office rented for 6s a week, then moved to Gerrard

Portrait of a Man, by Giovani Battista
Moroni. This sixteenth-century Italian
painting became familiar as the emblem
of the *Tailor and Cutter*, being
reproduced in every edition.

Street in Soho, where its neighbour was the notorious '43 Club', run by
Mrs 'Ma' Merrick, who achieved the distinction of marrying three
daughters into the peerage before going to prison.

In the early years, it was a technical journal laced with admonition,
stern encouragement and helpful adverts for patent needles,
consumption remedies, artificial teeth ('5s a tooth, self-adhesive') and
literature ('Overcrowding, its Evils and its Remedy'. One shilling.
Longman, Green & Co.). The prose is pontifical and humourless,
sometimes hilariously so, but Williamson had grown morose in
contemplating the evils of the trade and the weaknesses of its
practitioners. 'Long and irregular hours, together with the irregularity
of the trade itself, has gradually come to engross the thoughts, energies
of the whole man, while the cultivation of his mental faculties, as also
his home and social instincts have been neglected,' he wrote in 1872.
'Two hours in the cricket field woud prove a perfect cure for the chest
diseases and complaints so frequently manifest . . . or for the family
man to be able to go home at a reasonable hour so that husband and
wife may fulfil their natural and proper functions in the exercise of
their mutual sympathy.'

A year later, he was in despair:

> The trade is in a CHRONIC STATE of decomposition and decay. By
> the term trade we embrace all classes: the highest and the lowest; the

male and female; the aristocrat and the slopper; the most servile unionist and the lowest form of sweaters; those who are employed in the highest sections of the trade and those miserable mortals wallowing in squalor and degradation, struggling for bare existence by making overcoats for the Police . . . .

To versify his feelings, he had John King, the tailor poet, write in the first issue:

See: the star of freedom dawning.
Workmen only wait awhile.
Stand,
Fearless every danger scorning,
Then on you its light will smile.

Left
Continuity is assured as three generations work side by side in the cutting room at Poole's. Back in 1890, head cutter Garwood Dent made a comparatively princely £948, mostly from a ⅝ per cent commission on the garments he cut.

Not that the victims were mollycoddled. Correspondence was encouraged, but not criticism. Reader 'Mac', who had dared question an article, was told : 'Egotistical and cynical insinuations are invariably prompted by vanity, arising from a disorganized state of the nervous system, operating on an ill-balanced mind. We can believe that you looked at the article and probably read it, too, without comprehending it; your mind glided over the surface without conveying to the mental faculties a perception of the leading element permeating the writer's thoughts.' Reader 'Willie' was told: 'You are a little too conceited and opinionated; a week in the cutting room would lower you several degrees on the ladder of fame.'

One sin was abhorred above all others:

We have frequently seen a great deal of mischief done by the introduction of ale in the workshops. The vile custom should be speedily put down and there is no doubt that this could be accomplished if masters and foremen were a little more on the alert. Tailors, as a rule, are an intelligent class of people, but unfortunately we too often find the most learned among them to be the greatest profligates . . . is it not astonishing that despite the most assiduous cultivation on the part of the steady portion of tailors, some are found stubbornly ignorant and devote all their spare time to ribaldry and drunkenness?

That was in 1869. Three years on, Williamson was no less obsessed: 'The very abundant use made of strong drink has introduced into the ranks of journeyman tailors a class of men which has brought the more respectable body of journeyman tailors into much disrepute with the general public.'

Drink was, and remains, a tailoring problem. Some perfectly respectable master tailors with eminent clientele will 'go on the cod' with single-minded determination during a slack period and at least one substantial firm on Savile Row itself was all but destroyed by the 'Guv'nor's' alcoholism in very recent years. The tailors themselves suggest various reasons, which could all apply to other trades, but is it possible that the persistence of the house-of-call system through many generations and the grim conditions of nineteenth-century workshops unconsciously influence group habits to this day?

A hundred years ago, one person believed she had the answer and launched a crusade of such energy that some still talk of her Mill Street Mission as though it was yesterday. This was Angelica Patience Fraser, the Florence Nightingale of tailordom. Having suffered an unhappy love affair when young, Miss Fraser for no clear reason decided to dedicate her life to saving tailors. A tiny figure under ubiquitous bonnet, Miss Fraser arrived from Edinburgh after achieving the religious conversion of Donald Macallan, 'the infidel tailor' whose leadership of 'free-thinkers', secularists and socialists' in the Scottish capital had disturbed the godly.* In 1875 she began religious readings in the workshops around Savile Row, at the same time recruiting the help of the touring American evangelists Moody and Sankey. The Tailors Prayer Union and Total Abstinence Society was created, then its brother organization, The Tailors Evangelistic Deputation. Miss Fraser's main concern was the annual spring migration to the West End of hundreds of young country tailors. In March 1880 she called a conference in the Burlington Hall – site of the evil Lord Barrymore's theatricals – and then began regular meetings in the heart of Soho, home ground of the 'Carnaby boys', the old-style drinking tailors who lounged about the rougher pubs beyond Regent Street. As speakers, she invited divines and paragons such as Mark Knowles, a cripple who had risen from shoe-shop assistant to barrister.

The Fraser family organ was brought down from Scotland along with the Prince Consort's bed, so named for the honour bestowed upon it and upon the Fraser family by Albert himself (since when it had never been slept in). Thus armed, and boosted by a turn-out of 600 for a tailors-against-drink rally, Miss Fraser in 1885 founded the Tailors Institute in Mill Street, a few steps from Savile Row.

The cottage-like premises at 13 Mill Street became home to the 238 pledge-takers of the Total Abstinence Society, the workshop-touring gospel readers and the Mill Street Band of Hope, while weaker elements of tailoring society were encouraged to attend classes in a wide range of subjects or to use the reading room, which was open from 11 a.m. to 11 p.m., and all for an annual subscription of 4s. Miss Fraser raised £1,000 in six months to pay for it. When she approached Poole for £100, that cagey company replied that it would be 'more beneficial to the object in view to give a donation of £20, to be repeated each year the firm continued to approve of the scheme and that it appears to be succeeding in its design'. Poole kept contributing until World War I emptied the Institute.

Miss Fraser was accident-prone, a condition believed by some to be caused by 'the absorption of her mind and thought'. One day, when a

Above
Angelica Patience Fraser, the tailors' Florence Nightingale. Florence herself was headquartered nearby, in General Wade's old home, by then an hotel.

---

* As a high union official, Macallan provided much support for Miss Fraser, who kept his letters but ordered them to be burned after her death. Her biographer, W. G. Askew, performed the incineration and writes how he 'reluctantly consigns these outpourings of an honest soul to the flames and as he does so he fancies the smoke of them ascending as incense to the heavens where both these departed souls are sure to dwell'.

trap door in the reading room was left open, she disappeared into the coal cellar. When found by the caretaker, she was kneeling on a pile of coal, giving thanks to God. Such faith bore results, for the great Humanitarian Upsurge was underway and for every missionary saving souls in Africa, there was another eager to confront degradation at home. Social reform was in, and an 1883 pamphlet, *The Bitter Cry of Outcast London*, inspired an army of investigators to uncover every last morbidly fascinating detail of sweating.

Waves of Irish and Jewish emigration, increased use of female labour and a trend towards sectionalized garment-making had served the sweaters well. Some of the best West End bespoke firms had opened storage and distribution centres in the East End, while others used middlemen to tap the cheap labour sources. The system fed on itself, with some journeymen becoming sweating masters themselves; numbers of West End journeymen left the trade altogether and sought work in the docks. Tom Hood's 'Song of the Shirt' ('Work, work, work, till the brain begins to swim; work, work, work, till the eyes are heavy and dim . . .') was the anthem of the reformers, who competed over the horror stories, such as the tale of the distraught woman suffering from double vision, who believed that God had taken pity on her by enabling her to double her work.

Matters came to a head in 1888, when the House of Lords held committee hearings to investigate sweating. Poole, a focus as ever, sharply cut its reliance on outwork in the course of the hearings. Whatever faults that might have existed were put down to foreman error and a suitably villainous scapegoat was found in the person of one Vantini, an Italian living in Gerrard Street, a sweater of young girls. Witnesses credited Vantini with making £2,000 a year out of supplying Poole with trousers; he was said to receive 5s 6d from Poole and to pay the girls 1s 3d; another version had him paying the girls 5s a week. Vantini 'did not work', the committee under Lord Dunraven was told. 'All he did was walk about and boss the girls.'

Poole picked up some praise for putting its house in order. 'If all the other great firms mentioned would do the same, great assistance would be given in solving the problem of the sweating system,' the committee was told. Nevertheless, it was made clear that all the 'great firms' had

Above
Temperance meeting in the Exeter Hall, scene of Miss Fraser's annual rallies. Speakers were sandwiched between concert turns, 'and woe betide the artist who would seek to leave the hall without listening to the address', her biographer wrote.

become increasingly reliant upon sweating and the laughter that greeted one witness who questioned the origin of some of their lordships' expensive waistcoats had to be a little rueful. Conditions were such that a man was obliged to be a sweater or submit to being sweated on by someone else, one witness who sweated for Nicholl told the enquiry. He spoke of payment as low as 5d for a garment, with the worker having to pay for his own thread out of this.

Above
Site of the *Tailor and Cutter* and its tailoring academy is now a Chinese food store.

Above Right
This Carnaby Street workroom has been occupied by tailors since the sweating era. The cheery atmosphere under current guv'nor Brian Staples would have startled his Victorian predecessors.

The sweatshops were supposedly breeding grounds for vice, through their use of large numbers of women. The street-walkers of Oxford and Regent Streets were tailoresses 'whose minds had been poisoned by the indecent conversations carried on in the workrooms', their lordships were told. The sexism and racism that such cut-throat competition fostered was much in evidence in the displays of emnity towards women and all those deemed foreign. It was stated that girls could live more cheaply than men 'because they can do without so-called luxuries'. One witness was praised because his 'physique and respectable dress contrasted most strikingly with the appearance of the foreign sweaters'.

The Lords condemned sweating and, while this did not lead to immediate measures, the workers gained heart and began patching up ethnic and other differences. By 1891 they were on strike and the masters were on the defensive. The call was for improved working conditions and a uniform system of payment for all. Changing times were evident in the languages of some of the speeches – German, French, Yiddish – at a strike rally in Hyde Park.

The men made their headquarters at the Crown in Heddon Street, right behind Savile Row, while the nervous masters conferred round the corner at Poole's, where a mood of conciliation was set by the chairman Howard Cundey, who impressed the *Tailor and Cutter* as 'a fine speciman of a West-End gentleman . . . light moustache and a fine head of jetblack hair . . . clearly well fitted to take a leading part in public affairs'. Poole, once more, was in command. The masters agreed to talk and, by the end of June, they had accepted a uniform payment system based on a complicated log of rates and hours for every element of every item of clothing. They fudged on the working conditions issue, but won praise from some of the strike leaders. It was said that they 'took their beating like gentlemen'.

Three of the six signatories for the masters headed firms that still exist in some form today – Poole, Davies and Meyer & Mortimer. Bands and banners led the men from Heddon Street to a victory meeting in Exeter Hall, where efforts by some of the smaller firms to scotch the deal were stamped on by Cundey. The Universal Time Log for London came into force on Saturday, 4 July 1891.

The log remains, in a somewhat notional form, the basis of work-payment to this day, though haggling over the details almost led to a breakdown the following year. By August 1892 a union drive against outwork and employer irritation over the 'vexatious demands that usually usher in the busy season' culminated in an attempt at a national lock-out. London journeymen rallied to support their provincial brethren and a press report on 31 August alluded to a union warning of the danger of infectious diseases being spread by home-produced garments.

The trap was sprung twelve days later at the Trades Congress in Glasgow. In moving a resolution on outwork, Fanny Hicks said she was surprised that nothing had been done to make employers responsible for the sanitary conditions of domestic workshops. Then she casually mentioned the fever lurking near the Duke of York's trousers. When the clothes of royalty and the aristocracy were made under such conditions, how did people suppose the clothes of working people were made, she wanted to know.

So did the masses when the news broke next day. Revelling in the lifting of 'the curtain of mystery' surrounding such matters, *The Star* expostulated: 'We now know that the tailor who clothes the extremities of members of the blood royal sends the garments out to the tailoresses just as if they were suits from the windows of the ready-made shops, there to take their chance of picking up any stray fever germs that may be floating about.'

Miss Hicks gave the name of the Duke's tailor 'in confidence' to reporters, thereby ensuring maximum publicity for this juicy detail. It was none other than the venerable Davies & Son, who put up a stout defence. Yes, it admitted to sending out royal as well as other work, but it drew attention to a notice, dated 1839 and stating: 'Workpeople are requested to immediately inform the Cashier of any case of ILLNESS ARISING IN THEIR HOMES. The firm will undertake that they are at no loss by so doing.'

The workperson in question was identified as a Mr Granfield of Woodstock Street, on the corner of Oxford and New Bond Streets. Davies still has a copy of a statement in large cursive script that it issued three days after the denouement: 'Interview with Mr Granfield. He states that he rents *three* rooms:- lives in *two* and the *third* is a large Front room used as a workroom. *Miss Hicks'* statement is *absolutely untrue. The Story* of illness next door at the time the garments referred to were made is *also untrue*.'

The press tracked down Mr Granfield, who turned out to be 'an old soldier having seen long service in the 15th Regiment as regimental master tailor . . . as becomes an old red-coat his place is spotlessly clean . . . there is no carpet on the floor to harbour vermin and the boards are as clean as a Christian's conscience'. Granfield said he had done work for Davies for twenty years and that he now intended to quit the tailors,union in protest against the way in which he had been stigmatized. He admitted, however, that there had been diptheria next door.

Above
The Cheap Tailor and His Workmen. This Leech cartoon on sweating reflects anti-Semitic sentiments of the time.

Right
A page from the original log book of 1891, now in the possession of the Federation of Merchant Tailors.

LOUNGE JACKETS.

	Hrs.			Hrs.
Pockets jetted top and bottom	3		Fitting and marking up	½
Ditto, with welts	3	....	Two pockets with welts, flaps, or patched but without flaps, or jetted top and bottom without flaps	3
Ditto, patched	3			
Ditto, under flap	2			
		½	Sewing side seams	½
			Canvas	¼
			Padding lapels and stay tape	½
			Pressing canvas pockets and seams	½
Lining of side seam	¼		Basting over, including back lining or buggy	1
Ditto, to facings	½	....	Felling in linings	1¼
		¼	Sewing shoulder seams	½
		1	Making up raw edges or bluff	1¾
			Holes in forepart, each ¼ hour.	
			Buttons, ½ hour per ½ dozen or part thereof.	
		1½	Making plain sleeves, as morning coat	2¾
		1	Putting in sleeves	2
			Pressing foreparts	¾
		½	Closing	¾
Machining stand		½	Cutting and padding collar	1¼
			Pressing and covering collar	1½
			Putting on collar	1
			Pressing off	¾
				20½

Whatever the particular circumstances of Woodstock Street, the cat was out of the bag and union branch secretary T.A. Flynn was dancing a jig. Miss Hicks had said nowhere near enough, he maintained: 'Some time ago, the whole of the West End work was given to the best firms, who employed perhaps only a third of their hands outside,' but standards had deteriorated, so that now the work was contracted to men who used only outworkers 'and pay no wages at all to speak of – the worst firms in the trade are getting it and having it made in fever dens'.

The demise of various titled personages was quickly tied by the press to diseased garments and, under the headline 'HRH ALARMED', it was reported that the Prince of Wales had sent a telegram to his tailors (at this stage Meyer & Mortimer) 'asking the attendance of the head of the firm at Marlborough House'.

Reporters scoured Soho looking for the disreputable 'backshops' of tailoring's grand names. *The Star* kept ahead of the pack with its descriptions of 'evil, dark and dirty dens – all within two minutes walk of Regent Street . . . it is in these places that the clothing which covers the backs of the dandies of Europe and America is made'. It wrote of 'doors tight locked against a stranger in view of the recent disclosures',

Left
Embattled masters sought to deflect criticism by pointing to bad conditions in New York. The caption with this 1887 photograph charges that workers were locked into firetraps and fined 25 cents for washing their hands and similar misdemeanours.

of a human 'meat market' where scores of poor tailors huddled in all weathers in hopes of finding work, and of a sweathouse in Bridle Lane with ten people to a room, 'each paying 2s a week for his sitting and here he will bring the work from the best tailors of Sackville, Maddox, Hanover and elsewhere . . . and these are not Jews, not even pauper aliens, or "greeners"; they are "sturdy Scotchmen", "devil-may-care Irishmen" and "independent Englishmen"!'

The Chronicle found an ex-tailoress who had worked in a dilapidated Poplar garret where, she said, the Prince of Wales's waistcoats and plush Court costumes used to be turned out 'and perhaps still are'. This gruesome place was run by an Irish tailor – 'a filthy-looking object, with a shirt like a soot-bag' – who was said to work for some of the best West End firms. The garret's description was calculated to turn the reader's stomach: 'Three dirty beds and in a corner a heap of greasy paper cuffs and collars which, having been cast off by the workpeople, were used as occasion required as fuel for the fire . . . in this room twenty people worked unwashed squatting on grimy bare boards and took their meals of faggots, fried fish, black pudding, two-eyed steaks (bloaters) and saveloys, washed down with beer and shandygaff containing a dash of gin.' Nine people were said to have slept in the room each night, 'including one of the male hands who made himself as comfortable as he could on the pressing board' and children with measles and inflamed eyes oozing mucous. 'It was in this noisome den that she remembers some very fine waistcoats being made for the Prince of Wales – moiré antique, buff jean and white, and blue jean with white spot,' *The Chronicle* reported.

The death of a five-year-old girl in a Holborn outworker's home sent fresh shivers through the populace; the coroner called the place 'warm with scarlet fever' which, he added, 'cannot be propagated more easily than by infected clothing'. Doctors chimed in with letters to the papers about tending dying patients in clothes-filled sweating dens.

The Star pressed its 'Tailors and Death' investigation into the workrooms of the elite firms and it concluded that 'bad as are outworker conditions, some employer workshops are worse'. Hill Brothers' workshop in a cul-de-sac off Piccadilly was pronounced a rickety death-trap and Jones & Co. in Regent Street was accused of 'making magnificent uniforms for the military dandies in another tiny firetrap'. Despite the witchhunt atmosphere, some earned praise. Sandiland & Sons in Conduit Street had 'capital workrooms' while the Prince of Wales must have been relieved to read that 'everything is done to secure the health and well-being of the workmen' at Meyer & Mortimer – 'three well-lighted, well-ventilated floors contain about eighty men . . . sanitary arrangements are excellent and so closely does Mr Mortimer go into details that the stove in the workroom is on a patent principle, which prevents the heat escaping into the

Below and Far Right
John Jones, whose 'magnificent uniforms for military dandies' were made in a tiny firetrap, the press charged. The firm is today a part of Dege, whose director Michael Skinner here supervises activity.

atmosphere except when required for comfort'.

Frederick Mortimer admitted to farming out about 40 per cent of the firm's work. He explained: 'My workshops are full now and my men are busy. Suppose an American gentleman calls and orders ten or twenty suits, wanted immediately. I am obliged to give them to outworkers.

Evidence suggests that the Hicks gambit was a carefully worked-out strategy. If so, it worked to perfection. Miss Hicks was discerned to be no ordinary sweated seamstress, but a union leader 'with advanced ideas'. Her brother had recently returned from the United States, where Massachusetts had just enforced the licensing of home workshops. Copies of the Massachusetts regulations and licence forms were whisked before the masters (Mortimer said he was 'favourable' to them) immediately the storm broke. Transatlantic labour cooperation was evident in other regards. To obviate the slur of 'Jew sweaters' and promote the integration of foreign workers within the union, New York labour organizer Abraham Cahun was active in the East End and addressed at least one large rally.

Below Left
The Mill Street Mission, with Miss Fraser at the door. From here, she and her ladies' auxiliaries sallied forth to the tailors' workshops. Reaction was mixed, her biography suggests: 'Every man knew how she brooded over them, yearning for their spiritual welfare, and this knowledge naturally made many shy of coming into close contact with her.'

The Star got it right at the outset, when it declared that sweating and white slavery was one thing, but 'This great country draws the line at the Duke of York's trousers.' It even put it to verse:

Long years we've struggled to release
From cruel and galling fetters,
From poverty and pain and woe,
The slaves of heartless sweaters;
And lo! our efforts may be crowned
With victory, for now, sirs,
Within a fever den they've found
A royal prince's trousers.

In vain we told the awful tale
Of sickness and starvation,
And pictured fetid fever dens
And crime and degradation.
It passed unheeded, but, forsooth,
'Twill perhaps be altered now, sirs,
Because within a fever den
They've found a prince's trousers.

Folk had but little sympathy
For slaves in their own city,
Reserving for the heathen blacks
Their charity and pity;
But now self-interest points the way.
There'll be a change, I trow, sirs,
And we shall hear some more anent
The royal prince's trousers.

8

Edwardian Sunset

The Duke of York kept his trousers and stayed healthy. More important, he stood by his tailors and established a uniquely intimate relationship with them that was to last through his reign as King George V.

Davies created a room for his exclusive use – a sharp departure from the royal rule of having tradesmen call – and fitted it with panels and a tube like a hose pipe, which communicated with the tailors upstairs. It is to be assumed that by this time the fifth-floor shenanigans had abated, for King George was a respectable and dutiful monarch, quite the opposite of his frolicksome father.

The press having wrung all it could from the trouser scandal, the matter was allowed to drop, with an aftermath of petty bickering between Miss Hicks and Granfield's lawyer. New laws began to regulate the condition of outworkers and, by 1901, employers were made legally responsible for the sanitary conditions of all premises. Union activists continued to campaign over the outworker issue and scuffles in Soho led to some arrests.

The Sweating Exhibition of 1906 brought throngs of the righteous to the Queen's Hall, where high spots included a widow with four children who was said to earn 3s to 8s a week, out of which she had to pay for her own cotton and find rent of 5s. The exhibition was followed by the Anti-Sweating League Conference on a Minimum Wage, which in turn led to a formal government enquiry. In 1909, wage boards were set up and a minimum wage established for a quarter of a million artisans, including all tailors in the ready-made and wholesale trades. The rate was 6d an hour for men (what it had been 100 years earlier) and 3¼d for women, or 25s and 13s 6½d for a fifty-hour week. Savile Row was not affected, as retail bespoke tailoring was excluded from the order.

A badly planned strike in 1912 was to end all attempts to restrict outworking, for sentiment had swung towards the masters and the men were hopelessly divided. Along with a call for more 'inside' workshop space, the strikers sought a 2d increase in the log-hour rate. The masters, led again by Howard Cundey, called that outrageous and claimed the demand would lead to a 20-30 per cent increase in prices. They based their reasoning on the complexities of the log system, under which a log-rated hour was by their reckoning hardly half an hour of actual work-time; according to their sums, a log-hour rate of 7d was worth an actual 1s 1¼d an hour and a 2d log-rate increase would be equally magnified in real terms. Customers became alarmed and began to sympathize with the masters.

After five weeks, some marching to the 'Marseillaise' (in which the Anarchist League somehow got involved) and a half-hearted attempt to get Paris tailors to come out in support (Paris sent a telegram), the strikers gave up and returned at the old rate with the workshop campaign lost. On 4 June 1912 they filed into the London Pavilion and voted by 1,100 to 762 to go back to work. The journeymen of Savile Row would never unfurl their banners again.

The men had been at odds among themselves over the outwork issue and Poole had released figures to argue that even after reducing accommodation, it still had plenty of vacant workshop places. The exploitation of women became an issue when the charge was laid that some journeymen preferred outworking 'because of the unlimited opportunities it affords the unscrupulous man to exploit female labour'. An instance was cited of a union official making 'considerably more than £4 a week', partly through the efforts of a woman who worked for him for 25s.

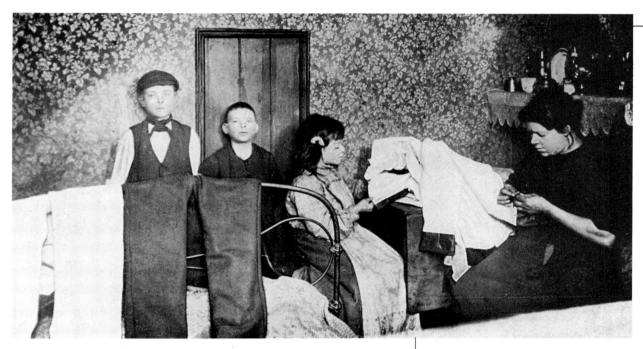

The shape of the modern trade, and of its problems, were defined in the strike's outcome. The *Tailor and Cutter* had earlier outlined these problems:

> A very great change has come over the way in which high-class tailoring firms are conducted. It will be within the recollection of many of our readers, that the heads of most high-class firms, not only personally attended to the get up of a large portion of the work, but themselves cut out some of the most particular garments. Even after old Mortimer had retired from the more active duties of his business, on his occasional visits to the shop, he has been known to take up a finished garment in his hand, and, admiring its excellent workmanship and finish, has ordered the cutter to give the man two shillings extra for making it, and to state further, that it was his wish that he should have it. The coin thus had all the charm of a certificate of merit or diploma; and thus men were encouraged and stimulated to turn out good work; but all this is changed. The heads of these same firms are for the most part non-practical men, and it is the commercial aspect of the business which now forms its chief interest and attraction.

Large firms had no place for apprentices and little interest in training, the trade journal lamented – 'a half dozen West End employers could not be got to attend a series of meetings to propound a scheme for starting a tailors' school'. Howard Cundey, himself a

Above
J. B. Johnstone presides in portrait over
the activities of great-grandson
Malcolm.

Below
Wells of Mayfair's citadel dates from
1829, but was rebuilt as a statement of
permanence in the traumatic year of
1892.

'non-practical' man, gained credit for Poole by responding with a five guinea prize for the best student of cutting, though it was politely suggested that more good might be done by offering such inducements to the needle-and-thread journeymen than those few marked out for pampered specialization. The *Tailor and Cutter* itself tried to do what it could through its Tailor and Cutter Academy, a rigorous place that helped make the journal's Gerrard Street headquarters a sort of secular twin to Miss Fraser's soul-saving Institute. The tone was highly moral. Just as the journal's staff were expected to begin work with prayers at 8 a.m., so the unmarried staffers and Academy students lodged in the Tailor and Cutter Home in Canonbury were required to be in by 8.30 p.m., with lights out at 10 p.m.

Such activities were warmly encouraged by the masters, but not the notion that they should themselves become involved in training – less and less so as more and more foreign labour kept arriving. The Jews were the most significant; to this day, some experts divide Savile Row style into two, that of the floppy English traditional and the more shaped cut that the Jewish emigrants brought from Central Europe.

The early arrivals were fleeing the Russian pogroms and German anti-Semitism of the early 1880s; further waves followed in the early 1890s and the early twentieth century. London's Russian and Polish population was put at 1,709 in 1881. In 1911, it was 68,420, and a substantial portion of these were tailors. They brought talent and new determination, but their availability in such numbers not only depressed wages, but ultimately led to a permanent reliance on immigrant labour.

By the end of the 1912 strike, the masters felt complacent enough to suggest it was up to the trade unions to look to the question of apprenticeships – unless, said one, they wished to see their trade 'pass, like the hotel business, into the hands of the foreigner'. Interviewed in the *Pall Mall Gazette* and identified only as the principal of a well-known West End firm, this master maintained that foreigners were being employed

because they are better trained and are more artistic craftsmen . . . .
But the Englishman is a more rational workman, and is not imbued with
Socialist views like the foreigner. Both for temperament and from
patriotic motives we would rather employ him than the foreigner. The
masters have been making overtures to the men for years on this
question of apprenticeship. It is for the men to wake up to the necessity
of training themselves to become as skilful as the foreigner.

Rectitude is the word that best describes the master's mood in these Edwardian years that were a last hurrah for the age of privilege. Queen Victoria's sixty-four-year reign had ended in 1901 and Bertie had nine years as Edward VII before all the good living took its toll and another bout of national mourning* marked the accession of George V. Between these bouts of strangulation in black crepe, 'more money was spent on clothes, more food was consumed, more infidelities were committed, more birds were shot, more yachts were commissioned, more late hours were kept than ever before,' as Virginia Cowles nicely put it in *Edward VII and his Circle*. It was the era of dressing for the occasion, and for every occasion, a different dress. 'A man's wardrobe is now almost as varied as a woman's,' the authoress of *Manners for Men* wrote in 1897. 'He has different costumes for walking, riding, driving, visiting, boating, hunting, shooting, golfing, bicycling, tennis, and cricket, dining, smoking, and lounging, football, racing, and yachting, to say nothing of uniform and Court dress, besides the now developing motor-car costume.'

Numbers are hard to come by, but during the 1912 strike the Association of London Master Tailors listed 169 member firms of 'Savile Row' rating, with a combined capacity of 1,492 'sittings' for journeymen in their workshops; no estimate of outworker strength was given.

The list includes numerous names familiar today. J. B. Johnstone was into its second generation in Sackville Street, where full-bearded Irish founder John Brown Johnstone had settled in the 1840s. Tom Brown had been in Conduit Street since 1887, having begun at Eton back in Brummell's schooldays; it was one of several Savile Row firms to farm the rich Etonian spawning grounds. John Morgan had begun in Cowes in 1820 and came billowing into London on the crest of the mid-Victorian yachting boom, reaching the West End in 1883. Now Morgan was tailor to the Royal Yacht Squadron and had a royal warrant from supplying liveries to Victoria's household.

Jones, Chalk & Dawson on Sackville Street were a trio of Hawkes employees who had quit to set up on their own in 1896. William Jones was Hawkes's head cutter, Chalk was also a cutter and Dawson came from the counting-house. The cutters are not only the surgeons of Savile Row, but also the impresarios: the people the customers identify with, so that their departure – often with their customers in tow – can cripple a firm. In this classic case, the ex-Hawkes trio quickly acquired a royal warrant and appointments to sixteen regiments largely through Jones, 'an acknowledged authority on military tailoring with an obliging disposition,' according to the *Tailor and Cutter*. Jones was of that legion of country tailors that Miss Fraser strove to save – a Welshman 'possessed of strong constitution, a striking personality and a passionate liking for hard work'. When he unexpectedly expired on a Monday early in 1906, the partnership was severely strained, but the firm held together and it prospers still.

The web of familial relationships that binds Savile Row together was already nicely entangled. Take the firms of Dege, Skinner, Wells and Cooling Lawrence, all on the 1912 list. William Cooling was briefly a partner with James Poole in the venture into Old Burlington Street, but he left to found his own firm at 47 Maddox Street in 1829. Cooling's daughter Jessie married a tailor named Lawrence, whose name was tacked on to the firm, and their daughter Jessie married their head cutter, John Byron Wells, who left to set up a rival concern just around the corner in Conduit Street. That was in 1880. Still another - third

Below
Sporting Bertie equipped for his final fun years.

H.M. KING EDWARD VII.
9501c Rotary Photo. E.C. Langhams

---

* Mourning was big business and national mourning the biggest - in 1799 the journeymen's wage was doubled 'in cases of general mourning'; the Victorians turned the formal celebration of death into such a palaver that the National Mourning and Funeral Reform Association was formed to protest its rigours and cost.

generation – Jessie married Fritz Dege, whose firm is today into its third generation in partnership with fourth-generation Skinner. The inter-marriage produced two firms called Wells (as there were two called Skinner), which were eventually to reunite to become the basis of today's Wells of Mayfair, which still occupies the same Maddox Street building that William Cooling moved into on the day he left James Poole. Wells thus holds the record for the longest unbroken occupancy of any Savile Row location.

Not on the 1912 list, because he was on the other side of what his son calls 'the last really decent tailors' strike', striker Bernard Weatherill could not find subsequent work because of his reputation as a troublemaker, so he set up on his own as a breeches-maker in Ascot. 'He was a hard taskmaster, who was dedicated to high quality, but I do believe that his greatest satisfaction was to seek out and buy those businesses who had refused to employ him when he was a journeyman – and to sack the bosses,' expounds his son Jack, who took the hint and became a Tory politician. The firm became one of the most prestigious Savile Row names in hunting and show-jumping. Jack became Speaker of the House of Commons.

An image was promulgated of progress the diligent way, the way of Miss Fraser's paragons, with the righteous assuming the burden of masterhood and exercising strict but fair rule over his fortunate workers. Henry Hill was the perfect example. The son of a country schoolmaster, he was born in Cullompton in Devon and apprenticed to a tailor. While still very young he headed for London, where he all but starved, and on a Christmas day was said to have 'approached the Thames', only to be stopped from jumping in by a kindly stranger, who gave him half-a-crown. He found work the very next day and saved until he had five guineas, which he invested in cutting lessons from a Frenchman. That got him a foreman's job and he kept on saving until, in 1845, he could afford to start on his own in a room at No. 3 Old Bond Street, just over the wall from the Burlington Arcade. Within five years he had somehow landed a royal warrant from the Prince Consort. Trade boomed; in 1855, he expanded next door and his brother came up from Devon to take charge of the business side. They opened a Paris branch and exploited the latest wizardry of telegraph and railway to gain a reputation for their speed of response to a suit order. During the Crimean War they fostered their fame by enclosing a bottle of port or brandy with each package sent to the troops.

Miss Fraser must have heard about this, for spirits were out and barrels of herring and packets of chocolate substituted in the Boer War. Henry lived stylishly in Brighton – he was an early commuter – and retired in 1880 to collect paintings and donate a stained-glass window to Cullompton Church. He had no children, so Harry Hill, a nephew, was prepared from childhood to take over the firm. In 1891, Harry became the first president of the association that the West End masters set up as the counter to the journeymen's effective unionization in the sweating crisis.

The path of patriotic opportunism did not always run smooth. In 1900 Poole and Sandon, a neighbour at No. 8 Savile Row, got together to offer some free uniforms for men volunteering to fight in South Africa. A nasty little crisis arose when it transpired that Poole and Sandon aimed to spread the generosity by getting their men to make the garments cheaply. The men were disgruntled and it quickly evolved into an arcane argument over whether an officer's jacket was a 'gentleman's outfit' – it was, after all, a Norfolk jacket in camouflage - or a military garment outside the log agreement.

An angry Howard Cundey gave his workers 'a rare towelling' and 'called them things which the men in the committee room over the

Below
Labour MP Keir Hardie dealt formal wear a mortal blow when he braved Parliament in tweed cap and plain black suit.

Duke of Argyll in Windmill Street considerately asked the *Star* man not to put into print', that paper reported. The union called the men out for a discussion and, when they returned, they found a policeman guarding the door. Cundey had locked them out. 'The war in the Transvaal has spread to Savile Row,' *The Star* declared, as 300 Poole men and 60 from Sandon were idled.

The minutes still exist of the stormy meeting that followed between the Masters' Association and the union. It was held on Saturday, 6 January 1900. Harry Hill presided and Cundey was on his high horse. 'What has happened is a thing that cannot be discussed with patience,' Poole's man barked. He had been motivated by a desire to help his country and his men and what had he got – a walk-out! He told the meeting: 'These are not the men I want and I shut the door in their faces!'

Four hours of strident talk achieved nothing, but later the union agreed to let Harry Hill arbitrate the dispute. It took him five months to get agreement on a complicated set of terms that the union, in a chirpy note to Masters' Association secretary William Cooling Lawrence, maintained were much the same as it had been ready to accept all along. The military jacket had been logged to the last stitch, through nineteen steps from 'Marking' to 'Pressing off', for a total of 20¼ log hours, or much the same as a Norfolk jacket.

A coterie of masters now formed an aristocracy within the trade – Hill, Lawrence, Cundey – particularly Howard Cundey, whose grand manner seemed to proclaim the preeminence of Poole with every

Below
Under the patronage of Bertie, leading men of the West End musicals began to influence style from the 1890s. George Grossmith instigated coats with turned-back jacket cuffs in *The Spring Chicken*. Grossmith parodied the elegant but fatuous stage-door johnnies and the johnnies loved him for it. Other style setters included Arthur Roberts and Seymour Hicks.

gesture. This extract from a 1905 note from Cundey to Lawrence says it all:

> I am personally responsible for the nomination of Mr French as a Vice-President of the Association of London Master Tailors. I suppose I ought to have mentioned to the committee my intention of inviting him to act if elected, but . . . I felt confident my recommendation would be approved by the Members, who, if they desire me to act as President, must grant me lieutenants, like Mr Forster, Mr French, Mr Goodall and yourself, who are congenial to me, and with whom I can work in harmony . . . . I hope you will see the matter in the same light as I do, as I desire to have the wholehearted support of my Colleagues in the responsibilities I am proposing to undertake.

The Boer War of the uniforms was not allowed to disturb Poole's annual dinner. With the journeymen locked out, Cundey invited his permanent staff to the Trocadero Empire Room, where 'the enjoyment of the banquet was enhanced by selections of music performed by Senhor Draghi's Orchestra, and later in the evening these were interspersed with songs and recitations,' the press recorded. 'The loyal and patriotic toasts were received with outbursts of marked enthusiasm, obviously evoked by the crisis through which the country is now passing.' Speeches addressed to the head of the firm were 'eulogistic'.

Next year, the humorous recitations and character songs 'were successful in keeping the risible faculties of the auditors in uncontrollable agitation'. In 1902, the loyal toast to the King 'evoked immense enthusiasm', for, soon after his accession as Edward VII, Bertie had decided to make it up with Poole. He reappointed the firm as his Court tailors and set it to work on a pile of scarlet and gold uniforms for his coronation.

The mood of reconciliation was catching, for 'numbers of the journeymen, smartly clad, and with beflowered buttonholes' turned out for Howard Cundey's wedding in 1903. So did 'several of the aged inmates of the Journeyman Tailors' Asylum'. Detectives were hired to guard the wedding presents. 'We would like to describe these in detail, but that is quite beyond us,' the *Master Tailor and Cutter's Gazette* apologized to its readers. 'They were, as a friend was heard to remark, more than ducal.'

One of the honoured guests was the ageing Angelica Patience Fraser, who was so transported by the occasion that she 'donned a distinctly wedding garb in honour of the bridegroom'. The end of the Boer War and Edward's coronation were occasions for joy that attracted record attendances at her annual mass tea party and tailors' rally at Exeter Hall. A Jubilee Fund to mark her fifty years of saving tailors raised £3,700, with Howard Cundey donating the first £100 and Harry Hill the next.

Back in royal favour, Poole snagged another exotic warranty in intriguing circumstances. Muzaffar-ud-din, Shah of Persia, had been promised the Order of the Garter if he would visit Britain, but Bertie the Stickler got obstinate and refused to confer his top order of chivalry on the infidel, even when it was pointed out that his mother had given it to the previous Shah. When the Shah duly turned up for his gong, the Foreign Secretary, Lord Lansdowne, was in a tizzy, but thought he had the answer when he had a version made of the Garter star and badge, lacking only the cross of St George. He rushed it to the royal yacht ahead of the Shah, but the sight of it so enraged the King that he threw it out of a porthole. The ersatz gong plopped on to the deck of a passing steamboat and was returned by a stoker, but the King did not see an omen in this. Lord Lansdowne resigned and the Shah had to be content with the consolation prize of an introduction to the King's tailor.*

Another conspicuous Poole patron was the Marquis de Soveril, known as the Blue Monkey for his baboon-like face and the tinge of his skin; he was celebrated for having exactly the same dumpy figure as his good friend the King, though he cooperated with Poole to much finer effect: from lustrous top hat to shimmering boots, he was a famous sight along Old Bond Street. The Blue Monkey and the King wore their frock coats unbuttoned, for reasons as obvious as the undoing of the bottom waistcoat button, which is curiously the most remembered of Bertie's many sartorial innovations. Then there was Lord Chesterfield, reputed to have the biggest wardrobe of all; in this case Poole shared the load with at least two others, one being Meyer & Mortimer.

Cracks in formality had begun appearing by the 1890s. Socialism was on the rise and Kier Hardie, first Labour MP, stormed the silk hats and frock coats of Parliament with a tweed cap and the black suit that was to become Labour Party uniform. Formal evening wear began to give way in the face of the necessities of a new, busier lifestyle. The theatre was expanding rapidly and there were not enough patrons able to commute to their new suburban homes to change and be back in time for curtain-up, so standards began to be eased.

*Though some time later, Britain's need for his goodwill was such that a Cross and Garter was sent out to him.

Above
The Duke of Argyll pub. In an upstairs room, a few yards from the long forgotten site of Pickadilly Hall, irate journeymen brought the Boer War to Savile Row.

Left
Edwardian sunset: tailoring would never see its like again.

Below
Moses Moses brought the old clothes
trade from Monmouth Street to Covent
Garden, where expansion celebrations
were a regular occurrence.

The King fought a spirited rearguard action (novel style and innovation was acceptable only if it emanated from himself) and was proud of what he made of John Burns, the first working man to become a cabinet minister. 'J.B.' petitioned to be excused from wearing Court dress when he was received at Buckingham Palace, but the King would not hear of it. It turned out that Burns had worked as a messenger for Hill Brothers when a youth; he went back to his old firm and got kitted out in perfect regulation costume. Bertie could never take Burns's politics – Burns favoured the abolition of the House of Lords – but he would boast how 'there never was a man at my levee whose dress fitted him so well as John Burns'.

On 25 January 1910 – her eighty-seventh birthday – Miss Fraser's life's work was recognized with a gift from the King of an enamel broach surmounted by the royal cypher and a citation commending 'the valuable services you have rendered unceasingly to a deserving class of His Majesty's subjects'. Three months later the King died, after a life dedicated largely to the products of that deserving class.

Where did they all go to? Those garment mountains amassed by the Victorians and the Edwardians? A sartorial version of the economic 'trickle down' theory certainly accounted for some of the sumptuous cast-offs. In 1906, a butler named Tiverdale, who had been fined for 'obtaining a situation with a false character', was found to possess five trunks filled with fifty suits. Among the two million servants required to keep Society in shape, Tiverdales surely abounded, but an innovative alternative in re-cycling had emerged out of the railway slums of King's Cross in 1860. The year Lincoln was elected was also the year Moses Moses got his start in second-hand clothes. It is the modest boast of the descendants of Moses that no British monarch can be properly crowned – and no formal function of any significance can take place – without assistance from the business he created.

A Talmud scholar with piercing dark eyes and wild, spade-shaped beard, Moses moved in on Savile Row's calamities, its 'misfits' and suits left because of debt, death or aristocratic whim. He also haunted auctions and deceased estates; since widows usually insisted that he take all or nothing, he'd take all, which led to an ever-widening accumulation. Moses made his headquarters in King Street, Covent Garden, had five sons and died in 1894, by which time his firm was called M. Moss. The accumulation was turned to advantage in 1897, when Charles Pond, an unsuccessful stockbroker, borrowed a suit to spruce himself up. He kept coming back for the suit until the sons – they called themselves the Moss Brothers – decided to charge him. Thus was born suit hire.

Moss Bros at the turn of the century was a cosy, crowded place with garments piled from floor to ceiling and spilling into the street on sunny days. Second-hand and misfit trousers cost from 6s 6d to 10s 6d and quality suits 35s to 45s. It was a tough area of market men and pub brawls. Cabbies were cultivated through the supply of cheap coachmen's overcoats. 'Constant supplies of beer and pies of all descriptions were necessary to the smooth running of each day, since customers often spent whole mornings and afternoons trying on suits and would send out for refreshments both for themselves and the assistants serving them,' company biographer Warren Tute relates.

The Boer War caused a run on a patent German gaiter, which set the brothers thinking. A military department was opened in 1910 and soon they were buying up stocks of khaki from cloth dyed in Germany. Savile Row could count on the custom of the Kaiser, but it took the Row's misfit handlers to anticipate the Great War.

9

Prince Charming and the Hollywood Connection

There was a solemn little moment in the Burlington Bertie pub after the 1988 Swiss avalanche that killed Prince Charles's equerry Major Hugh Lindsay. 'He was mine,' murmured Dege director Peter Day, over a mourning pint. 'Second one I've lost this month.'

Imagine, then, the impact of World War I, when chivalry and good form met the machine-gun. In one fell swoop, the entire emerging generation of sartorial elite was all but wiped out. Yet their age of privileged elegance was already mortally wounded, mowed down by the onslaught of wireless, films, the car, the aeroplane, suffragettes, ragtime – so perhaps the sinking of the *Titanic* in 1912 is most appropriate as a symbolic finale.

War was not all bad for Savile Row, which after all was built on martial foundations. Gieves tripled in size during a conflict in which the firm contrived to follow the Fleet wherever it went. This had become something of a habit. The first James Gieve and his partner, Joseph Galt, had fitted out a large yacht as a tailor's workshop and general amenity ship, loaded up with provisions, and sailed her right into the Crimean War.

After Crimea, Gieves concentrated on cultivating the naval officer, from cadet to grand admiral. It sent congratulatory telegrams to the homes of successful candidates for the Royal Naval College and followed up with a personal visit by a Gieves emissary in frock coat and silk hat, to discuss the boy's prospects – and clothing needs – with the proud parents. Cadets were met at Portsmouth by another member of

THE

"GIEVE"
Life-Saving
WAISTCOAT

In every branch of H.M.'s Services the "Gieve" Waistcoat has proved itself the one reliable means of safety in cases of sudden immersion through mine, submarine, or flying disasters at sea.

The GIEVE Life-Saving WAISTCOAT

Made to any size—price **50/-** net

PATENTED THROUGHOUT THE WORLD.

BUYERS and AGENTS apply

"GIEVES" Ltd., 65 South Molton St., LONDON, W.1.

The inflatable waistcoat – Savile Row's answer to the U-Boat.

staff, who checked the correctness of their dress before they boarded the tug that took them to the College on the Isle of Wight. The catch-'em-young strategy, followed in varying degrees and widely different circumstances by other Savile Row firms, worked like a charm for Gieves, who outfitted 98 per cent of the 3,967 cadets who attended the College between 1903 and 1921, when it closed. The same technique was applied to the college at Dartmouth.

Gieves managers were expected to be able to identify an officer, his ship and even his prospects for promotion on sight. Officers in those days were required to pay for their own uniforms, so Gieves introduced a credit system, with the navy cooperating by docking monthly instalments at source. The firm published books – *How to Become a Naval Officer* and *Customs and Etiquette of the Royal Navy* – and ran a carpenter's shop to make sea chests; it had an insurance department offering Life and Kit insurances; it maintained a launch service for ships offshore, ran a flower-delivery and theatre-ticket agency and attended to extraordinary chores for ship-bound clients, such as shipping a favourite Rolls-Royce to a naval attaché in the United States or a skeleton to a doctor doing anatomy studies at sea. It instituted a telegraphic code to simplify shipboard ordering – thus an officer cabling the single word 'alpenstock' knew that a new ball dress coat would be put in hand, and the word 'amblieroppy' told Gieves that a white uniform was lost and a replacement needed quickly. 'Alopecy' translated as 'send one new Regulation folding cocked hat'; 'Aloud' meant 'send a new pair of epaulettes', and so on.

Once when the Mediterranean Fleet was operating near Constantinople, a cheeky midshipman aboard one of the battleships placed an order for a single front collar stud. James Gieve II – 'Mr Jim' – saw an opportunity in this and told his Malta manager to devise a way of getting a man to the Fleet. A cable was sent to the Fleet commander asking him to post a notice in all ships saying that Gieves was sending a representative to wait on Midshipman So-and-so with a front collar stud and to advise personnel that any further orders would be gladly accepted. The amused commander complied, the representative and the stud reached the Fleet by a circuitous route that included two sea voyages and a train journey across Italy, and soon Malta branch was flooded with orders.

In 1911, Gieves was duly appointed naval outfitter to the sailor King George V; warrants from the rest of the royal males followed and Gieves's shop, then on the corner of Hanover Square, became a dressing station for officers changing into full-dress uniform for Court levees. That tradition carries on today.

The outbreak of war in August 1914 stretched Gieves and other military tailors to the limit. Workshops operated round the clock, and there are tales of tailors on duty for six or seven days and nights on end, snatching what sleep they could lying prone on their boards. Their thanks was an enamel lapel badge and a grandly signed Christmas message of congratulation from Mr Jim. Representatives of Gieves sailed with the Grand Fleet and with the Mediterranean Squadrons. A Gieves man was aboard the supply ship *Borodino* and resident representatives were based in Malta and Gibraltar. As a nifty way of cutting customer losses, the Gieves patent life-saving waistcoat was also deemed a sartorial success, since it looked little different from the standard uniform day vest, when not inflated. Another special feature was a pocket containing a brandy flask. Satisfied users included Commander Robert Dannreuther, one of six survivors from HMS *Invincible* at the Battle of Jutland, and the second Lord Montagu of Beaulieu, who stayed afloat when a U-boat sank the SS *Persia*.

It was commonly believed that Gieves did not require next-of-kin to settle the bills of officers killed in action. Though David Gieve cautions in his history of the firm that 'it is not clear that the whole legend is strictly accurate', Gieves did stand by an undertaking not to raise prices for the duration of hostilities. The war lasted for four years, where four months had been anticipated, and auditors estimated the cost of the rash promise to be in excess of £20,000, which Gieves sensibly wrote off to goodwill.

Goodwill at less cost was the lucky lot of Moss Bros, whose enterprise with Savile Row's cast-off clothes and cloths inspired a new egalitarian spirit in unexpected quarters. First Sea Lord 'Jackie' Fisher, a Gieves's hero, was so impressed with the crowded little shop that he brought along his daughter and chose an outfit. General 'Black Jack' Pershing, on his way from fighting Pancho Villa to leading the US Expeditionary Force against the Germans, bought a trench coat and shortly afterwards came back for as many more as Moss Bros could supply. America heard about it and the company's reputation went international.

The war that emptied Miss Fraser's Institute and dumped her charges in the mud of Flanders changed the survivors' expectations.* A lifetime of squatting cross-legged in a back room began to lose its appeal; the spring migration of the country tailors was over.

The age of the Lagonda and the dole queue began with a brief post-war tailoring boom that found the *Tailor and Cutter* coyly seeking to broker Savile Row's marriage with the new flaming youth. 'A man

Above
Making love with conviction. Dennis Bradley, a sprightly Savile Row personality of the inter-war years, commissioned this promotional painting entitled *Seeing Red and Feeling Blue*.

Above Left and Above
Navy style, East and West. The pre-revolutionary Chinese navy acquired a distinctly British look when Gieves sent out emissaries in the wake of a visit to Hong Kong by a British battle fleet. 'The Chinese said, "Cor, who's yer tailor?", but perhaps we were singularly unadventurous in our response,' reflects Robert Gieve.

*Despite its wartime growth and despite negotiating thirty exemptions from service for key staff, Gieves sent 127 men to the war. Even the biggest Savile Row firm would soon have a total complement of less than half that number.

cannot make love with any kind of conviction unless he is wearing a coat cut within half a mile of Piccadilly,' it advised. The tailors pulling out the old paper patterns of returning warriors discovered something remarkable. The codgers – the alteration tailors – were kept busy, for it was found that customers had become more 'manly' during the fighting years. The result was 'quite a different attitude of figure . . . the drill, physical exercise and open-air life have developed particularly the muscles of the chest and arms and upper parts of the body'

The stylists were working on this when rising costs and economic stagnation caused the boom to turn to slump; the government had made ready-to-wear, fixed-price 'British Standard' suits at 57s 5d available to all demobilized troops and many found that was enough, or all they could afford in the new times. The casualness of the new style-leaders was further cause for alarm. The *Tailor and Cutter* again, at the Royal Academy private view in Burlington House, asked: 'Where was the trimness, and elegance of garb of the well-groomed man? Where the suits that deserved sonnets? One looked in vain for the style and shapeliness of Stultz, the prestige of Poole, the hall-marks of Hills. . . . Can it be that men are turning to false gods and are lured by the slogans of mass-production?' The long rearguard action against sartorial slide was on. The country was going to the dogs, said Poole, and rising new star Frederick Scholte agreed. Yet there was little they could do to halt a trend towards simplified fashion and greater freedom, as exemplified by the sports jacket and the woolly pullover, or to stop the frock coat and morning coat from falling before the lounge suit, now so ubiquitous a male uniform that it became simply The Suit.

The new ideas found their champion once again in a Prince of Wales. This was Edward, David to his family and Prince Charming to the rest of the world, until the traumatic love affair that forced his abdication after the briefest of uncrowned reigns. In his delight in clothes, he was everything his predecessors had been, and he contrived to be wholesome as well. Whatever the Prince wore, every man of his generation wanted to wear, though trying to keep up with him could be as bewildering as it was expensive. He would not only appear in several outfits a day, but he could keep it up week after week. He led the revolt against the old ways and brought comfort back into clothes, particularly in getting men out of starched shirts and stiff collars. 'All my life, hitherto, I had been fretting against the constrictions of dress which reflected my family's world of rigid social convention,' he explained. 'It was my impulse, whenever I found myself alone, to remove my coat, rip off my tie, loosen my collar and roll up my sleeves.'

'As worn by the Prince' became the catch-phrase of the West End shops, and then of the world. 'His fair and clean-cut good looks were sufficient to make him an idol, considering his position,' an American critic summed up, 'but he possessed just that combination of conventional good taste and slight but never exaggerated whimsy to make him a fashion idol.' With perhaps a touch of exasperation, *Men's Wear* in New York reported that 'the average young man in America is more interested in the clothes of the Prince of Wales than in the clothes of any individual on earth'.

The gradually successful struggle the Prince waged with his meticulously conservative father George V (who said of his son: 'He hasn't a single friend who is a gentleman') neatly summarizes the period and its outcome. At the 1923 Chelsea Flower Show, the King was resplendent in pale grey topper, frock coat and spats. At the 1926 show, he caused alarm by wearing a morning coat and striped trousers instead of the usual frock coat; he also abandoned spats, a fact discerned too late by visiting Americans, who were said to have 'snowed under' the Buckingham Palace shrubberies with hastily discarded spats at a subsequent royal garden party. For the 1934 show, he wore a blue lounge suit and bowler, thereby authenticating the suit for all men everywhere and making blue the colour of the year. George V died in January 1936; for that year's flower show, the new King Edward VIII wore a straw hat with a black mourning band.

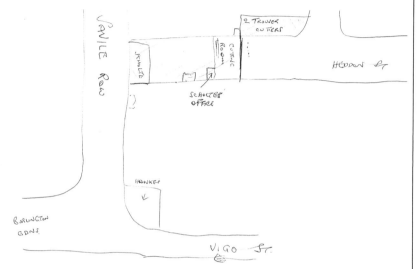

Left
Harry Errington doodled this sketch of Scholte's lair while describing life under the tyrannical legend, whose ruthless attitude towards clients extended even to royalty, Lord Mountbatten once hinted.

For Savile Row, a crucial moment in the struggle came early on, when the Prince enraged his father by turning up at Ascot in a grey suit. Ordered to change into a black frock coat, which he did not possess, Edward made a dash for his military tailor Scholte, who cut out a coat on the spot and had a tailor sit up all night sewing it together for the Prince to satisfy his father at the next day's races. Scholte was to stay the Prince's tailor for the next forty years, put a distinctive personal stamp on suit styling and influence a generation of cutters.

Scholte was a red-headed Dutchman with a red-headed temperament, who made his reputation as head cutter with Johns & Pegg, a specialist in military tunics much patronized by the smartest Guards' officers in the years before World War I. Scholte's most important client was Lord Athlone, King George V's brother-in-law. He started at No. 3 Cork Street, then opened opposite Poole. There he abandoned his speciality of officers' uniforms and inaugurated a new era in the cut of civilian clothes, largely by adapting the military tunic technique.

'The lounge suit is first favourite with prince and peasant, duke and dustman,' the *Tailor and Cutter* determined, and the 'lounge' promoted by the Prince was the 'London cut' as executed by Scholte, a new type of high-waisted, close-fitting, yet soft suit, its broader shoulders owing something to the phenomenon of the war-induced improvement in physique. Later, the square-shouldered effect would be accentuated with the draped back giving what the trade press called alertness and cleancut quality as of modern homes where the ivy has been cut away and the moss removed'. More to the point, it could make the fat man appear lean.

Anecdotes of Scholte abound and the few veterans still active who served him in their youth cringe at the memory of that awesome autocrat of the shears. It was the era of the thirteen-guinea suit, 'and if we didn't have a couple of lords come in, it was a poor day,' says

Harry Errington, a Sackville Street tailor who was a striker (cutter's assistant) under Scholte. 'He was a very clever man and hard as nails. You could always tell when he was present, the atmosphere was so tense.' Relief came twice a week in summer, when Scholte would leave at 4 to play golf. Errington takes a cloth merchants' note-pad and sketches the layout of Scholte's lair, an establishment stretching from Savile Row to Heddon Street in the rear, with Scholte's office strategically placed to spot customers arriving and to spy on his workforce. Scholte would be at the cutting-room door to greet the customer, paper pattern in hand, but woe betide any who tried his patience too far: there are tales of him slashing the legs off a pair of trousers that some impertinent customer had dared to criticize. Errington is ambidextrous and would cut the cloth with his left hand, while wielding the chalk with his right – until Scholte spotted it. 'I'm not having any left-handers here – use your right,' he instructed, and Errington obeyed, except on golfing afternoons.

The fate of the House of Scholte is a familiar one. The great man's son was more interested in wearing clothes than in making them and there was no strong personality to take over; the client list was plundered by staff who left to start on their own. Scholte died rich – reputedly as much from property investment as tailoring – and that was the end, except for his influence, which lives on in the men he inspired as he terrorized.

If the Prince of Wales was the world's best-dressed man and ultimate arbiter, the princelings of style were a new breed altogether – films and recordings gave performers vast audiences and influence accordingly.

Right
The image of the dashing cavalry officer is still assiduously cultivated. This one is from Dege.

96

Jack Buchanan, a tall, lithe Scot celebrated for his elegance in evening clothes, wowed the Americans to such an extent that to be called a 'Buchanan' was the supreme compliment that could be paid a dude of the day. It was Buchanan who in 1925 introduced on Broadway the broader-shouldered Savile Row look. Hollywood's notion of sophistication was the Englishman, and it imported Ronald Colman, Leslie Howard, Noël Coward and later Cary Grant to give its pictures swank. Even Gary Cooper, from the Bitter Root Mountains of Montana, was of English stock and had spent four years at Dunstable Grammar School.

But Hollywood was also promoting an American version of manhood – the tougher, meaner, Bogart man, or its more charming version, Clark Gable, who never took no from a lady and could not be imagined in a fitted waist. Gable had only to take off his shirt in *It Happened One Night* to change male underwear forever. Under such influences the broad-shouldered effect grew and grew to reach finally the gross proportions of the zoot suit, and then to rebound on its distressed initiators across the Atlantic.

The relaxed, easy image of the American dream was being fed into minds everywhere and with it came an acceptance of relaxed, easy clothes that could not have been more distant from the Savile Row ideal. For every person who taught themselves 'The Prince of Wales Foxtrot', there was someone learning their steps from 'The Tango as Danced by Valentino'. It is certain that more people worldwide mourned the death in 1926 of 'The Sheik', who was said to have 'dressed with the grace and distinction of an eighteenth-century

Left
Her Majesty's Body Guard of the Honourable Corps of Gentlemen at Arms emerges from Gieves to board a bus for royal escort duty. The tradition of using Savile Row as nobility's storage and changing room goes back to its origins.

courtier', than had ever heard of Beau Brummell. Valentino danced his 'Blood and Sand' tango in button boots bought COD from Maxwell's, now a part of Huntsman; George Cleverley, the fabled craftsman who made them, went into retirement with just two mementos from more than sixty years of shodding the mighty: a picture of some slippers he made for Churchill and a framed letter from Valentino.

American supplicants at the shrine of true style were sometimes made to wait. Fred Astaire's first London performance was in *Stop Firing*. When the Prince of Wales came down to the dressing room to congratulate him, he took it all in: 'He was dressed impeccably in tails,' Astaire recalled. 'HRH was unquestionably the best-dressed young man in the world, and I was missing none of it. I noted particularly the white waistcoat lapels – his own special type. The waistcoat did not show below the dress-coat front. I liked that.' Astaire learned that Hawes & Curtis made the Prince's dress shirts and waistcoats. 'Next morning I was there and asked if I could get the waistcoat like HRH's. I was apologetically told that it could not be done. So I went somewhere else and had one made like it.' Hawes & Curtis were not alone in shunning theatrical types, film stars and 'flashy youngsters'. Scholte ruled them out, just as he did not approve of such excesses as Oxford bags (fortunately for the Prince, he did not either). But Astaire had better luck at Anderson & Sheppard, whose portals he entered like a kid into a candy store: 'It was difficult not to order one of every cloth that was shown to me, especially the vicunas. They never wore out. I outgrew most of them.'

Astaire shrugged off that first snub to become Savile Row's dancing deity, its own preferred image of excellence. The energy of his performances never seemed to cause a crease, while, as the *Tailor and Cutter* put it, 'his slight, light frame ensures that his clothes never get too much of a bashing'. The picture of Astaire dancing in *Top Hat* – in a tail coat made by Kilgour, French & Stanbury – has become one of the icons of Savile Row.

Anderson and Kilgour were emerging powers fuelled in part by the immigrant tailors, who were beginning to assert the kind of influence that the German artistes had exerted in Brummell's time. The influence at Anderson & Sheppard was Scandinavian, while the old firm of Kilgour & French was revitalized by the acquisition of the Hungarian brothers Fred and Louis Stanbury, and by the elegance of cut that they introduced. Fred was an engaging personality who revelled in the creation of clothes; Louis was more of a martinet, with something of the Scholte in him. There is a hilarious story of Louis seizing a jacket and stamping furiously upon it to demonstrate to one of his tailors how much he disapproved of shoddy workmanship. 'Er, yes,' said his startled customer, who was supposed to be impressed by the performance. 'But what about my watch? It's in the pocket.'

Savile Row initiations could be traumatic for tailor and movie star alike. Bing Crosby tried Lesley & Roberts, which was doing enormous business on Hanover Square. He related:

> They took one look at me and whisked me into an inner room, a cubicle in the back. I guess they didn't want the clients to see such an apparition in their shop. I wanted to see some material. The salesman who waited on me was formal and starchy. He had on a wing collar, an Ascot tie and a cutaway. He began to lift down bolts of cloth and, as he unwound a big bolt, a moth flew out. 'Consternation' is a weak word for what ensued. People rushed from all parts of the store and went after the fluttering interloper with rolled-up copies of *The Times* . . . they were still spluttering and thinking up excuses when I left. I was glad to get away. It's embarrassing to witness the degradation and shame of a brave and friendly country.

Cooper and Gable went to Lesley & Roberts, as did Von Ribbentrop and other leaders of the Third Reich and the firm's six-storey premises were for a time so busy that they came to be known as the Lighthouse, for the lights being on at all hours. Dennis O'Brien, who is now all that is left of the Lighthouse, has equivocal memories: 'Showbusiness people are all over you one minute, gone the next – you upset one, you upset all of them.' He remembers with a shudder a Crosby visit when the press got a tip-off: 'It was terrible.' The firm's preferred method of stimulating a more traditional class of business

Below
George VI coronation uniforms being despatched from Savile Row. By this time, the horses were becoming a sentimental affectation.

was to canvass Oxford and Cambridge universities, where cash inducements would be used to lure undergraduates of good family.

Three structural developments of the 1930s were to have a lasting impact, two of which were detrimental to the Savile Row ideal. The trouser zip was accepted with equanimity in 1934 because it came with the recommendation of Lord Louis Mountbatten, who won over the Prince of Wales and his more conservative brother George. The tailors thereupon decided that zips made trousers hang better and helped reduce creasing. The only snag lay in the journeyman's log, where the zip, although far easier to install than a button system, could command a higher-rate charge, simply because it was never thought of when the logs were created. The first Savile Row trouser-maker to put in a zip was Nick van der Steen, one of three tailoring brothers of Dutch extraction. 'Being first, Nick said that for his skill he ought to get more, and being also a bit of a bolshie trade unionist, he got it,' recalls veteran unionist Ron Keston. The 1935 *Tailor and Cutter Yearbook* included extensive instructions on 'How to Make a Fly with a Zip Fastener', which suggests that there were teething troubles.

Y-front underwear and belted trousers were two innovations that Savile Row never could quite accept. The best bespoke pants are crafted in a lopsided manner to accommodate the male person – as it is called – in the natural state, something which Y-fronts and all-elasticated briefs deny. A belt likewise constricts and alters the way in which a pair of trousers hang; disastrously so, according to some purists, though others suspect that it is the ease of fitting the suspended version that most motivates the traditionalist.

The purists had plenty to worry about in a time when a Labour prime minister – Ramsay MacDonald – was audacious or ignorant enough to wear a bowler hat with a morning coat in the presence of the King. Nor were the Tories much better. Stanley Baldwin's cabinet was taken to task by the *Tailor and Cutter* for not realizing that 'the way to a lengthy stay at Westminster lies through Savile Row, Bond Street and the Burlington Arcade . . . it would be infinitely preferable, for example, if ministers came down to the House after dinner in full evening dress'. Baldwin himself was 'the worst offender – he has a liking for being unbuttoned'. Winston Churchill, then Chancellor of the Exchequer, was an indiscriminate patron of Savile Row and a profound disappointment to every tailor he turned to (in 1926 it was Poole). Kindly friends called his clothes sense eccentric; others were less polite. The only element of the trade to really appreciate him were the repairers of cigar burns. Savile Row had to be grateful, then, for the likes of Sir Samuel Hoare, perfector of the Foreign Office look of black homburg, rolled umbrella, crisply-cut three-piece suit, striped shirt and white collar – and the glinty-eyed half smile to go with it. Or Anthony Eden, of the 'Eden Silhouette' that the French so admired, with the homburg in his case worn slightly tilted to the left.

By the early 1930s the grey flannel suit had gone multi-seasonal and even women were seen wearing them – in Hyde Park! 'Many people of both sexes are turning up in our wonderful Rotten Row in costumes that were not only disgraces to our Royal Park, but to our country,' the *Tailor and Cutter* protested. Many were 'without hats, others in stockings and pullovers of every bright shade and variety'. It was time to take a stand. Degenerates dining out in the West End minus dinner jackets were warned: 'Such slackness in dress will in the long run make for slackness in behaviour, and it is not so wild as it sounds to say that society will fall to pieces, and man will revert to a state of savagery. A man who, alone in the jungle, changes into his dinner jacket every evening, does so to convince himself that he is not a savage.'

To cause further irritation, The Men's Dress Reform Party had been

Below
Fred Astaire dancing in 1934: from initial rebuff to the embodiment of Savile Row's self-esteem.

launched in 1929 to dispute Savile Row's most sacred precepts with a manifesto much the same as that of the nineteenth-century reformers. The founders were a priest and a painter, Dean Inge of St Paul's and Walter Sickert, who sported white bowler hats and loud check suits and considered the Savile Row product 'boring, uneventful, uncomfortable and tedious'. The Dean condemned trousers as ugly and unhygienic, and there was some support in the party for the kilt, for it was reasoned: 'Give a man the dress of a hero and he walks proudly in the light; clothe him in many a modern suit and he creeps in the shadows.' Shaw, still in his woolly combinations, lent support, but the party's only success seems to have been the introduction of tennis shorts.

Perhaps to convince itself that all sense of propriety was not lost, the *Fashion and Cutter* in 1929 appointed unidentified 'expert judges' and ran a 'What Style Does the Average Man Look his Best In' competition. The winner was a double-breasted suit with bowler hat; the runner-up, a traditional evening ensemble of tail coat and white vest.

Far Right and Right
The policemen (this one is about to round Anderson & Sheppard) took up residence in the worrying period just before World War II when Savile Row lost much of its privacy with the demolition of the quaint Savile Row Place.

It was becoming apparent, however, that Savile Row had to bend, just a little, and disavow some of its fancier conceits. There was a smug old story about William the Conqueror landing at Hastings and immediately extorting from the defeated Saxon nobles a letter of introduction to Poole's. Such images of prohibitive exclusivity (allied with an endearing reticence in pressing for payment) had become a burden, for blue blood was in shorter supply and the ledgers needed replenishing.

Nurturing the mystique while dispelling the less profitable misconceptions called for a lot of finesse, especially since the rules of superior trading ruled out advertising or self-promotion. Particularly rankling in the case of Poole was the story of J. Pierpont Morgan, who was popularly believed in America to have been turned away by the firm. Despite disavowals, the tale kept being retold with added embellishments. Eventually, Howard Cundey opened the firm's ledgers to the rude gaze of public scrutiny to reveal that J. Pierpoint was enrolled as a customer on 15 July 1857, upon the recommendation of his father, Junius Spencer Morgan, who had himself opened an account on 27 September 1854. Cundey then got down to the delicate heart of the matter:

I have myself read some very extraordinary statements to the effect that would-be customers were not accepted by my firm unless personally introduced by someone already on the books. Naturally this is the manner in which one prefers to extend one's business, as it is highly satisfactory to have one gentleman recommending another; but as the business has always been run (to some extent, at any rate) on commercial lines, it has never been the practice of the firm during the thirty-eight years in which I have been personally connected with it to refuse the order of any gentleman offering to pay cash or to provide suitable references.

An awkward, yet necessary, clarification. But what was to be made of 3 June 1927, when *Paris-Midi* came out with the headline, '*Londres se pronounce por la culotte*', then the stunning announcement: '*Poole a parle.*' The unthinkable had happened. Poole, in the person of Howard Cundey himself, had granted an interview to the French press. In asking for instructions from Savile Row, Poole's Paris manager wrote that he could not bring himself to accept the authenticity of the article. Was he to deny it, or ignore it? Howard

Above Left
All part of the service. Crimean-era sea chest designed for the navy by Gieves.

Cundey died soon afterwards, though there is no reason to connect the two events. Eulogized as 'the Paladin of the trade', he had dominated his fellow masters ever since the sweating crisis.

Through the years of economic depression, coaxing clients to pay up became ever more of an art; Gieves's manager Hubert 'The Archbishop' Quick was celebrated for the respectful effrontery of his assaults – 'Surely, my Lord, you do not expect Mr Gieve to accept an order for yet another uniform before you have paid for the greatcoat which you have been wearing these past two winters!' But the factory-based multiple tailors with their 'brass and glass' establishments were making such inroads that the *Tailor and Cutter* was driven to warn that 'it would be folly to ignore or deny the existence of these people', while the *Sartorial Gazette* raised the alarm over dubious products on the sorely stretched misfit market: it reported that faked labels were being sewn into garments 'which have originated anywhere but the West End' and that these were being sold as Savile Row rejects.

Moss Bros prospered. In Philip Debensky, an illiterate Polish tailor, it harboured the Scholte of the misfit world; Dubensky worked by 'rock of eye', the instinctual method from the days before the mathematicians, and was said to be able to alter any coat without the customer being present – 'he's there now', he'd say, with finger pointed to his head. With Savile Row prices rising steeply and nowhere near enough misfits, or even fake misfits, to go around, remarkable things were happening in the hire department. It was furtive at first, with customers retreating behind the clothing piles when acquaintances turned up, but it was observed how the aristocracy seemed less embarrassed than the middle classes to be seen emerging with one of the department's plain fibre suitcases. Nansen went hunting with the King in Moss Bros hire and Shackleton, then Elgar, popped in for Court dress ('All I need now is the cap and bells,' Elgar commented), while Michael Arlen helped advance the notion of rented polo breeches.

For Gieves, recession had come earlier, with drastic post-war navy budget cutbacks – £365 million in 1918-19 to £52 million in 1923 – and sharp reductions in personnel. Foreign businesses took up some of the slack. It is recorded that Mr Jim and an assistant once spent a night in the Old Bond Street shop, pillowed by gold bars 'which a loyal naval attaché had used to pay his country's debt to Gieves on the eve of the revolution which ended Imperial Rule in China'. Gieves had kitted out the Chinese fleet with an oriental version of what it did for the Royal Navy. In searching out new uniform business, Gieves exploited the rivalry of the crack Atlantic liners to garb their officers in a manner worthy of Jutland commanders. For what it called its 'flagship', it equipped 21 Old Bond Street with a front lounge furbished with all the staid grandeur of a London club.

By the mid-1930s, Gieves began to feel the benefit of Hitler, as rearmament got underway and officers multiplied. Others were not so fortunate. The impact on Savile Row of the Depression and its aftermath is difficult to assess precisely, but the average collection at the annual charity dinner dropped from £3,500 in the 1920s to £2,400 in the 1930s. For firms such as Poole, a noble image and a pile of dusty warrants were no longer enough. 'The name of Poole is a household word,' the *Tailor and Cutter* wrote in 1927. 'It stands out from all the other shops. There it is, solid, square and imposing; with brass rail and blind in the window; with an old-fashioned porch and seats, and a grand commissionaire. There is something pleasantly Victorian about its stucco front and flat roof, and its air of impeccable respectability. Above the centre window is a huge crown, resting on a cushion; and the inscription reads: By Special Appointment.' Twelve years later, the paper simply repeated that description – word for word – in reporting that Poole was taking over Hill Bros. It was a merging of the venerable against stern times ahead.

The accession to the throne of the best-dressed man in the world should have saved matters. Edward's coronation was fixed for May 1937 and Savile Row had just time to savour the prospects of a robe and uniform boom, and even to conjure with improving the garb of politicians for the great occasion, when Edward abdicated five months short of the event. That was the end of princely inspiration; the brother crowned in his place was of much more sober mien.

'Our King is gone, and with him a mixture of esteem and love,' the *Tailor and Cutter* declared, before making an abrupt loyalty switch. As the ambassador of men's clothing King George VI 'will be of more help to us . . . because he is always correctly dressed'. Court hosier George Izod said much the same: 'His Majesty is the perfectly dressed Englishman. The fact that his dress is conservative will not hinder our trade, rather it will be helped, simply because the average man likes to be quietly attired.' In fact, style leadership was gone and it became increasingly clear that popular taste, once directed by the British aristocracy, now devolved upon America, and Hollywood in particular.

The *Tailor and Cutter* was reduced to instructing businessmen on the perils of baggy knees, while on Savile Row concern was directed at the erection of a very large police station, which was set to dominate the tailors' domain and, so it was feared, usurp the very name of Savile Row. Letters to *The Times* and some hectic lobbying secured one concession: the great pile of Portland stone arose, but it was named the Central Police Station, thereby saving Savile Row from an identity crisis.

There was, however, a vibrant new departure in the endeavours of Bobby Valentine, who adapted the Continental curves of Stanbury to cater for the caprices of the dance-hall and smart restaurant set. His squared shoulders, wasp waist and billowy pleated trousers were a precursor of the pop age creations that assailed Savile Row thirty years later, and they brought Valentine success before he was twenty. 'I was a bloody lunatic,' he now says. 'I used to get carried away with things a bit.' As tailor-of-choice to ballroom dancing champions ('they used to bring the girl with them for their fittings'), band leaders, golfers ('Bobby Locke insisted on looking good at the beginning and end of his swing'), jockeys and all sorts of eminent eccentrics (he sent Peter 'Teasy-Weasy' Raymond to Ascot in a rose-pink morning coat), he was to endure as the elfish elder statesman of an alternative Savile Row.

Poole and Hill merged in January 1939. Uniform orders picked up as the year advanced, but the utilitarian now reached into warfare, with the cancellation of dress uniform and the introduction of an all-purpose battledress, lambasted as 'ugly, clumsy, unhealthy, expensive and very difficult to make . . . especially in a hurry'. By the end of August, cloth remnants were being made into blankets for stretchers and tailors' boards turned into splints. At Poole, sandbags and a big water tank joined the cushioned crown and a shelter to hold seventy-five people was reinforced against blast, with extreme measures taken to protect its precious patrimony of paper patterns dating back to Napoleon: thousands were compressed flat in the basement, then blankets saturated with soap and water were put around the doors to form an air-lock.

So Savile Row battened down for another war.

Left
Poole battens down for war, sealed, sandbagged and with precious paper patterns secured against blast.

10

War and Worse

Hitler had a fondness for English cloth and some of his minions were Savile Row men, but nobody told his bomber pilots; they flattened many of the Row's more venerable establishments and sent much of its history up in smoke. We shall never know the inside leg measurement of Lord Nelson or how much Beau Brummell owed his tailor, for pattern and ledger were blasted to oblivion from Piccadilly to the farther reaches of Conduit Street.

Gieves, unique in the extent of its empire, had fourteen workshops destroyed between 1940 and 1942 (its Malta branch three times), and a direct hit on 21 Old Bond Street gutted the 'bomb-proof' strong-room in the basement and fried all the firm's past to a cinder. Meyer & Mortimer was bombed out of Conduit Street in 1942 and found permanent refuge with Jones, Chalk & Dawson in Sackville Street. Sandon was bombed out of 8 Savile Row in the early hours of 16 September 1940; the offices and workshop were completely demolished and four battered fitting rooms were left standing. Miss Selleck, the secretary, placed her typewriter on some debris and tapped out orders on her knees in the street. Scholte got blasted into the rear of his building. At the north end of Savile Row, a single land mine wiped out ten firms next to the police station, which naturally survived. Dege was bombed out of Conduit Street in 1941 and found sanctuary in Clifford Street. So did Pope & Bradley, whose cocktail bar 'bathed with the starlight of actresses, writers, painters' had been the pride of tailor-novelist-impresario Dennis Bradley. The beautiful, bomb-damaged Georgian house that his son Pat moved the firm into had twenty-three holes in the roof, requiring twenty-three buckets when it rained. All in all, it was hardly surprising that during the blitz* the bowler hat recovered some of its popularity.

Military finery, such as full dress, undress and mess dress, was discontinued and the blouson-jacketed battledress instituted for all occasions, while fashion for men went into mothballs. One of the more endearing characteristics of the Savile Row product became a matter of patriotic pride. Longevity had always been Savile Row's long suit, with frequent records of garments lasting more than one lifespan, and now old clothes acquired cachet as an indication of their wearer's concern to conserve national resources. Lord Jowett, the Paymaster General, had an ancient Inverness cape unpicked by his Savile Row tailor and the cloth shrunk and cleaned to make a jacket and waistcoat. Admiral Sir Walter Cowans was likewise proud to wear a monkey jacket made in 1887 that was seeing service in its second world war (and

---

*Savile Row was to remain bomb-prone even after the war. The IRA in 1975 blasted replacement premises that Gieves found on Bond Street, and T. G. Hammond on Stafford Street was shut down for more than a year after a car bomb exploded on its doorstep and deposited bits of two Iraqi officials around the shattered shop. Hammond had slight consolation in reopening in time to catch some of the 1970s boom in Arab business.

*In America, eliminating trouser turn-ups was welcomed as a patriotic gesture and resulted in saving twenty million yards of cloth.

he went on wearing it after the war). Some felt, though, that the 'Old Clothes Conscious' campaign went a bit too far when the Mayor of Ipswich won the 'Britain's Shabbiest Mayor' contest with a pledge not to buy a suit or new underwear until victory was achieved.

Civilian trade dwindled with the introduction of the British utility suit, made in brown, grey or navy cloth with a low wool content and a government-enforced economy cut – narrow, single-breasted, two-piece with no pleats or turn-ups* and a minimum of buttons. The sartorial zealot could always find ways to individual expression, however, and there were some who bought trousers too long, so as to be able to create their own turn-ups. It is related, too, that the prototype of the Edwardian Look was made by a Conduit Street tailor for a young Scots Fusilier, who ordered it in the depths of the war 'as a protest against austerity'. The delivery date of the historic garment has come down to us – 19 January 1942.

Below
Poole in wartime made for the Free French and their leader Charles de Gaulle. US officers serving in Britain were also attracted by its reputation and ordered heavily for their return home: at the end of the war, there was an eighteen-month waiting list.

Eric Newby, a writer who grew up in the trade, was scathing of its contribution to the war effort. 'Some of the tailors, but not the majority of course, had gone as far afield as Wales where, raised to the rank of Sergeant-Major, they had set up shadow factories in quarries and churned out battle dresses and shrouds for the duration, returning at war's end to bore stiff those who had stayed behind with stories of the perils they had undergone from falling slate,' he wrote in his autobiography. The demobbed Newby went to his father's tailor for a suit. The tailor, one of the stay-behinds, 'had been blown up by a bomb when passing through the Burlington Arcade and was if anything in a worse state of nerves than I was – the lapels of the suit he had made me had an edge like a fine saw . . . .'

The end of the war found Savile Row in as bad a state as its tailors, nearly a dozen of whom had found temporary refuge in Poole's, with lesser numbers squatting in other foster homes, including the premises of cloth merchants like Wain Shiell and Holland & Sherry.

Couturier Hardy Amies describes wandering up Savile Row 'in the late summer twilight' of 1945. Just demobbed, he was looking for a place in which to fulfil his ambitious dreams, and he found it in the blasted hulk of No. 14. The one-time home of Sheridan and Brodie, of the Coke family and Viscount Dundas, was in a sorry state behind its handsome George II façade. Two near-hits by landmines during the blitz had blown out all the windows and destroyed the dome over the stairs, and years of rain and weather had been allowed to do their worst. The house had been left derelict, and it was easy for Amies to break in through the basement. He found 'wet slime . . . not one room in four floors was habitable', yet under the slime was a suggestion of Palladian grandeur: plenty of carved pine panelling and a splendid first-floor drawing room 'of a size to accommodate about 100 gilt chairs, which was what we wanted'. On 12 November 1945, he and a staff of eight moved into two rooms on the top floor; all they had were several rolls of brown paper, and with these they started to cut out patterns.

Amies had No. 14 restored to a state worthy of Lord Burlington; from the turned staircase balustrade to the egg-and-tongue plaster motif under the dome, the work was carried out in the original Palladian spirit. Combining charm with the uncluttered mind of the innovative entrepreneur, Amies had all the right instincts for success in the new environment. Tradition was fine, but only so far as it was good for business. Exports were right away made a priority and, by the time of his first show in January 1946, Amies already had his first American orders. By 1950, this engaging outsider from the women's trade was experimenting with the French innovation of the ready-to-wear boutique, having quickly surmised that fewer and fewer customers would be able to afford the increasingly costly bespoke product. It was the sort of departure that his tailor neighbours did not wish to know about.

Post-war recovery for Savile Row proper was slow and laborious. The new Labour government tried to provide all servicemen with a good demob suit and most were happy to step into the new uniform of chalk stripes, usually in blue or grey. Clothes rationing was maintained until 1949 and price controls set for non-utility bespoke clothing – tailors could charge their immediate pre-war price plus 110 per cent, or a maximum of £15 for a suit and £9 for a jacket. Make-do-and-mend remained important. Crews for the 1949 boat race had to borrow blazers from Old Blues. The Cambridge team sported one dating back to 1902.

The former Edward VIII, now the Duke of Windsor, was a rather equivocal figure in exile, while his brother was a man of duty, all too aware of his responsibility to set a frugal example in a time of austerity. In the war, George VI had worn old suits and had frayed shirt cuffs and collars replaced from shirt tails. In peace, he offered no lead at all and it took an indiscretion by a royal butler to reveal that he liked to wear a tartan dinner jacket for informal family occasions. This revelation of vivacity in so staid a figure aroused intense media interest, but it was the only snippet on royal style to be gleaned throughout his reign.

The sartorial vacuum had come at an awkward time, for if the old rule held about fashion following imperial power, then Britain's days were numbered. American influence was proving overpowering among the young, to whom bobbysoxer idol Frank Sinatra's crumpled look was particularly alluring. Zoot suits were sighted within half a mile of Savile Row: this extreme development of the drape shape had caused riots and arrests in the United States when adopted as the garb of ghetto rebellion. Modified, the zoot became the uniform of the spiv or 'wide boy', while back in the United States, *Esquire* magazine introduced the 'Bold Look', whose wide shoulders, broad lapels and boldly designed accessories cocked a zootish snoot at Savile Row orthodoxy. In Italy, too, a Senor Brioni was working on ideas of fine tailoring that would shortly result in a serious challenge to British dominance.

In Savile Row, it began to be felt that something needed to be done to maintain standards. The Masters' Association was another victim of the war, having merged into the National Association of Merchant Tailors (the term 'merchant' being preferred because it was felt to carry less of a whiff of the bad old days of sweating). Masters/ merchants attending their 1947 conference in Southport were warned that the bespoke trade was doomed unless they became receptive to new ideas.

The notion of promotion was raised and the *Tailor and Cutter* began campaigning for a little polite clamour by noting the French poet Lamartine's observation that: 'The Lord Himself needs bells.' A promotional body of great decorum was created and named the Men's Fashion Council. In October 1949, it staged what it called a 'style survey' at Brown's Hotel and showed the work of ten Savile Row firms, who thereupon became known as 'the big ten'. Davies, Hawes & Curtis, Kilgour, J. B. Johnstone, Jones, Chalk & Dawson, Poole . . . they were all familiar names. Though a bold and radical departure by Savile Row standards, the show was virtually ignored by the media, so that the Council retired to think again, after consoling itself with the thought that it was not easy to create headlines with garments made in such perfectly good taste. 'At least one "shocker" should have been introduced into the collection,' the *Tailor and Cutter* suggested.

Left
Amies brings feminine fashion to the Row: from his 1947 collection. The *Tailor and Cutter* was peeved and offered the opinion that 'all women's clothes are derivative and copies of male fashion from the skirt on'. Amies, Dior and others soon obliged by turning their attention to the males.

Right
The bomb-blasted hulk of No. 14 Savile Row as found by Hardy Amies.

Above
No. 14 as restored by Amies. He recalls having great fun, until scolded by his interior designer for trying to give the grand old house a dress-shop appearance – 'He then proceeded to decorate my office as if it were that of a solicitor: a rather unreliable, smart solicitor, I may add, which was just the effect I wanted.'

It was another three years before an individual tailor, Morley Jeffrey of Sackville Street, tried a one-man show along the lines of a couture collection. Despite the support and impeccably conservative location provided by the cloth merchant Wain Shiell, his efforts were ridiculed by most of the other tailors, who took special delight in pointing out that an innovative 'telejacket' (a sort of smoking jacket for television watching) had been buttoned wrongly. The *Tailor and Cutter* attributed this attitude to 'repression and inhibitions' caused by the fashion aspect of men's clothes having been 'viciously smothered' for a century. This did not help Morley, who shortly afterwards gave up his business.*

That improving journal of John Williamson and Miss Fraser looked as sombre as ever, but now was edited by a lively young iconoclast with the appropriate name of John Taylor. He tried to take some of the starch out of the stuffed shirts with editorials of wit and energy, but it was not easy.

'The world is looking to us to set the pace in men's fashions,' *Harper's Bazaar* declared in 1950, and it proclaimed 'The Return of the Beau'. With no prince to set the style, substitutes were sought in the likes of Jack Buchanan, who had added jewelled buttons to his midnight-blue waistcoat, and Cecil Beaton, whose waistcoats were very bright.

Success seemed to have been achieved with the reception accorded the New Edwardian Look, as ordered by ex-Guards officer customers of Savile Row, possibly acting upon the inspiration of the Scots Fusilier of ten years earlier. The outfit featured slightly flared jacket, natural shoulders, slim waist, tightish sleeves and narrow trousers; a curly-brimmed bowler set atop a longer hairstyle and long, slim, single-

* He joined Broderick, a firm specializing in the diplomatic trade that had been at No. 4 Savile Row since 1924. Broderick had a strong Egyptian trade, which never recovered from the fall of King Farouk.

breasted overcoat with velvet collar and cuffs completed the Look. Alas, Savile Row had no time to relax in self-congratulation before ghastly things began to happen. Clothing manufacturers seized upon the style and adapted it, so that by 1953 it had become the badge of the 'Teddy Boy'. Horrified Savile Row dropped the Edwardian Look like a hot brick, and there was a lot of mutual recrimination over their becoming involved in such venturesome innovation in the first place.

With its very long, loose cut and broad shoulders, 'drainpipe' trousers, fancy waistcoat, bright socks, crepe-soled 'brothel creeper' shoes and 'bootlace' necktie, the Teddy Boy variant incorporated something of the drape shape in achieving a dizzy combination of Edwardian dandy and American gangster. For Savile Row, it was a revelation. The proletariat could now adopt – and adapt – the styles of their superiors overnight. Once it had taken a generation or two, with the durable Savile Row suit descending through death to valet and thence to the second-hand trade. Now the factories had the machines and the masses had the spending power to oblige Savile Row to restyle far more often – or not to restyle at all.

Technology, frequently reviled and often defied by the bespoke tailor, was clearly becoming more of a menace. The first sewing machine had been smashed by a mob of tailors in the 1830s; the first gas iron was ridiculed in the 1870s and electric irons were rejected in some quarters well into the 1970s. Artificial silk lining had Savile Row in a tizzy after World War I, and when Terylene was introduced as the wonder fabric of 1951, the Bespoke Tailors Guild was so scoffing in its rejection that the *Tailor and Cutter* felt it 'pertinent to wonder how the early tailors reacted to the first man who began to cut garments from woollen cloth. Were his findings airily rejected by those who insisted that fur was warmer and woad certainly fitted closer?'

Similar negative ardour had met the advance of the suit itself, and the *Tailor and Cutter* had strong words on this too:

> For some strange reason tailors will always fight the introduction of a new fashion – in spite of the fact that the new fashions are the very life blood of their trade. The Drape Look, the Edwardian Look, the Military Look – all these produced sneers or airy dismissals from large sections of the trade. When the New Look was first sprung on women, the Federation [of Merchant Tailors] passed a Resolution condemning it. Luckily for the trade and for Fashion generally, Christian Dior took no notice.

Not only was technology improving the off-the-peg product of the factories, but more than half of all British males were by the late 1950s being dressed by the multiple tailors, now on every street corner with their made-to-measure choice of cloth and style speedily executed by efficient factory systems. Such formidable competition 'must obviously be dangerous to the bottom end of the bespoke trade . . . but competiton need not necessarily be a bad thing', urged the *Tailor and Cutter*, which reasoned that it could help 'by enlarging the general feeling for clothes especially made to fit'.

The Men's Fashion Council was attacked for 'sitting in secret' and limiting itself to the refinement of Savile Row niceties when, it was suggested, a bolder approach was needed. Why not discreet advertising, the *Financial Times* wondered, after finding the average man to be 'as much bewildered as attracted by the exclusive atmosphere that the West End has cultivated'. Tight, unyielding rectitude and 'steady orthodoxy' were no longer enough, the tailors were told.

'Light up your windows – it can help your business,' the *Tailor and Cutter* brightly suggested, and it launched a series on how to advertise.

It even suggested a little sex appeal might be a good thing: 'It is a paradox that the best tailored suits are the worst photographed; it is time this ceased . . . however attractive your tail coat may be, a pretty girl hovering in the background admiringly will help it – and attract male attention.'

The response was grudging and suspicious. A few Savile Row tailors still refused to be identified, far less interviewed, by the media. As late as 1955, one tailor would not permit a cuff style to be photographed, on grounds that such publicity was 'vulgar' and would reveal his 'secret'. The one big surprise of the 1950s to emanate from Savile Row came from the outsider at No. 14: Hardy Amies agreed to design for one of the big multiple tailors; if Savile Row scorned fashion, Hepworth's was determined to keep abreast of it.

But tradition was not all spent. In Teddy Watson, a new royal tailor had emerged with all the right credentials. Leaving school at thirteen, Watson trained under Scholte and worked with several big names before joining Hawes & Curtis. There he met a royal sponsor in Lord Mountbatten, who took him to India to organize the wartime manufacture of officers' clothing. Once back in Britain, he acquired his old firm, which had lost much of the glitter of its Prince of Wales's days. Watson was doing his own cleaning to save £3 a week, when Mountbatten brought along his nephew Prince Philip, then a Lieutenant-Commander. According to Savile Row lore, Mountbatten first had some of his old suits altered to fit his protégé; the work was evidently satisfactory, for Watson went on to tailor for a clutch of royals, including the Duke of Gloucester and, in time, the Princes Charles and Andrew.

Below
The success of the demob suit weaned many young men away from bespoke, while the war itself had a profoundly negative effect on traditional values. Rigorous clothes rationing, for example, encouraged the abandonment of the waistcoat, since an extra shirt could be acquired with the coupons saved.

As young husband to Princess Elizabeth, Philip briefly stirred the hopes of those seeking a new style leader, but these hopes were soon dimmed. This Prince put comfort before style, and Watson later ruefully admitted that it 'made things a little difficult, because as a tailor I am more concerned with how he looks than how he feels . . . but we built up a good relationship over the years'. Watson's notion of style was set within strict Savile Row limits. He disapproved of fads like wide lapels and kept cutting what he called 'the same classic suit' for fifty-seven years.

This record was more than matched by John King Wilson, the only tailor ever to cut for an American president and a British prime minister at the same time: John Kennedy and Harold Macmillan. 'J.K.' was a craggy Scot who trained on Savile Row before World War I, who fought in the great tank battle of Cambrai, and eventually came to head Morgan, where he was a two-time winner of the Dandy Trophy as Savile Row tailor of the year. The Kennedy and Macmillan connections were both of the dynastic sort – Morgan cut for four generations of Macmillans and for several of the Kennedys, starting with father Joseph when he was Ambassador to Britain.

J.K. developed his own cutting technique and was an innovator who aspired to what he termed 'ingenuity of style', but grieved whenever that style was 'prostituted by extremists . . . particularly in America'. Where style was everything, yet fashion an increasingly dirty word, defining the permissible was tricky, until the Dandy organizers came up with a prize for an act of tailoring which, in their words, exemplified 'progress without vulgarity'. This was J.K's meat, and he won in 1952 with an attempt at a convertible single- and double-breasted jacket of a design so complicated that even the *Tailor and Cutter* abandoned an effort to describe it.

Aged eighty-nine and dying, J.K. still contrived to complete a course of lectures at the Royal College of Art. His students included the present manager of Blades, Lawrence Willcocks, who says that he still views Savile Row 'in terms of his vision . . . He would say, "I will do this by rock of eye", and like a magician with his chalk as a wand, he would use the shape of his hand and the length of his forearm to create the perfect suit.' Dennis Wilkinson, who took over the Morgan business, says J.K. 'possibly wasn't the best businessman, for he had a benevolent attitude to life – he wasn't really concerned with obtaining money, or anything like that'. He recalls J.K. seeing Field Marshal Lord Slim across the street when both were well into their eighties, 'and just as they started into the road, the Field Marshal turned round and said, "Get back on to the pavement Wilson, get back. Retired field marshals are ten a penny, fine tailors are a great rarity."'

A strong personality remained the prerequisite for success on Savile Row and the the firm of Huntsman had in Robert Packer just the man to buck the trend, so that when the rest of the Row began to shrink alarmingly, Huntsman was expanding. 'He was a fantastic character,' says Brian Lishak, a Wells director who fetched and carried for Robert Packer when he was sixteen and Packer eighty. 'He had this talent – he loved clothes and he loved quality and he loved people and he put the whole thing together and people adored him.' What Packer put together was a formula for efficiency at any price. Whereas the traditional bespoke suit was put together by an individual coat-maker, trouser-maker and waistcoat-maker, Huntsman opted for a production-line system, with garments progressing along assembly lines of artisans in its two workshops. The system excluded the use of outworkers, upon which other firms depended to varying degrees, and afforded greater quality control at a cost of some individuality, at least in the minds of those customers who liked to imagine 'their' craftsman making their suit. To compensate for any perceived loss of romance, Huntsman stressed hand-crafted and traditional techniques, to the point of not electrifying one of its workshops.

Huntsman had been at No. 11 Savile Row since 1919, having grown in typical manner from a 'gaiter and breeches maker' who opened on Old Bond Street in Brummell's day; Packer took over from the Huntsman family in 1932. The product was as distinct as the process –

Below
The Men's Fashion Council was a decorous attempt at self-promotion by the top tailors. It described this 1950s offering as a masculine version of the trapeze line.

Above
Wren officer by Gieves.

its slim, slighty flared look spoke only of Huntsman, so that passing strangers on the steps of the Plaza in New York could pause and luxuriate in delicious recognition that they shared a famous tailor. And such an expensive tailor. Pricing was possibly the smartest decision of all – when you are more expensive than anyone else on the Row, you can never be ignored.

While Huntsman seized the high ground, poor Poole found itself exiled from the very street it had led to glory. The Depression years, war, death duties and the slackening of energies as dust settled upon the ancient warrants had reduced Poole's fortunes to a point where it had been obliged to sell its Savile Row freehold. Now, in 1960, the entire extent of Henry Poole's parthenon, from Savile Row through to Burlington Street, was being torn down to make way for a multi-storey car park, with a token fringe of booth-like shops for rental to tailors.

The police station had not been the last gross intrusion upon Lord Burlington's little urban village. Savile Place, the Row's quaint tunnelled access to the north, had been demolished to improve traffic flow and the blitz did the rest: such alien enterprises as the Ministry of Health were housed in the undistinguished office blocks that had risen on the bomb sites and Savile Row's surviving Georgian structures could be counted on one hand.

To Lucius Beebe, transatlantic chronicler of the Swells, we owe this description of the original Poole's in its last days:

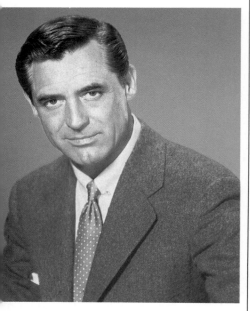

Below
Cary Grant had true Savile Row sensibilities. 'The role of the male is to serve as an unobtrusive background for the eye-arresting splendour of his companion,' he said in 1952. 'All it takes are a few simple outfits. And there's one secret – the simpler the better.'

Above Right
The Duke of Windsor in exile had an appropriately cosmopolitan wardrobe. He had sports clothes made in Rome and some business suits in New York, while Davies continued to make his evening clothes and some suits, despite the celebrated Scholte connection. Celebrities, like others, switch tailors more frequently than is popularly imagined.

A single storey finished in mustard-yellow plaster, some of it in a state of uneasy adhesion, it is without windows. In a recessed alcove in this imposing façade a red-and-gold plaster crown, also in some disrepair, might be taken to symbolize the estate of the royalty upon which Poole's once depended for a large measure of its business. A crepuscular entrance lined with dark wood panels and creaky floorboards suggests an almost primeval antiquity. The salesrooms, cutting rooms and business office, with open fires in wintertime, are roofed but not lit by glass transoms in which generations of dust were not even disturbed by the wartime bombing. Without in the least suggesting contrived archaism, Poole's is well aware of the uses of a venerable setting. An assortment of Court swords still glitters dimly in an armory in the main salon at No. 37. So does a representative selection of the blue-and-plum-coloured Court tailcoats, frogged in gold, faced with watered silk, buttoned in crested gold, mute reminders of departed levees in London and dinners at Windsor Castle. Hundreds of bolts of prudent fabrics are stacked on mahogany tables dating from the days of the founding Henry. In winter, a coal fire burns in the grate, its light reflected in the brass jockey scales on which the shrinkage and expansion of the peerage are recorded over the decades, and on a huge bronze eagle bought from Paris by Henry as a tribute to an exhalted customer.

Half-a-dozen cutters in jackets and waistcoats stand at cutting tables, and the whole is presided over by Hugh Cundey, first gentleman of Savile Row and a repository of overpowering, if respectable, magnificence. On the walls are about fifty framed warrants, testifying to the patronage of emperors, kings, sultans, emirs, czars, rajahs, archdukes, princes, lord lieutenants, and defenders of various faiths and keepers of privy seals past all tally or reckoning. 'If you were to go through the pages of "Burke's Peerage" or the "Almanach de Gotha", says Mr Cundey, 'from 1850 to the end of civilization in 1914, I think we could match you page by page with our old ledgers.'

The Cundey line was now represented by Hugh and Sam, sons of Howard, grandsons of the first Sam. They evacuated the business and its treasures round the corner to Cork Street, and premises once occupied by Pope's Dr Arburthnot. 'Life will never be the same,' said Sam, who soon concluded that this was no bad thing as he discovered how the polished treasures improved under lighting and visiting experts were surprised to find in the workrooms such innovations as 'modern work tables, all covered with a special type of linoleum for smooth working' and designed to accommodate a 'perch' posture, rather than the traditional cross-legged position, which after several hundred years of universal use had become discredited as demeaning and potentially crippling.

Was change on the way? For several years, the *Tailor and Cutter* had been harping on a theme of 'modernity with dignity'. It counselled its flock that 'although in itself the creation of a restrained atmosphere for this class of business is a worthy aim, in many cases the struggle for dignity at all costs has led the less imaginative to retain styles of interior decoration that were old fashioned at the coronation of King Edward VII'. In 1953, it reported a breakthrough in acclaiming what it called 'the first bespoke tailoring salon', just opened by the brothers Harry and Burt Helman. These premises, 'quite different to any yet seen', were designed in the manner of an elegant period drawing room, with handsome fireplace and chandeliers, and cloth samples stacked behind sliding-glass panels. Burt had wanted to go further and make it the first unisex salon, but Harry cautioned against this 'lest in attempting to please lady customers the men were frightened away'. They compromised with separate entrances.

The bespoke tailor was under mounting onslaught from mass-production products that were being steadily improved and marketed better. Designers were working in environments intended to soothe men into a buying mood and the *Tailor and Cutter* felt moved to warn Savile Row that it was 'no longer possible to sell clothing to men only in the archaic setting of the mock-Tudor club-room'.

That Savile Row chose to ignore this advice may be due to the one positive phenomenon of its post-war experience. The Americans arrived in droves. The sharp post-war increase in economic activity brought thousands of businessmen across the Atlantic, along with torrents of tourists – close to half a million in 1955. In Savile Row, they discovered all that America lacked in the way of elitist pretension and musty tradition, and so they grabbed at it, the more so when they discovered that old-world glories were dispensed at old-world prices. The very best of West End bespoke could undercut anything available back home. An awesome wage gap saw to that. In American terms, the

Above
The Queen's coronation in June 1953 taxed Savile Row to the limit. It also crowned the reputation of Moss Bros, who rented sets of utility robes for 25 guineas – coronet included – and variously kitted out more than 1,000 of the Abbey congregation.

London craftsman was making little more than $18 for a forty-hour week, which did not rise much above $45 for the most experienced veteran.

In 1955, the *Wall Street Journal* encouraged its well-heeled readers to try Poole's:

> Inside you'll see a musty showroom that hasn't changed since Dickens' days. Scattered around a well-worn carpet there's a stand-up reading stand bearing the London Times, an ancient weighing chair, several roll-top wooden desks topped with windup clocks and calendars where clerks still keep the company's books by hand. There's even a tiny gas flame and box of wooden splints with which gentlemen can light their cigars. And if you make a favourable impression on tall and solemn company director Hugh Cundey, you may get a peek at . . . .

Poole reckoned that its American sales increased five-fold in the first decade after the war. Others reported increases in proportion to their perceived venerability: thus Kilgour estimated its American clientele had increased by 35 per cent, while Huntsman said its US business was rising by 10 per cent every year. The moral seemed to be – keep it creaky.

Below
Amies and team set off for Buckingham Palace with an outfit for the Queen.

Where once the Prince of Teck and the Emperors of Brazil and France were the names to conjure with, a new brand of transatlantic celebrity put its sheen on the product. Whitley's, who had done some work for the Duke of Windsor, now dressed several film stars, among them Errol Flynn, whose proportions it considered 'pretty well perfect' (his vital statistics included a forty-four-inch chest and a forty-two-inch seat) for its squared, but not too squared, shoulders of super-cashmere. Huntsman made for Gregory Peck, banker Richard Mellon

Left
Macmillan and Kennedy shared a secret that was all too apparent on this occasion – the Prime Minister and the President used the same Savile Row tailor.

Below
A succession of Cundeys: Sam, brother Hugh and son-and-heir Angus in Poole's uncertain Cork Street days.

and 'Wild Bill' Donovan, founder of the Central Intelligence Agency. MGM boss Louis Meyer gave his custom to Kilgour, French & Stanbury, who also did for Cary Grant, Astaire and Joseph Kennedy, when he was not round the corner at Morgan's. Poole's haul included Clark Gable, Gary Cooper, the impossible colour-blind Crosby and jazzman Benny Goodman.

A prime example of the enthusiastic convert was Twentieth-Century Fox actor Clifton Webb, who fell for Savile Row while in London to film a thriller called *The Man Who Never Was*.* When he moved on to Rome to make *Three Coins in the Fountain*, he bought a piece of black silk, which he took home to Hollywood and then brought back to London, where it was turned into a dinner jacket by Anderson & Sheppard. 'The suits I have made over here are not as exaggerated as those in America,' Webb said. 'Shoulders are narrower and have less padding; an attempt's made to create a recognizable waistline; there's a better fit around the hips and the sleeves are slimmer. In a word, English tailors make clothes for gentlemen.' There was an unconscious irony here, for Anderson & Sheppard, though otherwise as conservative as any on the Row, was aiming its product at American tastes.

Above
Huntsman, at No. 11 since 1919: Savile Row's most expensive tailor and to many its standard-bearer.

---

* A film based on a real-life wartime episode in which the body of a drowned officer dubbed Major Martin was allowed to fall into the hands of the Nazis, along with some false information on the intended landing site of the Allied invasion. For authenticity, Major Martin carried in his wallet a bill from Gieves, dated 30 April 1943. Gieves was able to gain some discreet publicity out of the film's royal premiere, at which Major Martin was described as 'invented by the Admiralty, dressed by Gieves'. Savile Row contributed more directly to the war effort when Louis Stanbury's expertise in European tailoring techniques was put to the creation of clothes for undercover agents dropped behind enemy lines.

11

Beatles on the Ramparts

Right
The Beatles moved into No. 3, one-time home of the Duke of Wellington's brother, in 1968. When they began playing on the roof, some neighbours complained. Others crowded to watch.

Below
Lycett Green sketch of the Lycett Green line – 'Look less and be more.'

Macmillan said it – 'We have never had it so good' – but like Hitler before him, he clearly had not consulted Savile Row. The Swinging Sixties of jeans and jet travel ushered in a menswear boom, with London at the hub of a peacock revolution drawing its strength from the power of flowers and all things bright and ephemeral.

It was distressing for the guardians of propriety, not least because the nursery of flower power was in their own backyard. Carnaby Street, lair of the old-time drinking tailor and still a warren of little sewing workrooms, was suddenly a rival to Savile Row for global recognition. A small, shy, excitable young Scot named John Stephen had chanced upon Carnaby Street in 1957, when it had only one retail shop – a tobacconist – and rents were under £10 a week. He had the idea that there was a lot of money to be made in colourful, casual clothes that looked novel and exciting. Then came 'Love Me Do' and Beatlemania and the media did the rest. A new sort of elite patronized John Stephen – pop stars like the Beatles, Tommy Steele, the Rolling Stones and Herman and his Hermits. The fans followed and Stephen opened his second shop inside six months. Very soon he had nine shops on Carnaby Street and, with rivals crammed into the rest of the space, it became a place of pilgrimage for the world's youth.

The excitement set fashions churning faster and on an international scale never experienced before. Britain experienced a surge of European imports, with the Italians combining good tailoring with a new sexiness in their broad-shouldered, tight-trousered Continental look. Among the young, jeans and sweaters became the international uniform. 'Jeans are even worn at church,' *Men's Wear* reported. This

seemed to support the theory of leisure wear evolving with time into formal wear. If so, what fate awaited the Savile Row suit? A Savile Row-inspired 'London Line', with longer jacket and wider lapels, was the response to the Continental intrusion, but it was the big manufacturers who were setting the pace in innovation, with designers like Amies, Cardin, Balmain, Cassini and Pucci vaulting from women's wear to put their names on everything masculine from suits to umbrellas.

Burton, biggest of the multiples, began comparing its nineteen-guinea suit with the thirty-nine guinea creation of a bespoke tailor. Both products were identical in styling and cloth, and the company based its advertising campaign on a claim that most people could not tell the difference. There were protests. Burton withdrew the advert for a while, then ran it again with the re-phrased claim that people preferred its version. The point had been made – mass-production methods were so improved that even in the sensitive areas of shaping, shoulders and collars, the factory suit could have an expensive look about it.

In August 1965, Cecil Beaton gave Savile Row what he called 'a good talking to'. Said the high priest of haute couture: 'It is ridiculous that they go on turning out clothes that make men look like characters from P.G. Wodehouse. I'm terribly bored with their styling – so

Below Left
Nutters sought to lessen the shock of spotlights and mirrored walls by incorporating 'bits of old houses from a place in Isleworth' – specifically this old wooden portico and door.

Below
Tommy Nutter and first backer Cilla Black. Her enthusiasm was taken up by many others.

behind the times. They really should pay attention to the fashion produced by the young mods . . . the barriers are down and everything goes. Savile Row has got to reorganize itself and, to coin a banal phrase, get with it.' Beaton announced that he was so bored with Savile Row that he was going to give his custom to Pierre Cardin in Paris instead. The following year he was back, though he had one of the young mods do the design for the suit that he had Huntsman make up. The jacket had no lapels and differed in shade from the waistcoat and the high-waisted, cummerbunded trousers. Beaton said that he was very pleased with it – Savile Row craftsmanship was the best in the world; his quarrel was only with its disinterest in progressive styling.

Rupert Lycett Green was not a tailor, but he liked clothes and agreed with Beaton. 'As I wasn't doing anything at the time, I felt that I would like to have a try,' is how he disarmingly described his venture with Blades, a sally into bespoke tailoring under the slogan, 'For today rather than a memory of yesterday.' Blades was strategically situated on Burlington Gardens, at the top of Savile Row. The verve and connections of the owner-designer drew an eclectic clientele, from property developers to artist David Hockney, to savour what Lycett Green called his 'slim, but highly movement-conscious version of tailoring'. This consisted of a tight-fitting 'ergonomically perfect jacket' and trousers 'as slim as they can possibly be'. He also described it as a 'rather hotted-up traditional look' and spoke of people being able to play tennis in his business suits: 'I'm always trying to simplify our clothing . . . to look less and be more.'

Savile Row tailors tend to get tongue-tied, or retreat into platitudes, when describing the niceties of their style. Not Lycett Green, who could also talk up his customers to rare heights of self-congratulation:

> I think of my typical customer as being me, but in a variety of moods. He might be in a financial mood one day, a horse-racing mood the next day and he might be in a switched-on mood the day after that. The people we deal with are the people who can't be put into a mould at all. Our favourite customers are people with entrepreneurial qualities who have made money for themselves. We like them because they are more alive. They know what they want and they know what things cost. . . .

He was prepared to tackle 'anything but jeans' He pledged allegiance to a basic Savile Row tenet of faith – 'the fabricating is everything, really' – but allied himself with the designer world in changing patterns every few months.

Lycett-Green eventually got bored and went off to breed horses, but an unlikely partnership sponsored by the new pop culture was to have a more dramatic and lasting impact. Tommy Nutter and Edward Sexton met in the Burlington Arcade, where they worked for the same tailor in one of the quaint little two-storey shops: the craftsmanship was high, the atmosphere traditional and the clientele included the Luxembourg royal family. Sexton was the quintessential 'smart lad' with ambition; from a family of tailors, he had trained under the celebrated Fred Stanbury at Kilgour and took night classes in design. Nutter had started out as a plumber, when his eye caught a newspaper advert – 'Boy Wanted in Savile Row'. He got the job and found himself as trotter, running errands between workshops. By night, he frequented clubs like the Ad Lib, where the pop stars gathered, and with his gentle, engaging charm he struck up friendships with Brian Epstein, the Beatles' manager, and the singer Cilla Black. Clothes were a strong second to music in the pop consciousness and Nutter recalls how conversation got around to the notion of opening a shop on Savile Row, 'where you could get some design elements, which was the last thing any tailor would want to do, because you went to Savile Row not to be noticed'.

But that rule had already been broken in the most dramatic way by the arrival in its heart of Apple, the Beatles' company. On 22 June 1968, Apple acquired No. 3 Savile Row, former home of the Albany Club, and life on the Row was not the same again until 1972, when Apple departed, its open-plan interiors having strained the old building. In between, the Beatles recorded 'Let It Be' on the roof of No. 3 and caused extreme distress to at least one of their neighbours. 'Oh, those naughty boys!' Bobby Valentine recalls with a polite shudder. 'It didn't matter unduly except that it depleted the atmosphere – all those wild looking youngsters in beads. Sometimes we still have boys and girls praying at the shrine.' Valentine had his moment of revenge: 'When they started that ghastly blaring from the roof, I complained to the police and two policemen marched from the station; there was no more rock music thereafter.' The police station at the end of the Row had finally proved its worth.

A pioneer of sorts was already in place in Michael Fish, who had opened an audacious boutique with wide 'kipper' ties and the like on Clifford Street. With Mr Fish providing encouragement, Cilla Black and her friends providing backing, and Sexton there to provide technical strength, the House of Nutter opened on St Valentine's Day 1969 at 35A Savile Row, on the very site where Henry Poole had masterminded the Row's rise. The investment came to just £5,000. Cilla and her husband put in £2,000, Peter Brown of the Beatles' company Apple, lawyer James Vallance White and Tommy himself contributed £1,000 each. As the neighbours watched aghast, the first open window in the history of Savile Row tailoring let in light where light had never been before and revealed to the common gaze such shock elements as concealed spotlighting and a mirrored wall. The carpet was a tastefully sombre chocolate brown and, to lessen the shock further, the whole was framed by bits brought from a demolished ancestral home in Isleworth. The partnership was particularly proud of the front door, which was so genuinely old that it was warped and tended to get stuck.

Far Left, Below, Below Left
Mick Jagger, Bianca and Twiggy all Nuttered out, though Twiggy's manager Justin de Villeneuve evidently went elsewhere. The Jaggers' matching suits did for Nutter what a matching set for the Duke and Duchess of Alba did for Henry Creed before World War I – subsequent Creed clients included the Infanta of Spain, singer Mary Garden and Mata Hari, who went to her execution in Creed. Nutter's other ladies have ranged from Joan Collins to Lady Montagu. Also Barbra Streisand – 'I think I went slightly to pieces with her,' he confesses.

Most of Savile Row now agrees with Tommy Nutter's assessment of the venture: 'It was something different. Things had become terribly staid and one wonders whether they could have gone on without a bit of fresh air. Besides, they knew that I was from the Row and they knew that the quality would be there. I had some ideas in my head and I knew they would work.' Sexton recalls: 'We were more or less dismissed on the spot. Everybody said they'd give us six months. Well, we took off. It was the perfect time. Hair was long, ties were big, real estate was zooming and he did something quite revolutionary with window displays and we made a style that knocked your socks off – big, wide lapels.'

This is Nutter, twenty years later, talking about his creative genesis:

> Everybody was wearing a narrow suit at the end of the 1960s; it was a sort of ordinary nothing look, so I just went wild with the lapels and cut them as wide as you possibly could – enormous – and it was terribly flared at the jacket. So that was my first look, and it was different from anybody else. That look kept going for quite a while, then I changed quite drastically into very big shoulders, padded shoulders which I've stuck with ever since. I went very boxy, no shape at all, a drape chest on the jacket with very close hips without any flare or vents at all and very very wide trousers, very voluminous with very deep pleats and it was sort of based on a mixture of the 1920s, 1930s, 1940s, 1950s all thrown in together, yet it didn't resemble any of these periods. It was in fact my own look.

He used plenty of tweed and braid, which became something of a trademark.

For the next half-a-dozen years Nutters was an integral part of the 'London Scene', providing finery for the likes of Mick Jagger, the Beatles (three Nutter suits adorn the 'Abbey Road' album cover), Eric Clapton and adventuresome aristocrats like the Duke of Bedford. Girls, too, after Bianca Jagger walked in and demanded a suit just like Mick's. 'He wasn't very pleased, because he treated me as his tailor,' Nutter recalls. 'He was slightly old-fashioned like that.' Bianca was not happy with the first effort, which she considered too feminine – 'she took my jacket and put it on and she said that's the way I want it, so we cut her a man's jacket and that whole look started with her. I remember she had hair to her waist and she had that chopped to go with the look. Then I had all the girls coming in for their suits.' Prominent among them were Joan Collins, Diana Rigg and Twiggy. It was enough to keep the neighbours permanently glued to their wire blinds.

Success brought respect. The one-time plumber's mate had an 'elegant Mayfair apartment befitting his image' and his opinions were courted. 'I like clothes a little bit different from everyone else's,' Nutter told an American interviewer; one of his favourite outfits was in pink velvet.

Nutter and Hardy Amies found themselves curiously paired on the American best-dressed list of 1971, alongside Lord Snowdon (of the Nehru jacket), Angus Ogilvy and Yul Brynner! To the American *Men's Wear*, Nutter was 'tradition spiced with daring'; it hailed him as 'a member of the new establishment . . . one of a new breed of young businessmen in Savile Row', and it credited him with helping to bring about a resurgence of all Mayfair. 'Whereas the traditional Savile Row tailor is still doing well by doing nothing to change his image, Tommy Nutter is doing well by doing something,' *Men's Wear* determined. It mentioned the presence of the 'very able Edward Sexton with traditional tape measure draped round his neck', and it reported how

Above
Alien encroachment: only the plaque of royal tailor Hawes & Curtis recalled its existence until that, too, disappeared shortly after this picture was taken.

Sexton 'translates Tommy Nutter's style ideas into "how it should be"'

Nutters gave Savile Row the nudge it needed. Surprisingly the first to shed its frosted glass and let in the decorators was Poole, which tarted up its Cork Street reception area in green and gold and put actual garments in the window. It was Poole's first rush of blood since Henry bought up all that bronze from the Great Exhibition. *The Times* gave its benediction: 'Today's gilded youths, lost to Savile Row for too long, are returning. They have brought with them their ladies and a less tolerant attitude to traditions of dress and decor. Wisely Poole's realize it [and] others would do well to note it, for today when we buy expensively we expect the package to reflect it.'

A handsome fourth-generation Angus Cundey was now on hand to speak hopefully of a more fashion-conscious generation swinging back to traditional values, but clear glass and a coat of paint were not enough to start the stampede needed to avert crisis. Costs and prices were doubling every five years and there were nowhere near enough gilded youths to fill the thinning ranks of the faithful. Each *Times* obituary column dealt a fresh blow. A process of retreat and merger gathered pace, so that firms' names grew longer even as they grew smaller.

Despite a certain return to elegance among the youth, it was chic to go shoddy and the British Clothing Manufacturers Federation in 1975 branded the British male as the worst dressed in Europe. About the same time, a cartoon was published of a jean-clad, crew-cropped youth being told: 'For something a little out of the ordinary, here's a jacket with trousers to match; it's called a suit.' About the nearest thing to a royal style leader was the Queen's cousin, Patrick Earl of Lichfield, who admitted to owning twenty-six suits and appeared to feel it necessary to offer the excuse that he was, after all, a fashion photographer. All hope had been abandoned of the Top Royals providing a lead, and there had to be a touch of resignation in the way that *Men's Wear* in 1977 hailed the Princes Philip and Charles 'for their unique contribution to men's fashion in their lifetimes . . . neither wishes to become a tailor's dummy or a trendsetter, but to be well dressed for the occasion in the finest British fabrics and in clothes which are best-suited to their own personalities. The menswear industry, no less than the nation, could wish for nothing more.'

Not that Savile Row could have coped with a sudden reversal of fortunes – recruitment was near to nil and old journeymen were dying off even faster than their customers. 'Our image is deplorable,' Angus Cundey admitted. 'Boys and girls imagine long hours and dirty hovels to work in.'

It was no new notion. A meeting called in 1910 to discuss 'the decay of apprenticeship' was told that 'an increasing dearth of good workers is understandable in that the trade has no attraction for boys'. Some delegates concluded that the practice of sitting cross-legged was the problem, but the *Sartorial Gazette* demurred. It was 'monetary conditions and social surroundings', the *Gazette* suggested. ('My master would hit us with a yard stick if we sat straight-legged,' James Forsyth, a tailor who began learning the trade in an orphanage about this time, long afterwards recalled. 'In fact it was the most comfortable position to work in.')

Even at that time, the trade was becoming largely dependent on immigrants – along with succeeding waves of Jewish tailors would come Scandinavians, some Italians and a flood of Greek Cypriots; but then the sources began to dry up. Women, a major component of the workforce since the sweating era, also drifted away. By the 1950s, lack of recruits was becoming a serious worry and the long search for a

Above
Gieves & Hawkes exude an air of permanence, but this pairing of famous old names only goes back to 1975.

solution had begun; Huntsman announced that it was modifying its training methods 'to try and attract boys of better intelligence'. But a vicious circle of decline and reduced opportunities had set in, so that by 1978 royal tailor Teddy Watson could retire with the pronouncement that 'bespoke tailoring is dying' and that he was advising young people not to come into the trade. 'Certainly I have had a good life from it,' said Watson, who certainly had. 'But now it is on the decline and I can see no way of stopping it.'

Watson sold Hawes & Curtis to shirt-maker Turnbull & Asser, which was in turn bought by Harrods. Soon all that was left of Hawes & Curtis was a brass plaque, somehow forgotten when an Italian design house took possession of the premises on Burlington Gardens. Eventually that was removed too.

Poole in the mid-1970s had about fifty-five people involved in making around 2,500 suits a year and was struggling to achieve even a marginal profit; many others threw in the shears, either selling out or retiring into oblivion. After 'friendly discussion of the advantages of mutual support', Poole took over the small firm of Squires and then absorbed Sullivan, Woolley, whose customers had ranged from Viscount Montgomery to Rex Harrison. The *Financial Times* called it 'a neat piece of invisible patching'.

Gieves and Hawkes became Gieves & Hawkes in another piece of patching. Gieves had struggled with fortitude against the ravages of lost empires. Pax Britannica was gone, and with it sartorial sovereignty over much of the globe. A contract from the Imperial Ethiopian Navy and the enthusiastic personal custom of Emperor Haile Selassie was small consolation for the loss of so many colonial and dominion contracts. That it was a more hazardous world became apparent with the great Peruvian débâcle. Gieves's agent was waiting in his Lima hotel room for a summons to the presidential palace to present the results of eighteen months' work on samples and estimates for a complete redesign of the country's army, navy and air-force uniforms. As he idly watched a procession pass in the street, machine-guns opened up, the president fell, and in an instant all the work was, in Gieves's words, 'reduced to the value of outdated newsprint'. It was a foretaste of such misfortunes as the fall of the Greek monarchy and revolution in Baghdad, both of which left Gieves grieving the loss of good customers.

Revolution of another sort had more lasting consequences. The ritual of the fitting was proving irksome to the young, even to those who could afford it, for officers spending a weekend in London wanted a new suit to wear right away. 'The Saturday trade,' Gieves called it. So starting in 1947, some ready-made suits were placed in a wardrobe outside the manager's office; they were kept under lock and key, like some shameful secret.

Extended credit had always been a feature of the service, but an accumulation of £600,000 in outstanding debts by the mid-1950s obliged the firm to make an unprecedented appeal to customers, who responded with £150,000 within a few weeks. 'We all know about the debt this country owes to the navy, but what about the debt the navy owes to Gieves,' one senior officer commented dryly. What Gieves called 'a pleasing tribute' came from an old admiral, who died leaving an unopened envelope with his tailor. In it was found a small life insurance policy and a note. Having spent the greater part of his life in debt to Gieves, the admiral had not cared to contemplate dying in the same state, so he instructed that the proceeds of the policy be used to settle his account, with any surplus to be retained as a modest token of his gratitude.

But naval debts were becoming much less of a problem, for there was much less of a navy. Mr Jim, on his last visit to Malta branch, had the pleasure of seeing two battle squadrons anchored in Grand Harbour. When the branch was forced into closure in 1972, the British presence was reduced to a lone inshore minesweeper. That was the year in which Gieves decided to risk the ghostly wrath of Old Mel and to concentrate its West End activities on ready-made clothing. However, this sacrifice to necessity was no instant success, so it was in some desperation that, in 1974, Gieves bought Hawkes, who had also been relying less on bespoke tailoring. The attraction was the best address in Savile Row – No. 1. Gieves refurbished it as a palace of superior clothing, as grand and elegant as most of Savile Row was small and dingy, and in that way sought to compensate for any loss of status occasioned by its retreat to general outfitting.

Other Savile Row firms sought safety in numbers, and windows became encrusted with the legends of firms in shared 'sittings'. A few sought savings of scale through acquisition. Wells of Mayfair was the product of multiple amalgamation and Dege bought busily from the late 1960s, starting with Rogers & Co., a military outfitters dating back to 1774, and ending with Pope & Bradley.

Kilgour, French & Stanbury was bought by a clothing group looking for a venerable name to stick into its prospectus as it went public; as the 'craft tailoring division' of the Lincroft Kilgour group, it lost in liberty but gained in resources.

Not surprisingly, the most hectic adventures befell Nutters in its various manifestations, for Tommy Nutter quit after seven years. The protagonists of this first Savile Row squabble of the pop age are coy about discussing the details. 'There was jiggery-pokery going on and I felt I didn't want any part of it,' says Nutter. 'I had reporters chasing me down the street, but I kept quiet about it because it was so messy.'

Above
Elton John in 1976, with fine suiting fighting the psychedelia. A dozen years later, he remains Tommy Nutter's ideal client: 'Other people come for what I give them, but he'll come in and we'll have a sherry together and I'll have a chance to play around with ideas.'
A plethora of pop stars can cause problems. When Andy Williams walked in, he was mistaken for Perry Como.

Sexton's version is that he found his partner 'too theatrical, too extreme . . . [he was] frightening away a lot of serious clients'. Sexton also hints about 'some of us working harder than others'. Sexton carried on Nutters with two other partners – John Chittleborough and Joseph Morgan, who suggests that the magnetic Nutter was too much of a luxury for a small firm. 'When the three of us took over the liabilities, things were grim,' he says. A crash export campaign – Sexton roamed through France, Germany and the United States – was credited with saving the situation; it was observed that notices insisting on an advance deposit appeared in the reception area. 'We have learned that cash down is absolutely vital,' Sexton told *Men's Wear* in 1978.

So Nutters survived without Nutter and pop and rock stars kept coming to Savile Row. 'We did lots of them without Tommy around,' Morgan remembers, and reels off the names: 'Elton John, Paul McCartney, Kate Bush, lots of people on the BBC, Charlie Watts of the Rolling Stones. . . .' No longer simply 'Tommy Nutter's cutter' and finding acceptance in his own right, Sexton waited five more years then parted company as well, choosing to do so in the depths of the worst trade slump in years. 'I wanted my own identity, pure and simple,' he said. Against great odds, he was to flourish through aggressive marketing and publicity, directed mainly at America.

As for Tommy, in his own words, 'I took a year off and became a down-and-out. I had some very nice friends and they looked after me. It was that fabulous summer of 1976, so I got my timing right. Then I ran out of money, so I approached Kilgour and they said, right, go and stand in the shop and see if it works. It was a bit of a nightmare after having been a star, but I managed it somehow.' Tommy's star was soon glinting again: the media rediscovered him and old customers proved loyal; he then got backing for his own shop from an entrepreneur looking for a Savile Row investment.

So it was that in a period of retrenchment bordering on collapse, three different enterprises had sprung from £5,000 of pop culture seed money. Tommy Nutter's main contribution to the rejuvenation of Savile Row lay in the publicity that he generated and in the motivation he gave others. 'He's a brilliant PR, a charming, lovely chap, and let's be honest, he's done more to revive Savile Row than anybody,' is Edward Sexton's summing-up.

Right
Dougie Hayward fits Michael Caine. The relationship was to ripen into friendship, as can happen in Savile Row: sometimes with unexpected combinations. Nutter, for example, has an enduring friendship with some of the Sainsbury family.

Image apart, Nutters arrived in time to ease the path of an awkward technical adjustment that was giving many of its neighbours sleepless nights. Since the era of the artistes of St James's, Savile Row had crafted clothes of substance, clothes made of heavy worsted wools, sometimes thick as a rug. Cloth weights had been declining over the years, but American needs and the increasingly influential fashion end of the ready-to-wear industry had intensified pressure upon Savile Row to produce truly lightweight suits. This had many of the Row's practitioners aghast. Some saw it as a defilement of 'refined elegance'; others rued the loss of structure and considered a lack of lining improper. Some also confessed to technical inadequacy in the new discipline. With the heavy cloth of the past, a cutter could hack out a suit and rely upon the tailor to put it into shape, but the light fabrics were less forgiving and demanded much more precision from the cutter.

'Weight is very important for many of our overseas customers, who understand the problem, but still want well-cut clothes,' said Sexton. 'The soft jacket is very easy to wear, but it was going against the grain, against the Savile Row tailoring image. It was difficult to tailor light cloth, and besides, it's what you are paying for – all the hand-padding and so on. But they got over it. . . .'

Nutters was first to heed the trend and Sexton in 1978 announced that he had the solution in an ultra-light jacket made for 'a very important New York antiques dealer', who had wanted something very cool for hot climates. The pioneer suit was made in pure linen, 'but it could have just as easily been tweed . . . it's very practical for travelling and the design gives a natural drape, a 1950s look, if you like,' said its creator, who saw it as essentially 'a beautifully tailored shirt'.

A pontifical blessing came from Angus Cundey, who declared at a trade gathering that it was right for the cloth merchants to 'thrust the tropical worsted on us' and to oblige Savile Row to master the new cutting techniques that the lightweights demanded.

On 1 September 1979, Savile Row's last direct link with the days of Brummell was severed. A fortnight earlier, Davies & Son had got out its grandly scrolled notepaper to alert customers to its first change of address in 175 years. The Hanover Street firm that had survived the scandal of the Duke of York's trousers had been vanquished by a mundane rent rise. It took what it could – doors, a carpet, some fitting-

Left
Off-duty moment at Huntsman, with a rail of ready-to-wear at rear. When in 1981 the Savile Row standard-bearer began to sell clothing off the peg, purists were aghast, but 'it's worked out quite nicely,' says director Colin Hammick. Nicely enough for some observers to question the firm's future direction.

room chairs, a fender and fireplace screen – to recreate what it could of the old atmosphere in smaller premises nearby. It left behind the small room set aside for the King, still with its painted panels and speaking tube; likewise an extremely ancient bath and a rickety firewatcher's hut on the roof. The fifth floor, where the dubious bedrooms had once been, had ended as the domain of Ted the codger, the alterations hand. Treasures unearthed in the move included grimy ledgers revealing strange transactions, such as barter payments of sherry and claret for suits, and the sartorial histories of kings and cabinet ministers. Robert Peel's bill for 1829 was £128, while the Maharajah of Cooch Behar had treated himself to a tan goatskin motoring cap (£1 5s) and two pairs of matching gauntlets (18s 6d each) in 1902.

Davies could boast an honour roll as richly varied as any on Savile Row – Sir Oswald Mosley and Lord Alexander of Tunis, Field Marshal Haig and Irving Berlin, Sir Henry Campbell-Bannerman and Georgie Fame, Bing Crosby (who certainly got around) and Joseph Kennedy (ditto) had all graced the velvet-curtained fitting rooms. Yet the client balance had swung to almost 90 per cent foreigners as the £50 suit of 1959 became the £300 suit of 1979. Davies received a letter from former British spy chief Colonel Edward Boxshall, who confided that he was still wearing a suit made for him in 1935; not entirely by choice, for he wrote: 'I am unable to afford your present prices.'

The *Toledo Blade* of Ohio had a correspondent investigate the state of Davies, and of Savile Row in general. He reported: 'The era of the Flying Tailor is well underway – if they don't come to you, the only thing is to come to them.' Davies put it more decorously in its change-of-address letter: 'Our business was built on the clothing requirements of the aristocracy of Europe and Great Britain. Today our business is mainly with the affluent and famous abroad; an ideal commercial profile, we are advised, in times when exports are of prime importance.'

When, in mid-1981, Huntsman began selling ready-to-wear and across the street a cash-and-carry operation began selling Italian suits at bargain-basement prices, some thought they detected a death-rattle, but wisely not *Men's Wear*, who called the one event a 'logical development' and the other 'an indication of some of the subtle changes going on'. Ready-to-wear suits had been available in Britain since the 1850s, and it was exactly 100 years since Daniel E. Ryan had brought over an exhibition of American ready-to-wear garments whose 'excellence of workmanship and careful thought, combined with skilful cutting,' was reported to have 'proved of very great interest to both the West End and City cutters'. Top quality ready-to-wear had been introduced to Britain by another American, who in 1937 set up the Chester Barrie factory in Crewe. It was this factory that was now making for Huntsman, who aimed to lure back lost customers by offering a ready-made item that looked very much like the Huntsman bespoke suit, at half the price.

Savile Row's most expensive suit-maker was facing up to reality in the wake of a year in which it had reported heavy losses. In five years, its prices had doubled to £800, and the domestic contribution to its bespoke sales was down to 30 per cent. Poole and Kilgour had still greater dependence on exports and, with a few small newcomers to the Row, it threatened to become 100 per cent.

It was a rare English gentleman who now patronized Savile Row. More likely, he went to Marks & Spencer.

12

American Deliverance

We have pleasure to announce that Mr. B. Hall will be at the cities listed overleaf.

He will have with him samples of materials for Suits, Sports Coats and Blazers, Evening Dress Wear and Riding Wear. Mr. Hall will be at your service and will esteem it a favour to keep any appointments. Also he will have with him a large selection of shirting fabrics, many of which are made specially for Huntsman, from which orders for Custom Made Shirts can be taken.

H. HUNTSMAN & SONS.

INCORPORATING   LTD

CARPENTER & PACKER

TAILORS

11. Savile Row, London, England

ESTABLISHED OVER A HUNDRED YEARS

TELEPHONE: 01-734-7441   CABLES: "CARPACK," LONDON

Left
Huntsman's advance visiting card ascribes to the theory that royal warrants impress Americans. This decorative barrage of credentials go all the way back to Bertie.

Considering that three out of four Savile Row suits adorn foreign bodies and that most of these bodies reside in the United States, the relationship with that former colony has always been marked by a certain tension. Take 10 October 1986 – the day celebrated in America as the 100th birthday of the tuxedo. Not only had they misnamed the dinner jacket and taken to wearing it at weddings and on other unsanctioned occasions, but here were those confounded Yankees claiming to have invented the thing. The claim was based on the exploit of tobacco heir Griswold 'Grizzy' Lorillard, who on the above date in 1886 walked in upon the swells of the Tuxedo Club in Tuxedo Park, New York, wearing an evening jacket minus tails.

'Griswold Did It' was the theme of a lavish advertisement campaign, and the American Formalwear Association was adamant – 'America invented the dinner jacket.' Though it had adequate time to demur, Savile Row preferred to sulk, perhaps deeming it impolite to join in a bragging match with such an important client nation. 'I fear we are missing out on this,' Angus Cundey ventured when it was too late. 'But the dinner jacket is older than 100 years. We made a short smoking jacket for the Prince of Wales as early as 1865. . . .'

The trail of the tail-less jacket is confusing, but it seems to lead back to Savile Row, whoever was the first in America to wear one. Candidates other than Lorillard include Evander Berry Wall – he of

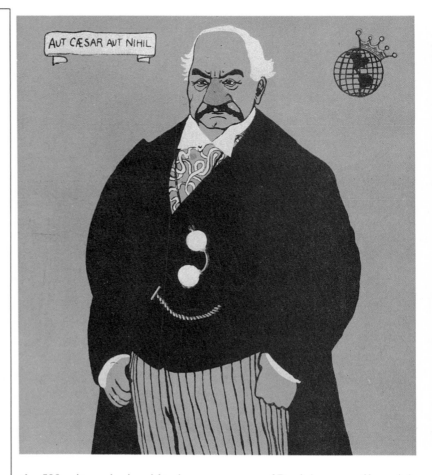

AUT CÆSAR AUT NIHIL

Right
Pierpoint Morgan illuminated the way for the big spenders.

the 500 suits – who is said to have worn one of Poole's sawn-off specials in Saratoga, two months before Grizzy's debut. Another account authenticated by a Tuxedo Club member of the time gives the palm to New York financier James Brown Potter, whose beautiful wife Cora had caught the eye of the Prince of Wales while the couple were in England; Bertie invited the Potters to Sandringham and mentioned that he wore short coats for dinner in the country, so Potter consulted Poole, who executed a rush order. Back home with a royal weekend under his belt, Potter was said to have impressed fellow Tuxedo Club members enough for them to copy the sartorial souvenir that he brought back. Hence the tuxedo.

Once invented, it was no contest when it came to product development. It is recorded that Grizzy's was bright red, and a further century of American inventiveness saw the tuxedo evolve as far as the Day-Glo yellow number favoured by Andy Warhol. It is in such delicate areas of interpretation that tension tends to arise.

'Do not, I beg you, leave a situation at fifty shillings a week to go to Canada or the United States,' *Tailor and Cutter* editor John Williamson urged his charges in 1872. 'American cutters are conceited, and their customers have been trained to wear garments with broad shoulders and a great deal of wadding. Remain where the felicity of your talents may be appreciated by higher mentalities and superior tastes.' For those who would not be dissuaded, Williamson had a few chilly words of consolation: 'You will have a great amount of prejudice operating against you – though perseverance and moral rectitude will overcome in course of time all such obstacles.'

Traffic in the other direction raised few objections, particularly when it brought such garment gluttons as Berry Wall. For the rich American, the lure then was as it is now. Brooks Brothers in New York might boast how President Lincoln, upon the occasion of his inauguration for a second term, wore a Brooks Brothers overcoat lined with twill silk embossed with the image of the American eagle bearing the words 'One Country, One Destiny', but this could seem a little provincial when stacked against the anecdotes of emperors and princes who patronized the likes of Poole.

So the Tuxedo Club members got themselves London tailors. Tales were told of millionaires like the busy captain of industry, who had his measurements taken and then set about ordering with gusto. After twenty minutes, he glanced at his watch. 'The devil,' he exclaimed. 'I can't spend any more time here today. How many suits do you make it?'

'Seventy-four, sir.'

'Guess I'll have to come back to order the rest. What time will suit you?'

'Shall we say this time next year, sir?' was the plaintive reply.

When American protectionist sentiment led to the imposition of the Dingley tariff in 1897, Savile Row felt able to react with haughty disdain, especially to reports that some firms planned to dodge the duty by opening branches in New York. 'A VAIN AMERICAN BOAST', the London *Daily Mail* jeered. It quoted Poole's manager David Belinfante:

> We have never contemplated doing such a thing and so long as I live I hope and trust that we never shall. We have been asked many times to send travellers to America for orders, but, of course, we would not do so. The best people in America come to us and if they have proper introductions we are happy to receive them. But they will always come to us and, no matter how high the tariff that may be imposed, we do not need an American establishment over there. America will come to us.

Belinfante was more subdued when he told the *New York Herald* that the reasons for not moving into America were 'purely business ones' – the cost of importing British cloth and higher American wages made it impractical – and he observed how an American who patronized an English tailor 'expects to get English clothes – English material and English-made'. Besides, he reasoned, 'the class of customer who comes to us would order all the same, tariff or no tariff'.

He was right; tariffs did not work, though protectionist skirmishing continued on and off and tempers became as frayed as King George's collars in the uncertain period after World War II, when the Hollywood influence appeared to threaten seriously 150 years of Savile Row style leadership.

'Men are still looking for manhood and not for costumed dandyism,' the *California Men's and Boy's Stylist* declared in an all-out assault on what it called the 'droopy-shouldered' English look. 'Women are used to our padding . . . they like the easy masculine drape of our coats. And we like it too. In California-made clothes a man will still be a man, not an Oxford grey mouse. We reject grandpa's suit!'

The *Tailor and Cutter* dubbed the top-heavy Hollywood style 'the Gnu Look', and became so concerned over its creeping influence that it lobbied against a move in Parliament to oblige American servicemen to wear civilian clothes when off-duty. 'The great American tragedy is that US clothes have always appealed to the worst side of British nature,' it warned. 'The present trend in London in men's clothes is towards a military smartness. Put the US soldier in his own civies and you will produce in London an apparent increase in vagrants.' Then it tried to go to the source by supporting Adlai Stephenson

Below
Sir Douglas Fairbanks: a Savile Row booster all his life, like his father before him. The *Tailor and Cutter* lauded Fairbanks Sr for 'embracing the stylings of London' while 'not surrendering that imaginative flair for clothes which many Americans are lucky to possess'.

Above
Veteran traveller Brian Lishak with Savile Row strategist and colleague Robert Bright. Note how the uniforms match.

('elegant . . . smacks of the British Foreign Office') in the 1952 presidential race.

Every little helped, for Anglophile sensibilities were soon fully aroused, so that by the middle of 1952, the *Tailor and Cutter* was reporting a trend away from the Gnu Look and Douglas Fairbanks Jnr felt able to assert that Savile Row had 'recaptured the tailoring supremacy of the world'. 'This is to be expected, of course, as Britain sets the style and the world follows,' the *Tailor and Cutter* clucked contentedly.

By the mid-1960s, *Esquire* was finding evidence of 'the London line' in everything from the roll of hat brims to the ribs on socks ('British explorers were always pictured wearing them on safari in Africa . . .') and it saw Savile Row setting its stamp on American suit styling, in which 'one of the interesting phenomena of the '60s, the growth of the natural shoulder . . . can be traced back to a leading old-line tailoring house in the West End of London'.

Above
First class to New York aboard the *Queen Mary* – a happy hunting ground for the travellers.

The notion of not going out after business was always an affectation of the few, and they grew steadily fewer. Flocks of tailors accompanied by cavernous trunks were a familiar sight on the Atlantic liners throughout the century – men such as C. Stuart Lawry, who made 130 transatlantic voyages for Davies and successfully defied the U-boats of two world wars. By the time Lawry died in 1955, he had sold and measured for Savile Row in France, Holland, Belgium, Germany, Brazil, Uruguay, Argentina, Cuba, Costa Rica, Guatemala, Colombia, Panama, Trinidad and Jamaica, as well as the United States and Canada.

From camp followers on imperial campaigns, Savile Row's tailors came to awe the natives in many an odd place. Among Meyer & Mortimer's stack of royal warrants is the Order of the White Elephant of Siam, which, company legend has it, was substituted by a lesser order when it transpired that the bearer could claim access to the royal harem.

Japan discovered Savile Row almost as soon as it opened to the West, and nowhere was the impact more profound. The first Savile

Row tailor reached Japan in the 1880s. No one is sure what happened to him, but lounge suit in Japanese is 'Sabiro', pronounced 'Soy-be-roh', a corruption of the holy name itself. The first Japanese ambassador to the Court of St James's made a bee-line for Poole. When the Crown Prince was on his way , Poole's sent out a man to meet him; the fitting took place aboard a Japanese warship at Gibraltar.

Poole had a workshop in Addis Ababa for a time in the 1950s and found the local tailoring talent 'very cheerful, willing and adaptable'. Cutter Ted Mitchell came back saying how wonderful the light was. Two Lawrence brothers, one a former Poole's cutter and the other from Wells, set up shop in Alexandria, where one became tailor to King Farouk and was charged with making a suit for every day of the year. He won a prize with a pair of jodhpurs he sent back to London. A photograph shows him looking stern in a fez. The *Tailor and Cutter* was providing complicated instructions on 'What to Wear Around the Globe' as late as 1955 ('Red Sea kit for Aden . . . worsted suits for Nairobi with evening dress on Saturdays . . .'), but the loss of India was the first of a series of retreats that made Savile Row turn more and more to America.

'It was a terrible tragedy for us when the Indian Raj packed up,' sighs Malcolm Johnstone, great-grandson of J. B. Johnstone, who founded an empire-girdling tailoring house with branches in Delhi and Lahore to serve the Indian Army officer class and fabulously rich princes like the Nyzam of Hyderabad, whose ordering was as munificent as his hospitality. Johnstone's representative would be provided with his own elephant while waiting upon the Nyzam's pleasure. With India gone and bad times at home, Johnstone also turned to America.

The camaraderie of those days was tremendous, according to Brian Lishak, a Wells director who made his first trip to America for Huntsman when he was just seventeen. It had to be. Journeys had an epic quality – five to nine days at sea, then two to four months or even longer hauling a mound of cabin trunks and suitcases all over the United States. Customs procedure was arduous, then the travellers – a dozen or more to a ship – would usually stay together for a fortnight in New York before going their various ways.

It was popular to sail on the *Queen Mary* or *Queen Elizabeth* immediately after Christmas and celebrate New Year at sea. Some splashed out on custom-made Louis Vuitton luggage and at least one sumptuous set of Louis Vuittons went down in a U-boat attack, though no Savile Row traveller was lost in the Battle of the Atlantic.

Once ashore, the rail system was their highway and most based themselves in hotels close to Grand Central Station. There was the Murray Hill Hotel, and later the Biltmore, whose twenty-first floor was Savile Row West; also the nearby Roosevelt. Group ritual extended to the first evening meal ashore, which was celebrated at Sacher's, a Madison Avenue restaurant run by a stout and homely German woman. Breakfasts brought everybody to Child's, opposite the Biltmore, where the waitress Helen was hard of hearing and so served everybody the same. In the evenings, there was The Rose in the East 50s, known for its bathtub gin martinis and beef-ends. On Sundays, it was The Brass Rail on Fifth Avenue.

Savile Row's envoys were treated as exotic pets, even by the police, who were known to extend understanding to any found weaving up Fifth Avenue late at night. For they were different, as different as their clientele expected them to be. 'Yes, the image was important,' says Lishak. 'We realized we were ambassadors and most of us were very much aware of the gentleman image. We were proud to do it and our

Bottom
Adlai Stephenson was Savile Row's choice for President.

Centre
When Clark Gable got around to Savile Row, he used the same tailor as Tyrone Power and other Hollywood heroes.

Below
C. Stuart Lawry, doyen of the travellers, had a client list headed by Harry Truman.

customers enjoyed it. They were Anglophiles and they loved everything English.' Lishak recounts a rummaging customs officer's surprise on discovering his supply of stiff collars: '"Stiff collars! What are these, bud? Let's have a look in here". . . then he called around his chums to see this guy with the stiff collars.'

Malcolm Johnstone has at the age of eighty-three only recently given up regular American expeditions. The great-grandson of J.B. is a Cushman on his mother's side. A Cushman? Genealogy is always a Savile Row delight: 'Of course I got on very well in America because they're awful snobs out there and they discovered that I was a direct descendant of Mary Allerton, the youngest lady on the *Mayflower*. Her boyfriend Robert Cushman followed on the next ship and thereby generations of Cushmans came down to my great-grandmother who came over to London and married a Muspratt of Muspratt Hall. . . .' Surely this was enough for any red-blooded American to buy a J. B. Johnstone suit. Those who did ranged from New York mayors to cowboy film hero Tom Mix, who satisfied another Savile Row obsession by riding a horse into Johnstone's Sackville Street shop (Henry Poole is credited with facing down a disgruntled client mounted upon a steed, and even Moss Bros has a horse-into-shop anecdote).

The publicity-minded Charles Emms enjoyed his American romps after the war. One moment he was advising that 'no man in a tuxedo is a fit companion for a lady in an evening dress – men should wear tails', and the next he was promoting his 'wonderful new paper vest . . . wear it and toss it away', and even chancing to add: 'I made one for the King.' Back on the Row, eyebrows were raised.

Poole's globe-trotting director Joseph Mead (who dared call him a travelling salesman, even if he did appear loaded down with several thousand cloth samples?) was always careful to refer to his biannual visits to places like Detroit as 'courtesy calls' on old London customers and 'friends they have introduced', for the image of exclusivity was precious, wherever the market. Yet even he would sometimes get giddy and talk to the press which he would never do at home. American males could not wear the shapely garments of the Englishman because their anatomy was different, he told the *Milwaukee Journal*. 'The American has high, square hips,' he commiserated. He also maintained that while the average Englishman drooped on the right shoulder, Americans tended to droop on the left.

Stuart Lawry was the doyen of the travellers. He carried a silver-topped cane. 'Clients considered it an absolute honour to be dressed by Mr Lawry,' says Brian Lishak. Lawry sailed first class on the *Queens* and was famous for the orders he secured on each voyage. Once in the States, his client list started at the top, with Harry Truman. Then there was Bill Richardson of J. C. Wells, who petrified even colleagues with his brusque retired army officer routine – 'He was very stern with customers, and they adored him for it,' Lishak recalls. Robbie Robinson, who travelled for Jones, Chalk & Dawson, was another artist in elitism – 'We were admiring this skyscraper when a young traveller boasted, "I've got 500 customers in that building", and Robbie turned round: "I've got one – the president."'

The comradeship was such that trust was absolute. 'I couldn't understand it when I first went over,' says Lishak. 'Here were all these competitors, all so friendly, it was extraordinary. There was absolutely no worry about looking after each other's customers – I went to Houston for Bobby Valentine, and once when John Wells* left all his orders behind, I brought them home for him. We'd even send customers to one another – if a customer found Huntsman too expensive, I'd direct them to a colleague. . . .'

Below
The Grangers. An Anglo-American alliance and probably the only husband-and-wife team ever to ply the American circuit.

*John Wells is a descendant of William Cooling Lawrence, the nineteenth-century master-negotiator, and like him became Lord Mayor of Westminster.

The rail networks made the whole thing possible. 'It really was luxurious,' recalls Lishak. 'You could work Philadelphia one day and pick up the train in the evening to land in Pittsburg and be open for business by nine the next morning. We used to visit thirty-five cities that way.' Mostly, they plied the eastern states and let the wild west alone.

Despite the obvious difficulty, even tiny one-man firms began to ply the States. Among the most successful was Jim Welshman, who arrived in New York, collected a list of delegates from the United Nations and, with a bag of dimes, began trading from a telephone kiosk. He had been spurred on by Fred Lintott of Huntsman, who told him: 'When you get to the other side, whether you're Huntsman or Poole or Welshman doesn't matter — we all start equal.' Among current voyagers, Malcolm Plews embodies the Welshman spirit.

Brian Lishak still travels America, but the circumstances are changed. Now he makes four trips a year, fast coast-to-coast dashes designed around airline schedules and a need for speedy service with a product that defies speedy service. 'A Savile Row suit is a want, not a need,' lectures Robert Bright, Lishak's colleague and centenary-year President of the Federation of Merchant Tailors. 'We need to achieve delivery when it's still fresh and exciting. The problems and cost are enormous.' So are the rigours. Aircraft may be faster, but there is nothing like the old Railway Express Company to porter the baggage, and cab drivers can become enraged at the approach of Savile Row tailors under full load. Back strains and worse come with the territory; perhaps it helps explain why Brian Lishak was inspired during a visit to Chicago to take up marathon running when well into his forties. Curiously, though, one firm has been effectively represented for the past thirty years by a man bound to a wheelchair. This is Ian Gregarson

Above and Left
Sexton's brightly beckoning window is a beacon in the Savile Row night.

of Stovel & Mason, tailor to Douglas Fairbanks and, at various times, Clark Gable, Tyrone Power, Charles Chaplin, Grace Kelly and Marlon Brando. It seems that even New York cab-drivers have hearts – 'they take pity on me,' he says.

Gone are the days when an English accent was enough to charm a customer into a change of clothes. 'Not all that long ago we were dealing with a very small group who were the equivalent of the American aristocracy, and the rest were very tough businessmen who made a lot of money very quickly and still used spittoons,' says Lishak.

'Frankly, a lot of our customers were in awe of us. That's changed.' Kilgour's Peter Ferguson-Smith did the bowler hat and rolled umbrella routine on his first Los Angeles trip in 1979, but hasn't since. He insists that, 'We're not trying to sell pinstripes to Texans – they dress less formally and so we must make less formal.' His regular circuit takes in New York, Washington, Dallas, Palm Beach, Beverly Hills, San Francisco and Chicago.

Who knows what an Adlai Stephenson victory would have done for menswear, but a reversion to conservative garb heralded by the election of President Reagan was a lifesaver, coming as it did with the dollar low enough to make struggling Savile Row a bargain attraction for Americans. The only snag was a revival of protectionist sentiment, which made it impolitic for certain leading figures to parade in foreign finery, even Savile Row finery. Kilgour is credited with dressing several of the Reagan cabinet, but Gieves hints at 'presidential associations' which fell foul of protectionist sensibilities; yet it adds darkly: 'Where there's a will, there's a way, especially when you're dealing with eminent people. If it's the way they choose to dress, they will, be it smuggled round the back door.'* The nomination of Senator Lloyd Bentson as a candidate for Vice-President drew a shrug and an 'Ah well, I won't be seeing him again,' from his tailor Lennie Logsdail. Likewise, New York Mayor Ed Koch quit wearing Savile Row, apparently as a precaution against potential embarrassment.

The American who is drawn to Savile Row today tends to be an enthusiast and is liable to treat his London tailor as a hypochondriac does his doctor. Magazine cuttings and scribbled notes on style ideas land on cutting boards from customer-zealots across the States, while the occasional Midwest doctor or Chicago surgeon will think nothing of phoning up for a spur-of-the-moment chat when the mood takes him. In contrast to the rarefied relationships of Savile Row tradition, American clients are more likely to encourage personal friendship. Lennie Logsdail of Sackville Street remembers reflecting on this when being entertained at the Capitol in Washington – 'It suddenly shook me: there was I, a milkman's son, being entertained by these two US senators who were interested to know my opinions of the Thatcher government.' From theatre tickets to honeymoon trips, the client in America has been known to oblige.

'Americans are different; they know what they want and those interested in clothes know about clothes – they'll tell you about some particular stitch they want and they'll know all about that stitch. It's the same with the cloth. . . .' This is Conduit Street tailor Sammy Stewart talking. Sammy's brother Henry went to New York fifty years ago and became a celebrated Savile Row transplant; at the age of eighty-four, Henry makes for Robert De Niro, Paul Newman and sundry billionaires who hold him in near-religious respect. He has been called 'a magician who defies the laws of physics and optics'. Americans get lyrical like that when describing their favourite tailor. Sammy is still on Conduit Street and a little disillusioned. 'The British are ignorant and disinterested,' he says. 'It's sad to see all the best work going abroad, but there it is.'

Bespeaking Americans at long distance is more difficult than it used to be, and not merely because snob appeal is not all that it used to be. American taste used to run to what was aptly called the sack suit, and Savile Row was happy to oblige, for the deep armholes and broad, rather shapeless cut allowed for plenty of latitude for error. The taste is now for more stylized clothing, more form-fitting and consequently more demanding.**

A few bright ideas have helped. Brian Lishak believes he was first to augment the tape measure with the camera, which enables the cutter back on Savile Row to get a sense of the body that goes with the measurements. His first camera used flash bulbs – 'it was an absolute menace, but the results were tremendous from the start'. Kilgour's Ferguson-Smith is one of several who use polaroid cameras – 'to the cutter, it's as good as having the man standing in front of him, because he can see whether and where he drops and so on'. Model fitting jackets in various sizes are another innovation that serve as a double-check and help pinpoint physical eccentricities not always obvious from measurement alone. Gently directing customers away from difficult-to-tailor fabrics also helps, while some of the travellers have come up with marvellously individualistic measuring devices, such as a converted car aerial. It still isn't easy – 'I'm sure every travelling tailor has felt his heart sink when he sees the man with the box under his arm and he wonders what's happened, but we all have a good success rate considering the circumstances,' says Ferguson-Smith. 'Obviously if we didn't people wouldn't put up with it.'

It is simpler for small, free-spirit outfits like Manning of Maddox Street, whose proprietor-cutter Stuart Manning makes at least four American trips each year; he likes Boca Ratan in Florida, so he includes it on his circuit, reasoning that 'You've got to weekend somewhere.' Manning flew to Hollywood to fit actor Richard Chamberlain on a Wednesday, was back on the Friday and, along with a substantial suit order, landed the bonus of an Emmy Award – television's equivalent of an Oscar – for an outfit Chamberlain wore when playing Nazi foe Raoul Wallenberg. Manning also has a tailor-brother in the States. He thinks New York's tiny custom tailoring equivalent of Savile Row suffers from ethnic overkill – 'They all look as though their main clients are the Mafia.'

Among the medium-sized, no firm is more wedded to America than Norton. Its origins are early-nineteenth century and it made clothes for the Kaiser, but since 1970 it has been owned by the patrician-looking John Granger, who has been spurred by the acquisition of a young American wife schooled in marketing into an intense concern for packaging the old image in smart new ways. His coda is, 'We still sell British tradition, but you have to change – business changes, attitudes change, everything changes. . . .' The Norton shop at 16 Savile Row has certainly changed. It now exudes the cute coziness of a yuppy clothing boutique in the Hamptons of Long Island, and in fact an East Hampton shop was the first to market the Norton Field Range, a collection of costly ready-made outfits for the American hunting-shooting-fishing set, upon which the firm is staking its future. Granger worked on prototypes for Hardy Amies's early menswear ranges and Amies is Granger's entrepreneurial ideal.

When a Norton ran Norton, he would sail on the *Queens* twice a year; the Grangers fly together to the States five or six times a year and go to places off the traditional Savile Row circuit, like Raleigh, North Carolina. Taking along the wife is something new to Savile Row. 'Irit's presence only increases sales,' he says, and she agrees vehemently.

The quintessential Savile Row exporter is Edward Sexton, now operating from a slickly designed salon in which the entire process of suit-making is on display and turned to visual effect. 'We're probably 85-90 per cent an export company, so a lot of our work is made without any fittings,' he begins, popping myths like so many balloons. His client patterns are so good that 'there's no guessing, it's very precise'. He uses model jackets and squiggles complex instructions on order

*For reasons of duty-dodging (at present it is a hefty 30 per cent) as well as patriotic pressure, all manner of subterfuge has been resorted to at times – delivery via Mexico, for instance.

**Differences in national clothing styles are greater than people realize. American trousers, for example, are cut much straighter in the seam. The English like them slacker in the leg – it's easier to climb stairs that way; but then, Americans tend to have less stairs to climb.

charts that he faxes back to base as he moves across the States: 'It's so simple – if you've got modern technology you must use it.'

Neat, nimble and with a well-honed ego, Sexton talks a language that Madison Avenue can understand. He is, he says, 'somewhat more contemporary than the rest of Savile Row . . . a little more emphasis on the shoulder . . . a little more expression into the chest area. . . .' As the first to hire a Manhattan publicist, he has received attention from the gossip columnists as well as the fashion scribes. 'Easy elegance is what Sexton is all about,' billowy blonde Suzy of the *New York Post* tells readers. A while later, Suzy describes how he 'flew off to Los Angeles for a last-minute fitting on sexy Michael Nouri, one of his favorite clients and dearest friends. . . . Sexton hand-carried Michael's gorgeous new dinner jacket and arrived just in time to suit up Nouri for the premiere of his new movie . . . .' Suzy can be relied upon for a paragraph most times that Sexton's in town. Few *Post* readers are ever likely to buy bespoke, but the effect is cumulative. In a country that sometimes finds difficulty defining the difference between Savile Row and King's Road, name recognition counts, and Edward Sexton can count upon getting a mention whenever English style is under review in the US media.

Above and Far Right

Fallan and Logsdail, neighbours on Sackville Street and companions in America, where Logsdail found a wife. The wedding in Philadelphia was a Savile Row occasion.

Above Right

TV production *Poor Little Rich Girl* gave Sexton a showcase the traditional way – through a recommendation. Here Woolworth heiress Barbara Hutton (played by Farrah Fawcett) luxuriates in the arms of one of her Sexton-garbed husbands (Amadeus August).

In *Poor Little Rich Girl*, a TV mini-series about the much-married Woolworth heiress Barbara Hutton, Sexton landed the perfect showcase through an impeccably Savile Row process of referral – series producer Lester Persky was a personal client and through him Sexton got the job of garbing the co-stars who play Hutton's many men and making suits for Farah Fawcett, who played Hutton. It was made-to-measure publicity, and Lori Simmons Zelenko Communications did not let their client down. 'Savile Row Tailor Re-Creates Cary Grant Look', the *Los Angeles Times* reported across an entire page, while the *Daily News Record* splashed it as 'Sexton Appeal'. There is nothing bashful about Edward Sexton. He told one interviewer: 'When the actors put on these clothes, they got an erection.'

And so he progresses, a news point wherever he goes. In San Francisco, there are the clothes he is making for Mayor Dianne Feinstein; back in New York, he is being photographed in the '21' club cellar, among wine stocks held for members ranging from Richard Nixon to Ivan Boesky; in Denver, it seems there is nothing remarkable to report, so the *Rocky Mountain News* has him talking about 'the cream of society' turning up to be fitted for his 'Rolls-Royce' clothing. Judiciously dropped snippets of gossip liven the interviews: readers learn how he made matching white jumpsuits for John Lennon and Yoko Ono, how Joan Collins likes her shoulders well padded, and how Cary Grant 'had small, sloping shoulders and a big head'.

To extend his American business, Sexton has explored beyond pure bespoke and sanctioned some local tailoring of his 'London Line', using his master patterns and cloth selections. Next step is a licensing deal for an off-the-rack Sexton menswear collection, to be manufactured in America. 'The old school was so snobbish,' he tells a Los Angeles reporter. 'Rather than sit on our backsides waiting for someone to push open the door, we're much more aware of marketing.'

A no-nonsense approach to selling straight Savile Row to a clientele unconvinced by silver-top canes or clipped accents is evident in the exploits of Keith Fallan and Lennie Logsdail, rival neighbours on Sackville Street, but partners when on the road in America. Logsdail explains: 'It's a very lonely business, a very hard business. You're out there three, four, five weeks and you sit in that hotel room all day and sometimes don't see a soul. A few have turned to drink and other devices. . . .'

Logsdail and Fallan turned to each other. They met in the Biltmore

Above Left
Anderson & Sheppard shuns publicity to the point of refusing photographs. This was shot through the window.

lobby, never having exchanged words on Savile Row, even though their shops are only a few yards apart. 'We just started talking and we got on well together and then we started arranging itineraries together,' said Logsdail, who is the tall one and plays the straight man to Fallan's wicked, deadpan humour. For six years, they have operated in America as a team, achieving substantial economies in the process, even while maintaining totally separate businesses – 'We help each other out all the time and we don't pinch. If you're confident, there's no problem.' Fallan finds endless mirth in Logsdail's large nose – 'it's like the Concorde' – while Logsdail makes a big thing about enduring Fallan's vanity as they work from East Coast to West and back again. 'We're there to make Britain great again, and to see if we can make a little bit on the side as well,' Fallan explains, deadpan as ever.

Fallan likes to debunk. 'I think it's a lot of bull, all this about styling,' he begins. 'I don't know what the hell a designer is in gents' tailoring, but what we've done is to be in the right place at the right time.' As Fallan describes it, his first trip was an eye-opener. He found a trade based on what he calls 'the old New Englander type', a dying breed schooled to be content with baggy, ill-fitting garments, such as he had been unwittingly making through years of working on American bodies he never got to meet. 'I held up my hands. I couldn't believe it. To my mind the clothes were terrible.' So he set about rescuing America with what he modestly calls 'a modern type of suit, slim-fitting in the jacket and pleated trousers'. He found a ready response, mainly among younger men 'in a senior-enough position to be able to afford one of our suits, but still young enough to be vain'. These are the people that Sexton calls his 'high fliers' – doctors, lawyers, investment bankers and the like, whose discovery of one or two of the more obscure, but more energetic, firms has shaken up the Savile Row pecking order. 'Americans have kept English tailoring alive; if a tailor tells you otherwise, he isn't doing business,' is the definitive word from Peter Harvey, Fallan's stay-at-home partner.

Fallan encourages the American tendency to be on first-name terms and keeps things as personal as possible, shunning cameras or other artifices and shuttling to and fro across the Atlantic with half-finished suits. He echoes Sexton: 'You've got to be more modern, you've got to chase, you've got to go there more often, you've got to be more intimate . . . not this old Savile Row thing where somebody comes in and you say, "Oh, no, sir, this is the way we do it and if you don't like it, too bad." That to my mind is finished.' Pausing he adds: 'Except for Anderson's. It works for them.'

This is a grudging acknowledgement, for Anderson & Sheppard contradicts all his reasoning and the wisdom of all those who insist that Savile Row needs to change to survive in the modern world. But Anderson & Sheppard is a marvel of contradiction.

Diaghilev was a customer, as was Fred Astaire, and Leslie Charteris suited The Saint there; now they do double-breasteds for Prince Charles – not that there's a hint of a royal warrant about: that would be too common. Anderson & Sheppard is the most secretive of all the Savile Row houses and the most hidebound by tradition, even though it does not have a particularly aristocratic clientele. Shunning publicity, it consequently gets a lot of it. Which may be the point, for America laps it up. The Anderson coat, and it will make it no other way, is roomy and soft, so soft that it has been likened more to a woolly cardigan than a suit jacket. Elegantly sensuous to the cognoscenti, it might appear a trifle limp on some bodies.

'To be honest, I don't like it,' said Keith Fallan, thereby flaunting a Savile Row taboo against ever criticizing one of their own. Neither did Professor John Karl, head of the menswear department at the Fashion Institute of Technology in New York. In a notorious episode that amused rather than shocked the rest of Savile Row, the Professor judged a copy made by a Hong Kong tailor named A-Man Hing Cheong to be superior to an Anderson & Sheppard original. He did rather lard it on when he suggested Anderson's stitching looked as if it had been 'done by an orangutan'.

Apart from its fast-and-cheap reputation, Hong Kong does have a few tailors who make quality bespoke at a price below that of Savile Row, though not spectacularly so. Yet Savile Row has Hong Kong customers who insist that the cut and the cachet is worth the 10,000-mile journey to visit their tailor. Numbers of Europeans also continue to patronize the Row, though it has long since abandoned the custom of the Continental branch shop. The Dutch are traditionalists who like English cloth, and there is a type of Frenchman who feels the same way about London tailoring as certain Englishmen feel about French food, wine and women. 'If I go to the best tailor in Munich, I feel like a well-dressed German, but if I buy a good suit in London, I feel well-dressed,' said one leading German diplomat, in explaining why he chose Savile Row.

Above
The likes of Senator Lloyd Bentson and New York Mayor Ed Koch appear lost to Savile Row out of fears of political embarrassment, though others are said to resort to back-door methods.

13

Decay and Renewal

From the Thistle in Vigo Street to the Burlington Bertie at the end of Old Burlington Street is 325 paces, or three minutes of brisk walking by a thirsty man. The route encompasses most of what constitutes present-day Savile Row tailoring, while in either pub can be gleaned the latest of its gossip.

In the Thistle, there is a bottle of champagne on ice from a case donated by the Duke of Devonshire, in celebration of the fifty years that he has enjoyed the services of Jarvis & Hamilton. Everyone has a drink on the Duke, who, it is agreed, has been an ideal customer blessed with an ideal figure, only lately going a little saggy. The host is the Jarvis & Hamilton guv'nor, John Reed, who looks a bit like one of Dickens's more raffish characters: in tight, black cutaway jacket, hard collar, dove-grey waistcoat, striped pants, paisley tie with matching handkerchief, diamond pin and red carnation, he is one of the few on Savile Row to dress the role. His client list – 'a lot of Debrett and City people' – is more traditional than most. Fathers still introduce their sons and are offered a 10 per cent discount on the first order. 'What I like about this business – the whole bloody thing's a family,' Reed says and quotes Harry Helman to the effect that it doesn't matter where the customer goes, so long as he is not lost to Savile Row.

In the Burlington Bertie, Harry Helman is leaning on a cane topped by a magnificent silver fox and giving one of his theatrical, roguish winks before confiding some piece of ancient tailoring lore to a little group of disciples huddled around. Harry has been a regular here since long before any of them were born.

To call Harry rotund is to do injustice to so circular a figure. It is hard to imagine him upon a horse, yet he is credited with matching the hunting exploits of a Jorrocks. As for his other social accomplishments, he is honoured among the greats at such resorts as the Casanova Club. Harry is often called the Godfather of Savile Row: in his eighties, he is its outstanding personality and its most caring. When young Malcolm Plews made his first American trip, Harry was on the phone to Lord King to try to get him a better airline seat; when Lennie Logsdail married the girl he met in Philadelphia, there was a bottle from Harry; when Edward Sexton was striving to create the Cary Grant look for an American television series, it was Harry he turned to for advice. To Harry, they are all 'lovely boys . . . lovely craftsmen'.

Harry and his brother Burt have tailored, and argued, together for sixty years. Born in Soho, where they opened on £2 a week in 1929, they are at once the soul of the trade and a superb double-act as they bicker through their days at No. 10 Savile Row. From the spot where Jeannette Marshall once peeped through the curtains at her doomed admirer, Harry and Burt kept an eye on Sexton, Plews and other young turks across the street.

Above
Harry Helman, genial Godfather of
Savile Row, holds court in the
Burlington Bertie. Protégé Malcolm
Plews dons Helman's signature hat and
wields cane in playful mimicry.

The Helmans have no need to travel: the world comes to them, or a sufficient well-heeled slice of it, in search of the look of quiet confidence that they regard as their hallmark. 'The first suit I made was just the same as we make now,' says Harry. 'Always a nice furl to the lapel.' 'You do your best to make a man look a little better,' says Burt, an artist at disguising stomach spread and shoulder droop. As consummate craftsmen, they win the ultimate accolade, which is the praise of their peers. While the client range extends from Swedish royalty and Rothschilds to actors like Terence Stamp, John Hurt and James Fox (even Muhammad Ali once, when he was voted best-dressed US sportsman), the Helmans' most onerous duty has to be that of tailors to the leaders of the Jewish establishment, for some have enough of a tailoring background to set the most exacting standards. If they have a favourite client, it has to be Lord King, 'a real stickler for the classic British look', who has stayed with them for thirty years.

They normally ask a month to make a suit and they are cagey about accepting just any old stranger. Burt says that 'Some shops in this street will take anybody on and some take only the people they think are right. I agree with this, because certain people drive you crazy.' As a convenience, they will sell a customer a pair of braces, but accessories are otherwise scorned. Though their premises are large by Savile Row standards, they have just ten craftsmen on their books and their production is low, while their prices are high. Burt again comments, 'I always say, rather do good work and make less, then you're producing something worthy and not getting too much aggravation.'

The Helman ethos is about as traditional as is practical these days, but for how long? The summer of 1988 was alive with rumour over the future of their business, for it was common knowledge that they might consider retiring if the right purchaser came along. But what value to put on a business so utterly dependent upon the craft and personality of its existing owners? And at such time of uncertainty? As ever, there was hope of a revival in the domestic market through a resurgence of conservative values among the young, yet it went with the sad reflection that any sharp upturn in trade could not be met by the little entity that is now Savile Row. 'You can't find the people,' is Burt's and everybody's lament.

Before the ready-made revolution of the late 1950s and early 1960s, there were hundreds of firms within that area which the tailors used to refer to as the Golden Mile: Savile Row proper and its generic zone bounded by Piccadilly and Hanover Square, Regent Street and Dover Street; at the time of writing, there are around fifty, and the majority of these are tiny concerns, often a lone cutter-proprietor carrying on a grand old name with the help, perhaps, of one or two sewing tailors in the shop and the rest of the work sent out. In a business as blessed with longevity as symphonic conducting, several of the loners are very old and unlikely to carry on much longer. Accurate statistics are hard to extract from a still secretive trade, but a union official put the number of tailors working for the West End bespoke firms at around 500 – all but about 150 of them outworkers, with not more than 200 fully qualified in all aspects of their exacting craft. The proprietors' federation puts considerably higher the total number involved in all aspects of the trade – at least 3,000, it suggests – and claims a combined annual production of well over 30,000 suits.

More than half of the firms are on the Row itself, while the outer marches are all but abandoned. The old tailoring thoroughfare of Hanover Street is totally bereft of tailors and Princes Street has only Tom Brown, now into its seventh generation of serving Old Etonians; the incumbent Brown is a schoolmasterly presence with a bassoon voice, whose abiding faith in the old ways has survived even the shock of a son going into advertising. Maddox Street is left with the enduring citadel of Wells of Mayfair, and Bryan Manning in a building opposite. Conduit Street, once a tailoring beehive, has a fly-blown air – hard times and rent rises drove Cyril Castle to the rear of his shop, with the front sub-let, and Sammy Stewart was likewise forced to retreat from a rather grand street-front location to the second floor of the building next door; across the street, Castle's friend and rival, Anthony Sinclair, ended his career in more humiliating circumstances, at the rear of a novelty store decked out with false bottoms and other rubber obscenities.

The process of forced integration is exemplified by St George Street's four survivors, who lodge together at No. 1, with the incumbent firm of L. G. Wilkinson (which incorporates the defunct Morgan) playing host to Jarvis & Hamilton, Joce and Johns & Pegg. Chatty, imperturbable Dennis Wilkinson sings out, 'Mr Johns, for you,' or 'Mr Reed, please,' depending upon the associations of the visitor, and thus they proceed with their various enterprises in an atmosphere of enduring civility. At the Piccadilly end of the territory, redevelopment on Sackville Street has driven out all the tailors, except for a pocket of survivors who cluster in a similar manner in the south-

Below
Bobby Valentine toasts kindred spirit Tommy Nutter across the generations: 'There are certain things about a name. For instance, my name happens to be musically attractive. So is Tommy Nutter's. It's a familiar, playful young name. It creates an image. . . .'

east corner.

The *Tailor and Cutter* has gone,* as have the Tailor and Cutter Academy and other supporting institutions. It was once said that no man might regard himself as truly a celebrity until such time as his clothes had been criticized by the editor of the *Tailor and Cutter*. Though enjoying a unique status as the most quoted trade paper in the world, its circulation dwindled to a point in the 1970s where it was no longer viable.

Abandoned, too, are the tailoring contests that had been popular since the June day in 1811 when Sir John Throckmorton won a 1,000-guinea wager by having the wool of two Southdown sheep turned into a four-button coat before the sun set. One or two of the old Dandy Trophies still gather dust on shop shelves, and there are those

Above Left
Dennis Wilkinson and John Reed in genial cohabitation. Four guv'nors share these premises on a corner of the square where the Four-in-Hand Club once gathered. Opposite is St George's Church.

*The Federation of Master Tailors continues with efforts to revive the title as a quarterly periodical.

who can recall with pride such triumphs as the occasion in 1962 when the Helman brothers won seven prizes with a jacket they had to be persuaded to enter; but there is no longer the sponsorship to foster such events. Without the *Tailor and Cutter* to keep an eye on things, 'best-dressed' contests have strayed far from the Savile Row standards. In 1980, the Menswear Association of Britain nominated a soccer player, who said that he left it to his wife to choose his clothes; at least he wore a suit when picking up his prize of a Japanese watch. By 1982, winner Anthony Andrews was wearing an off-the-peg blazer, and by 1984 the organizers were actively promoting the sacrilegious view that a tailored suit was not a prerequisite for best-dressed status.

Above

A Poole tailor of the 1940s. 'Tailoring is very hard work and it takes tremendous sacrifices to become fully skilled. You get paid for the stitches you put in, and unless you get the speed up when you start, you'll never get it and you won't be able to make a living at it' – union official.

Beyond the social fraternities of the pubs and other watering holes, which still retain some of the functions of the old 'houses of call', Savile Row's organizational structure is limited to that afforded by the Federation of Merchant Tailors, which is a national organization regarded with lukewarm enthusiasm by many on the Row. Wells's chief Robert Bright is a lay preacher in private life and an evangelist when it comes to Savile Row and its future. As a perennial senior official of the Federation, he has encouraged his reluctant brethren to invest more on training and to promote themselves to better effect.

It is not easy; when the Federation marked its 1988 centenary with an open day, much of Savile Row shut its doors on the event and the public response was equally dismal – it might have been the climactic scene from *High Noon*, so few turned out. Craftsmen from half-a-dozen firms combined to make a chalk-stripe suit for a BBC newsreader, who was to wear it in television appearances, but other firms considered such public display to be inappropriate, and at Anderson & Sheppard they viewed it as positively damaging to Savile Row's image.*

Savile Row is family, in every sense – the bickering and the petty-feuding included. With the partial exception of the self-isolating Anderson & Sheppard, the interrelationship of personnel is intense. For example, the book-keeper at Fallan & Harvey is the mother of the proprietor at Alan Bennett. The genesis of Fallan & Harvey and Burstow & Logsdail is instructive and typical. Keith Fallan was apprenticed at Huntsman and learned cutting at Wealeson & Leagate, where he met his future partner Peter Harvey. When Wealeson had a heart attack and died, Fallan and Harvey kept things going for a year or two until Hambros Bank, which had been a customer, bought the business and then sold it to Sullivan & Wooley.

Alan Burstow did much the same when Welsh & Jeffries was sold over his head; he left with youthful colleague Lennie Logsdail and they set up on their own in a workroom on the second floor of a rickety old Carnaby Street building. The ceiling was unsafe and they had only about a dozen clients between them; they did alterations for ready-to-wear companies to make ends meet, while gradually their client list

Left
BBC announcer garbed in formal glory for early radio broadcast. Savile Row failed in an attempt to sustain this spirit when television came along.

grew. After seven years in Soho, they jumped back across the great psychological divide of Regent Street and took shared premises in Sackville Street. Their rent quadrupled, but their turnover doubled and within a further ten years they had absorbed faltering room-mates Denman & Goddard and Carr, Son & Woor, venerable names with 150 years of tailoring behind them.

*Thirty-three years before, the Federation of Merchant Tailors tried to persuade the BBC to oblige all its television announcers to wear dinner jackets. The campaign was dropped after the BBC suggested the tailors bear some of the cost.

So this primeval process of decay and renewal still holds in Savile Row, if at a quickening pace, as do the dark arts of client capture, for after all the truly faithful customer has always been something of a myth. To retain respectability, a little subtlety is expected: one time-honoured tactic is for an absconding cutter to send out Christmas cards to the customers of his late employer.**

The economics of Savile Row are the sum of a collection of exceptions – how each firm survives or thrives is as individual as the way in which it puts together its suits. There is absolutely no limit to smallness, unless it be in the enterprise of a Mr Graham, a noted tailor of odd-shaped people, who once said of his brain that 'it just seems to guide the chalk to man's contours'. Late in life, he was accorded a sitting at Wells, where he was credited with a production rate of one suit per year.

There are no statistics. The Federation of Merchant Tailors in 1987 estimated the total turnover of all Britain's bespoke tailors at £25 million, with £17 million of this in exports, but it was only a guess. One-man firms are common, with the proprietor-cutter having all his work made up by outside coat-makers, trouser-makers and waistcoat hands, who in turn employ specialist finishers, etc. Two-man firms are even more common and enjoy an obvious logistic advantage. Only the top half-dozen are of any size: it was not until 1984 that the turnovers of either Huntsman or Poole passed £1 million. A little business can do nicely on a one-suit-per-day production rate, so long as it shares premises and operates with minimal permanent staff – ideally none at all. Peter Moore is one of the Row's loners. 'What threatens to happen is that the cost of producing the article becomes greater than its value,' he says. 'A large part of that cost is in overheads, and there isn't the volume in tailoring to cover the sort of overheads the bigger tailoring companies incur. I think it will gradually end up as individuals either working in communal premises or from home – there has to be a way they can cut the overheads.' Overheads like doubling rents, or the high cost of constant travel that reliance upon America brings. Subtract the overheads and the arithmetic becomes attractively simple – at 1988 rates, for instance, a coat-maker charged about £100 to make up a jacket and an average suit-length of cloth cost the tailor almost as much. So pricing becomes the most critical decision, and here Keith Fallan poses the question: 'If you make one suit a week at a high price, or ten suits a week at a medium price, who's the better off?' Always assuming, of course, that you have ten suits a week to make.

Fallan & Harvey could be judged a medium-sized success. They made 237 suits – at 4.55 per week – in the grim year of 1980 and 243 in 1981, since when they have bounded forward on their American success to achieve a rate of 15.36 per week in 1987. With a staff of five tailors, a shared machinist and presser and some outside help, they reckon to have a capacity to produce comfortably twenty suits a week; much more than that and they would need to hire sales help. The rent has just doubled, but a bespoke shirt firm and another tailor have a share in the premises. 'To have a computer would be like Utopia, but we haven't got as far as a typewriter yet . . . we're still long-hand,' Fallan chuckles as he sculpts shape into a suit section with his iron. Growing bigger means more problems, while staying static carries the danger of gradual decline. There is no easy option.

Anderson & Sheppard, for all its irritating aloofness and fuddy-duddy dedication to the Limp Look, is by general recognition the most

Below and Centre Right
Tom Brown III (died 1852), IV (died 1874), V (died 1906) and the seventh and last of the line contemplating an uncertain future. The family shop at Eton opened in 1784 and is still run by a cousin.

**Seeking custom through modern marketing techniques is not quite Savile Row, and John Kent in Old Burlington Street was as much startled as delighted when an American customer, who happened to be in mail order, recently sent him a prime mailing list of the Beverly Hills set. 'It's a cracker,' said Kent, who does not travel and was pondering how to exploit it.

successful firm of the late 1980s. 'It is undoubtedly working for them,' Robert Bright confirms. 'Anderson & Sheppard say "we don't want publicity because it damages our image". Yet it's all a form of marketing. No marketing these days is a form of marketing.'

Anderson is nothing if not contrary. Despite its vow of monastic silence, it is more open than most of its secretive brethren in its financial reports. These reveal a fascinating scenario. The firm is controlled by Volga Investments, a Jersey company, and its board is chaired by Josie Rowland, the wife of entrepreneur and media mogul 'Tiny' Rowland. Thus secured by big bucks, its day-to-day activities would appear to be left to a consortium of cutters, who have places on the board. In the year to 31 January 1987, it reported a pre-tax profit of £318,000 on a turnover of £1,540,000, and it gave this market

Above and Below
Sign in Japanese greets Japanese customer entering Blades. Nineteenth-century drawing of the same spot, with rear entrance to the Albany on left. Since 1803, the Albany's unique set of chambers for 'bachelors and widowers of the nobility and gentry' have afforded instant access to their tailors for many famous names, beginning with Byron and Macaulay and continuing today with Savile Row fan Terence Stamp.

breakdown: home £433,663, America £873,865, Europe £124,524, rest of world £107,926. It achieved this with a staff of twenty-five, two being administrative and the rest defined as 'production and distribution'. This indicates a substantial reliance on the traditional, self-employed craftsman. To appreciate fully the significance of the American customer to Anderson, an expatriate and visitor factor has to be extracted from the domestic tally.

Anderson may stay pure, but other firms of size have had to compromise to some extent, if only to protect themselves from the risks of too great a reliance on foreign sales in an era of volatile exchange rates. The dollar rate is a constant breakfast-time trauma, and at somewhere around $1.80 to the pound, it is time to take out the smelling salts. For all his affection for Savile Row, the American customer is highly cost-conscious and a soaring pound sours sales; likewise the stock-market crash of October 1987 left lots of unclaimed orders on the racks. Anderson's results were thought to have taken a dent, along with the others.

The response has been a quickening of enthusiasm for franchising and know-how and name-selling deals in general, which help to even out the trading bumps and reduce the perils of reliance on the one bespoke product. Gieves, with the greater resources of its garages-to-printing parent company, launched a global 'brand marketing' operation. Bespoke is now a minor part of Gieves's activities, but it provides the lustre. 'It's a slow, carefully planned expansion,' says Robert Gieve. 'Wherever we are, what you see here has to be mirrored. It has to be prestigious and oozing good taste.' It took three

Above
Empty shop housed the Burlington Arcade's last tailor. Uncertain times claim another victim.

years for the resident of No. 1 Savile Row to find the right address in Hong Kong – No. 1 Statue Square. Prestigious promotion is a Gieves's speciality. It will throw an eightieth birthday party for Sir John Mills (after all, he played Scott of the Antarctic, an old customer) and fill the place with film stars, admirals and generals; it will also make Bob Geldof a morning coat for a visit to Buckingham Palace, explaining, 'we didn't want him to meet the Queen in scruff order'. But then, Gieves even advertises on taxi cabs.

Dege has also diversified as much as dignity will allow, with military contracts, a cricket sweater business, a design contract in Oman and its 'Foxhunter' range of accessories – cufflinks, ties and so on – bearing the house logo of a fox mask with crossed brush and hunting horn. Managing director Michael Skinner delightedly displays his Dege boxer shorts and talks of financing a public relations representative from the proceeds of a Japanese design contract. He alarmed his partner John Dege by trying a computerized mail shot, and was rewarded with eighty orders in January, always the worst month of the year: 'Think of that – eighty orders. Eight-zero! The truth is, if you don't promote yourself, you die. . . .'

Franchising the noble names throws up some curiosities. For example – how does the layman tell the hand-made article from a factory-made suit bearing the Kilgour name? The answer is that the real thing carries no label, just a discreet ticket hidden in the inside pocket; only the version made by a factory in Allentown, Pennsylvania, carries the Kilgour, French & Stanbury label. Kilgour's Peter Ferguson-Smith stresses the value of regular 'feedback' visits to the US manufacturer, but his powers to influence are limited; the Savile Row firm has no control over this American operation, since the brand name was sold. Says Ferguson-Smith: 'You'd be surprised how many people walk in and say "Oh, I've seen your name in America, so I thought I'd come in while I'm in London and have the real thing", so there's a spin-off both ways.' Yet there may be cause to worry when a mass-produced representation of a famous Savile Row name is marketed, as in Barney's famous New York store, alongside the best from other countries.

Even Poole is available as a ready-to-wear label in Japan, and the Japanese can buy cufflinks, tiepins, crocodile skin belts and shirts bearing a Henry Poole logo (based on Napoleon III's coat of arms). Japan would seem to be a sufficient distance from Savile Row to permit such a descent into merchandising, though perhaps the question to be asked is whether Savile Row is a sufficiently safe distance from Japan.

The Japanese have a Savile Row beachhead at Blades, which is now part-owned by Ginza Yamagatawa, an affiliate of the Japanese Sewing Company, which makes 500,000 suits a year. Here is purveyed the 'Easy-Order' suit, so named for its popularity with busy Japanese businessmen. Easy-orders come with the same fabric selection as pukka Savile Row and a guaranteed six-week delivery date. The garments are individually hand cut, but otherwise the tailors are machines – a computer spits out the appropriate pattern from the measurements fed into it and then the suit is engineered by sophisticated machines that simulate the hand-work. The cloth is English, but manufacture is in Denmark, a hotbed of quality clothes engineering. The 1988 price was about £100 below Savile Row's absolute minimum; a more expensive version features some hand-tailoring of the jacket. Particularly good results are claimed for lightweights made by the process, technically known as computer aided made-to-measure.

Savile Row's reaction has been to try to ignore the Japanese welcome sign at the top of the street.

What it has been unable to ignore is the advance of quality ready-to-wear, not just the expensive, craft-made Chester Barrie version, but the engineered suit. Far fairer than the highly subjective Hong Kong's Best versus Anderson test was a *Guardian* newspaper comparative appraisal of a Huntsman and a state-of-the-art engineered suit from the Oscar Jacobson factory near Göteborg, outwardly similar and costing perhaps a fifth of the price. About the time that Huntsman determined to champion handcraft with no concession to cost, Jacobson pinned its future on computer-controlled machinery, constantly improving with each technical advance, forever striving for the feel as well as the look of the hand-made product and improving on its sizes with ever more sophisticated analysis of body types. It takes the factory 3¾ man-hours to make a Jacobson suit; at Huntsman the fittings could even take that long. An expert could spot the little differences right away – in the edge stitching, the lapel, the wrist buttonhole – but how many in a generation no longer schooled in the ritual of bespoke are prepared to pay that much more for its subtle delights?

Left
Bob Geldof, a candidate for worst-dressed man of the decade, was coaxed into a morning suit for his investiture as an honorary knight. 'I thought it would be a shame for him and for the order he was to receive from Her Majesty if he was to be seen in scruff order,' says Robert Gieve. 'He told me, "I'll always look like an unmade bed, but you've done me proud."'

14

Savile Row under Siege

Above
Nutter apprentice Jude displays a dash
worthy of his master.

Top
'The whole history of the West End is
foreign labour coming in,' says retired
union organizer Ron Keston (right), who
fled Austria just ahead of the Nazis.

The one thing that did galvanize Savile Row as nothing else had in a hundred years was a government edict, enacted by Environmental Secretary Nicholas Ridley in August 1987, to relax controls on property use in the West End, and thus to make things easier for developers. Affected, too, were other skilled creators of the luxury goods that make Mayfair such a mecca for the international big spenders, but it was the tailors who were felt to be primarily at risk as the West End's last surviving light industry.

The tailors had been grumbling about rising rents for decades – in 1948 they passed a resolution expressing 'dismay' and seeking rent control – but they enjoyed some protection from market forces, since their back-shop workrooms were in a light industrial category that was low-rated and secure from takeover for office development. The new regulations scrapped this category.

Coming from a Tory government, the blow was perceived as a cruel stab-in-the-back, hardly lightened by a ministerial expression of confidence in tailoring's 'flexibility'. *The Times* called it the most serious threat to Savile Row since designer jeans. Robert Bright spoke of a 'death blow' and warned that Savile Row could be 'gutted' inside six years, with the tailors scattered to the winds by the developers and greedy landlords. He became quite good at depicting the shiny, soulless wasteland of a redeveloped Savile Row – 'for a decade, tourists will still wander down, wondering what once was there'.

For once, there was unity in the face of adversity and Anderson & Sheppard, unlikeliest of all agitators, instigated a write-in campaign by its American customers, who fired off scores of protest letters to Britain's Ambassador in Washington Sir Anthony Acland. 'Can you get at Mr Ridley for us?' Anderson director Dennis Hallbery asked one interlocutor. Anderson's had a personal reason for discovering a group conscience. It had a six-year lease, but then it faced the possibility of being ousted from the site it had occupied since the 1920s.

The *New York Times* gave the matter front-page treatment, reasoning that 'anything that affects Savile Row is an international affair', and the American television networks came to interview Robert Bright, but just as he began to speak hopefully of 'rattling the Foreign Office', the order was put into force. When a delegation of tailors tried to impress upon the Environmental Secretary the sanctity of their little clump of streets and their need to be conveniently placed for their clientele, he is said to have suggested that they relocate in Hounslow, that being hard by Heathrow Airport and, by inference, their export markets.

The fate of Savile Row remains in doubt; whether it relocates elsewhere, as the flower, fruit and vegetable merchants of Covent Garden did, or whether it survives in place, may not be clear for years. Some big landlords, led by the Prudential Assurance, own large chunks of the territory and lease renegotiation has become a traumatic affair. A stretch of the west side of the Row is the largest section penciled in for possible office development.

Angus Cundey shifts uneasily in a deep leather chair, worn shiny by generations of prestigious bottoms, and estimates that twenty establishments are under some sort of imminent threat. Robert Bright talks of having three to four years to stitch together a concerted plan of action, but is pessimistic of success. His fear is of a diaspora:

> Our moves in the past have been based on the home trade. Now we need to know where the overseas market expect to find us. Currently they expect to find us here. If we're not here, where are they likely to look for us? That's the question. Who knows; it might be the docklands, if docklands develops and attracts the new hotels and the international visitors. But whether these trends are firm enough when the decisions have to be made is problematical. If there were enough of us doing it all at once, then it would be easier. If, as I suspect, it's going to happen over a period, with different decisions being made and with us becoming dissipated, then not only London and Britain, but the world will have lost something.

Even presuming the worst, Savile Row could yet prevail as a tailoring Harley Street, an accumulation of brass plaques and shared consulting rooms: after all, the doctors do their operations elsewhere, so why not the tailors? But to Bright, the workshops have to be close at hand or all is lost, since each firm exists in a symbiotic relationship with numerous mutually dependent craft activities that make up the peculiar eco-system of Savile Row and Soho. To the casual visitor, the routine of daily life around Savile Row is indistinguishable from that of any other set of West End streets, yet to a trained eye it is a self-contained village, with the constant criss-crossing of woollen merchant and buttonhole lady, trimmer and presser and trotter sustaining the work process and providing a hot and fast flow of essential news and gossip.

Tailors' workshops had been closing for years, with the support crafts falling away in a tail-spin of rising rents and fewer tailors. It was more than ten years since the Duke of Edinburgh had attended a Soho Society dinner to launch an appeal fund for the creation of a craftsmen's centre. A survey had found that 63 per cent were on the point of being forced out of their existing accommodation, yet the scheme failed from lack of support. Some outworkers are now solitary beings, operating from home.

With immigrant sources dried up, and fewer firms taking on fewer apprentices, the average age of the workforce had reached fifty by the late 1970s, and there were shortages in all sorts of specializations. Reduced workshop space, rising costs and poaching had all contributed to lessen enthusiasm for training among the very few firms to undertake it. A government-backed training scheme eased matters, though only slightly. It produced more than a dozen recruits a year, but not all of them stayed. Monty Moss, great-grandson of Moses, gave the trade only twenty more years, unless there was a change of heart and each firm's owner undertook personal responsibility for recruiting and training. That was in 1985. At the London College of Fashion, tailoring lecturer Colin Stovel is hopeful of a response and points to Alan Bennett, Malcolm Plews and Andrew Ramroop as three ex-students who now head firms.

The persistence of primitive conditions can only be explained by the attitude of the workers themselves, and in particular their pride in their craft. 'If by some mad decree they were dispersed, their skills would

Bottom
Douglas Hayward at home in Mount Street.

Centre
Paul Sexton (right), guv'nor's son, currently active in Savile Row.

Below
Savile Row is the sum of much scuttling about by numerous individuals on minute but crucial missions. Here a few lengths of cloth are outward bound from merchant Wain Shiell A diaspora would eliminate much of the personal nature of the business.

vanish from the face of the earth,' Eric Newby wrote in his autobiography. 'I still remember in our own model workroom . . . the quiet, withdrawn expressions that they wore, expressions of an incommunicable satisfaction.'

The workers in this case were women, once an integral part of the bespoke trade – in trade jargon, they were known as 'kippers' – but now reduced to fifty or sixty sempstresses, of whom only one is a true tailoress, according to veteran union organizer Ron Keston, who explains: 'What happened was that conditions were so bad that no mother would let her daughter become a tailoress. The old ones started dying out and young girls found far better ways of making a living than stitting in all that dust and grime.' For the tailoress always had second-class status, as a poorly paid assistant to her journeyman – 'almost a tailor', is Keston's description.

It is only in the last twenty years that electric irons have replaced charcoal-heated flat irons in some workrooms, and Huntsman maintained a gas-only workshop until quite recently, mainly because the foreman preferred it that way. When the ancient irons corroded away, an international search was undertaken to find a replacement source. 'I remember when my husband took over. He was horrified to see the tailors working on the floor around the stove which heated the irons,' recalls Dorothy Donaldson-Hudson of Hogg, Sons & J. B. Johnstone. 'He installed electric irons and cushioned benches, but they quickly got back on the floor again.' So it was at Anderson's, where Dennis Hallbery remembered the advent of a tailor with a wooden leg and the manner in which he made room for himself among the cross-legged crew on the floor: 'I'm going to throw my peg-leg in the air and where it lands I'll sit.' And so he did. 'If people only knew what their garments went through before they put them on,' reflects Maurice Sedwell, who finds romance in the past; 'I can still smell the gas, and the snuff that permeated everything; I can still sense the gas light, a lovely warm glow and the pleasure of a new gas mantel. It was a good, kindly light. Now you get bombarded by neutrons . . . .'

Some of these journeymen lived forever; shortly after World War II, a coat-maker named Sven Svenson was still working in Savile Row at the age of ninety-two and a Mr Child was still crossing his legs for Dege after sixty-two years' stitching. Of independent spirit despite their dependent status, they suffered from the arrogance of the cutters, who could hire and fire the tailors they used, and had a plentiful choice in the years of Continental influx. Everyone has stories of cutters keeping men waiting all day for work they then ordered to be ready the following morning. That has changed. Nowadays, a good trouser-maker has to be wooed, a coat-maker cosseted – and a good waistcoat hand has been known to work for as many as twenty firms! Likewise, the master-journeyman wars have long since sunk into a turgid truce, born of necessity. 'We realize we're both on the same side, basically,' says Ron Keston. 'We're there to get a suit made, because without that there'll be no money for anyone.'

'There were more characters in the past,' Keston reflects. 'Oh yes, they used to have a habit of going on the cod and wouldn't turn up for three or four days. Why? As one cutter explained, the trade drives you to drink. A man comes into the shop; he orders a suit; he tries it on three times, then he goes away for six months, comes back, he's lost three stone and complains that the suit doesn't fit him and he wants it done for free.' He pauses. 'They still do go on the cod sometimes, unfortunately. I've come across one or two workshops on a Friday afternoon when most of them are drunk . . . .'

If there is weakness in tradition and continuity, it is also where Savile Row's strength lies. Ties with the distant past are strong and enduring,

so that sometimes it is difficult to distinguish then from now. The handing down of skills could not be more personal, so that in a real sense the celebrated craftsmen of the past live on. Keith Fallan, as a typical example, uses particular techniques learned as an apprentice under Paddy Rice, an Irish coat-maker who worked for the great Hungarian Fred Stanbury.

Then there are the likes of Ron Pescod, spiffy boulevardier of the 1930s and still following a lifetime's routine of 8 a.m. starts to a morning's cutting and running the business, and thence at noon to client-cultivation in his favourite Swallow Street wine bar. Ron Pescod is Adeney & Boutroy, and thus the last in a line going back to the mid-eighteenth century (to which he claims descent on his mother's side). His mentor was J. P. Thornton, a marvellously self-important nineteenth-century figure who was still around in 1935 to autograph Ron's technical college graduation copy of the Thornton *International System of Garment Cutting for Coats, Trousers, Breeches, and Vests*; this monumental tome still has pride of place on the Pescod workshelf.

The pity is that there may be no one to follow Ron Pescod and to inherit the wisdom of the creator of the Thornton-sleeved Raglan, the Thornton Combination Breeches, the Thornton Dress Coat Front, not to mention Thornton's Calculated Waist Suppressions for Ladies. Behind many a Savile Row name is one ageing individual, and the tradition of family inheritance has faltered. In all Savile Row, only one firm – Sexton's – currently has a son who has gone through the rigours of apprenticeship to become heir-apparent to a father-master.

Christopher Morgan is a publicist who was briefly hired to try to promote Savile Row, and he has sad memories of the experience. His 'Master Tailors' Information Bureau' quickly folded for lack of financial support. 'A business that can't afford a fiver a week shouldn't be in business,' is his comment. Yet he remains a believer – 'it's a wonderful craft' – and he argues for the government to take a more direct role in its preservation: '£50,000 a year for promotion would be enough.'

Morgan's first bespoke suit was made by Douglas Hayward – 'I wore it for a date. It was blue hopsack and it felt fabulous. Funny how you remember these moments. . . .' Hayward is the last Savile Row tailor to live above the shop, and he does so in a style that befits the favourite of the Swinging Sixties' set. 'All my friends of that time, David Bailey, Vidal Sassoon, Michael Caine, people like that . . . it's as though they dragged me along with them,' he says, his Cleverly-shod feet propped up on a low table in his cosily plush Mount Street flat; he has just returned from a week in Barbados and Mustique with Lord Lichfield ('an old pal') and he is feeling a bit grumpy. 'It was too long and too far.' A shopman's a shopman, no matter how well-connected, and people do not order in his absence.

His father washed buses for a living and his mother worked in a factory; when he was fifteen, they told him to find a trade. He became a tailor because his uncle knew one and because he thought it was a good way to get his clothes cheap ('yes, it was as silly as that – I had no feeling for it whatsoever'). When he finished his apprenticeship, he trudged Savile Row looking for an opening, but was told his cockney accent was too strong. His luck was to find work in a shop in Shepherd's Bush, just when the BBC television studios opened there; friendships with personalities like Spike Milligan and Eric Sykes were a prelude to his subsequent achievements as a celebrity tailor.

Some Savile Row tailors boast of never having addressed a customer by his first name. No such frosty servility for Dougie Hayward, who has thoroughly enjoyed the social benefits that can go with the job and dabbled in such pursuits as owning an elite restaurant. Brian Staples,

Ron Pescod, heir to 200 years of tradition, in Saturday stripes with former *Tailor and Cutter* editor Taylor. Pescod bears an uncanny resemblance to his mentor J.P. Thornton, who signed this picture for him more than half a century ago.

his one-time manager, sounds a note of awe in describing the impromptu parties above the shop – Sam Spiegel, Edgar Bronfman, Sammy Cahn, Sammy Davis, Tony Bennett, you name them, they've all been up there. . . .'

Hayward is, however, the classic example of a tailor tied to his own generation; now a big, tweedy philosopher, he professes disinterest in being trendy any more – 'You work towards a sort of simplicity in more or less everything you do. What I want to do now is be very simple, and to rely on line and look, not detail. I'd just like to make five or six really beautiful suits a week. . . .' He does the New York-Los Angeles circuit, but in his own way, and not on a regular enough basis to become trapped by it – 'I stack up about sixteen suits in a bag and it seems to make a good trip.'

Hayward is located round the corner from Harry's Bar and Beau Brummell's old home and so is isolated from the rest of Savile Row, which is just how he feels about the community aspect of tailordom: 'They all get together and have a bunfight and nothing gets done; it's all very social, but no one faces the fact that in ten years' time there's not going to be anyone left . . . unless someone faces up to the facts.'

He believes that Savile Row has to compromise, and he believes this most strongly when he is driving around Ealing or Lewisham, looking for a buttonhole lady, a breed that is dying off. Despite the delights of the hand-sewn buttonhole, Savile Row will have to accept the machined hole sooner rather than later, and he argues: 'Basically, you've got shoulders, collars and sleeves, which is where the coat hangs and gets its look – that all has to be done by hand. But the tailors that are left will have to find machines to do the boring jobs and leave them with the creative work. This is what everyone is holding out against.'

He talks of a dozen Savile Row tailors getting together to buy a building and operate a joint office and workshop; that way, they could acquire the latest machinery and achieve all sorts of efficiencies and economies of scale. 'The style, the individuality a person comes to you for, that wouldn't change; you would still impose your own look on it, but without all the mundane, boring stuff.'

Hayward is a star of the trade and has savoured the rewards, but there is a bittersweet quality about his reflections. 'Everyone else seems to make money easier than I do, without the hassle and headaches. . . .' There is no hint of tailoring about his shop, which operates as a small exclusive outfitters, and Hayward ruefully observes how he can make more in a moment from selling a ready-made raincoat than from making a suit 'for somebody who's probably been to twenty tailors before he gets here and who's an unhappy, difficult man who needs lots of fittings and lots of energy and costs a fortune to satisfy. . . .'

But satisfaction there is, 'and as one gets older that becomes more important. The sad thing is, you can't tell young people how rewarding doing something good with your hands is. . . .'

15

Pomp and Changed Circumstance: Royals and the Row

Above
Prince Charles in the soft embrace of Anderson & Sheppard.

Left
The Yorks: the perfect matching pair. 'They're great. I think they're very much in love,' is their tailor's considered opinion.

Below
Up from the basement: royal tailor John Kent.

Hamlet and Savile Row have this much in common: neither would be the same without the prince. To an extraordinary degree, the Row's fortunes have been bound up in the fortunes of a succession of royal heirs, in particular the three Princes of Wales who became George IV, Edward VII and Edward VIII.

It was not surprising, therefore, that the present Prince of Wales was hardly out of his nappies before he was being promoted as the future style leader. The *Tailor and Cutter* persisted in placing the infant Charles on its annual best-dressed list (for his caps and rompers) until persuaded to desist by media ridicule.

Charles turned out a determined individualist, but not in the way that had been hoped. One theory holds that the royal males were cowed into abdicating style leadership by what happened to Edward VIII at the hands of an American seductress. 'Mrs Simpson's arrival on the scene turned everything upside down,' John Taylor has written. 'Resentful royals retreated into contemptuous regard for what seemed the only thing that Mrs Simpson and her Prince were good at: fashion became anathema.'

Then there is the theory of royal oscillation – one generation cutting a dash and the next withdrawing into sobriety: the sober Prince Albert had fathered the brightly bedecked Bertie, who fathered the severely conservative George V, who fathered the fashion-focused Edward VIII, who was succeeded by the serious George VI . . . but there the

theory encountered problems. 'Will the Duke of Edinburgh become Britain's new style leader?' *Men's Wear* wanted to know upon his 1948 marriage to the future Queen Elizabeth, though the answer was even then apparent. Prince Philip had no interest in becoming a fashion plate; instead, he became a tough customer for Savile Row, as rigorous in his quality standards as in his preference for sober comfort over élan. He stayed with Teddy Watson at Hawes & Curtis, the tailor Lord Mountbatten had started him on, and, in due course and in the time-honoured way, Hawes became tailor to his sons.

The Duke scored one for the egalitarian age when, in 1955, he paid for his valet to have an identical Savile Row suit to his own (it was a two-piece with large pockets) and he was largely let alone by the clothes' critics. Not so Charles, whose casual approach to clothes brought the trade to the brink of exasperation once he had married the magnetic Diana. 'He seems all too eager to let his wife steal the limelight,' *Men's Wear* moaned. 'Prince Charles is unfortunately the perfect example of the British man almost going out of his way to display no interest in his clothes.' Charles responded with good humour; in 1971, he turned up twinkle-eyed for a black-tie Savile Row dinner dressed in a shabby sports jacket and (to relieved cheers) changed into tails as he sat down. Guests of honour at these annual dinners have a tendency to traumatize their hosts: Norman St John-Stevas told the 1983 gathering that he could not afford bespoke, and the following year Royal Academy President Sir Hugh Casson brought low moans by admitting that he had not had anything made for thirty years.

Below
The Prince and Mrs Simpson in 1936. Did their fateful love affair traumatize the royals into a fear of fashion?

In one respect, Charles followed the example of past Princes of Wales in quietly breaking with his father's tailor. Unlike the others, he did not opt for an innovative stylist, but for Anderson & Sheppard, uncompromising purveyors of the lived-in look. 'Some swear by it. Some swear at it,' Anderson director Dennis Hallbery has said, which may account for some of the confusion in the press, as demonstrated in 1985 by the same suit being starred in two newspapers to very different effect. The *Daily Mirror* had Charles 'stunning historic Moreton-in-Marsh with an equally historic suit' featuring 'creases, wrinkles . . . even good old-fashioned turn-ups'. The self-same suit was used by the *Daily Mail* as proof of Princess Diana's beneficial influence: 'fashion experts will note the distinct '50s cut . . . one that is rapidly becoming high fashion – the previously almost obsolete ticket pocket, with the slightly exaggerated shoulders, the extra-wide lapels and the baggy trousers complete with turn-ups. . . .' In offering itself as arbitrator, *Men's Wear* suggested that the truth lay somewhere in-between: 'turn-ups are fashionable, four-inch lapels are acceptable on a double-breasted, but the suit does have a curious look to it. The cut is rather surprising for what appears to be a light tweed and loafers are an odd choice of footwear. There will be no best-dressed man award for Charles – yet.'

Shortly thereafter, the quest for a royal leader turned to Prince Andrew, whose 1986 wedding to a wholesome redhead crowned his popularity as a warrior and virile youth. Gieves produced a family tree to prove that the new Duchess of York was a tenth-generation descendant of the third Earl of Burlington, builder of Savile Row,* and the indefatigable John Taylor speculated that here might be the long-awaited leader. 'Prince Andrew could be our man,' he wrote in *Men's Wear*. 'He comes from the right "generation-swing".' Taylor saw in extrovert Andrew something of the spirit of Edward VII and VIII: 'it is an attitude which could well fit him for style leadership, now that tendencies are once again towards the elegant and the classical. For when fashion becomes esoteric, and its study is detailed, there is no need for flamboyance or vulgarity in innovation. And vulgarity and flamboyance must be avoided at royal levels.' Or roughly what Prince Albert had told his son Bertie a century before.

Andrew's tailor is John Kent, an energetic cockney who attends his charge with enthusiastic pride. 'I think he really loves clothes, and she does too,' Kent says of the Yorks. 'She influences him – not a lot, but she'll just say, "Why don't you have this," and between them we usually discuss it and get somewhere near what they both like. I think they're great.'

Kent chats on about the potential of Andrew as a style setter. The Prince is 'very into double-breasted', and he has just had a double-breasted sports jacket made from a specially crafted cloth. 'Now that's something that is a little different,' he contends. Then there was the tweed suit he made, again with a one-off cloth design, with matching skirt for the Duchess. He bubbles over: '. . . it's fun when you're there – you do your job properly, but it's a great atmosphere, it's not that stuffy sort of atmosphere. We have a laugh and we end up hopefully getting it right. It's terrific.'

How John Kent from Bethnal Green got to the Palace is a measure of the degree to which the traditions of service and succession still hold. He worked as a cutter under Teddy Watson for sixteen years and, upon Watson's retirement and in fulfilment of Watson's wishes, succeeded him as tailor to the Duke of Edinburgh. Watson had

Above
Charles got his own back at Savile Row carping with this practical joke jacket.

Below
Prince Philip as a newly-wed. The diffidence soon disappeared, but he resolutely refused to be a style leader.

*The Earl begat Charlotte, Baroness Clifford, who begat Lord George Augustus Cavendish, who begat William Cavendish, who begat Lord George Henry Cavendish, who begat Susan Henrietta Brand, Viscountess Hampden, who begat Margaret Brand Ferguson, who begat Colonel Andrew Henry Ferguson, who begat Major Ronald Ferguson, who begat Sarah Ferguson, Duchess of York.

Above
The Sultan of Oman's camel-mounted, Savile Row-accoutred pipe band.

meantime lost Prince Charles in some undisclosed dispute, but the other Princes, Andrew and Edward, followed their father to Kent. The contrast between Anderson & Sheppard, with its cabal of cutters, and the little enterprise of John Kent dramatizes the extent of Savile Row's variety. Stroll along Old Burlington Street and glance down into the basement beneath James & James, and the chances are that there will be John Kent measuring or animatedly advising some customer. Round the corner, window shopping is hardly encouraged at Anderson's and crossing the threshold certainly not. A stuffed stag stares out across hummocks of cloth, beneath which attendants huddle like ghillies on a grouse moor. Those who pass muster with the ghillies are escorted into the interior; the act of creation at Anderson's is sacramental and not for the rude gaze.

Savile Row is cluttered with royal warrants of every provenance, yet the two firms most intimately concerned with current day-to-day needs do not carry a coat of arms between them. Anderson stays absolutely mum about its relationship with Prince Charles – though it surely benefits from everybody remarking upon that fact – while Kent's simple basement bears no hint of royal connection. Welsh & Jeffries is the latest royal signing, having succeeded Johns & Pegg as Prince Charles's military tailor. Here again they are not boasting about it, but rather adopting a cautious attitude, at least until they feel more confident about retaining the trade.

Royal warrants have been around for 800 years. At the time of Queen Victoria and her vast family, they spread like weeds and consequently lost much of their distinction. At Cowes, convenient for the royal retreat at Osborne, so many shops had a royal customer that the one to stand out was an unwarranted butcher, who had the wit to erect a sign that read, 'By Appointment to Her Majesty's Subjects'.

Warrants may be issued by the Queen, the Prince of Wales, the Duke of Edinburgh and the Queen Mother to any supplier who has served them for at least three years. The proliferation comes from the variety of services that qualify for acknowledgement – anything from kitting the Yeomen of the Guard in their beefeater uniforms (Dege) to the subcontractual claim of a firm that supplied socks to Billings & Edmonds, sometime tailor to royal juveniles. 'When it comes down to a few pairs of socks, it does become a bit strange,' reflects gentle-spoken Colin Edmonds, who made the school uniforms of Charles, Andrew and Edward, and still glows with the memory; he stays hopeful that one day 'we'll see Charles's lads'.

Grand as it sounds to be 'appointed into the place and quality of tailor' to a royal figure, 'it's a lot of worry and rushing around and there's no money in it anyway,' as one warrant-holder remarked. The routine of royal tailoring has changed little since the days when Meyer answered summonses to the Prince Regent in Carlton House. Except on very rare occasions, a royal does not call upon his tailor; his tailor calls upon him, wherever he may be. Fittings usually are arranged for early morning, though the call can come at any time. 'I've been called out at all different times and all different places – Windsor, Balmoral, wherever,' says Kent. 'That's what being a royal warrant-holder means. It's giving a service.'

Colin Edmonds recalls how 'Teddy Watson used to go down in his Rolls-Royce and I used to go down in an old banger', and he chuckles over the days when they attended upon Charles at school and then at university. Schoolboy caps clutter his pokey office, which is brightened up by the incongruous image of a blonde calendar girl spilling out of a tight rugger jersey; a faded photograph of Winston Churchill guards the safe. In pondering the rewards of royal appointment, Edmonds thinks American trade might be boosted a bit, but otherwise feels them to be mostly mental: 'It's just that feeling of honour, really; it's a delightful feeling.' The aldermanic Robert Bright, the conscience of Savile Row, softens perceptibly when vividly recalling his personal store of royal encounters – of the Duke of Gloucester showing him his collection of model elephants and of the young Princess Marina, Duchess of Kent, so many years ago, stooping to help him pick up and fold away a load of cashmere sweaters that had tumbled to the floor: 'such grace . . . she knew just how to put me at ease, because I'd wanted the earth to open up. Of course, they were past-masters at coping with tradesmen. They were schooled in it and knew just how to do it, very relaxed and easy. . . .'

Despite their obsession with discretion, tailors talk among themselves and at such times the anecdotes flow freely. The royals have an intensely loyal, yet unsentimental, set of subjects on Savile Row. It seems that Charles is not an easy figure to dress – he has a long

Left
Colin McNaughton confides the secrets of braid and plume to Alan Bennett, his successor in the ambassador business.

body and short legs – and that his father is a difficult man to satisfy. Maurice Sedwell, an old crony of Teddy Watson, speaks admiringly of the Queen, who has been known to appraise and compliment work that drew no comment from the Duke. Some royals earn low marks for skinflint recourse to 'cut-downs and hand-me-downs'; but then, even the dandy Duke of Windsor 'rarely seemed to buy a new suit', according to the Duchess's memoirs. The tartan dinner jacket which launched America on a tartan craze in the 1950s was discovered by the Duchess to bear a label showing that it had been made for George V in 1897!

Royal wardrobes are tended with such care that it is hard to imagine anything wearing out. Kent struck out on his own only after consulting the Duke of Edinburgh, and he suspects that the Duke placed his first suit order more as a gesture of moral support than out of any real need – 'I thought it was great of him.' He thinks the Duke's critics are ignorant: 'He knows what he wants and – I'll be very honest – my tummy sometimes turns over as I'm going in there, because he demands perfection and you can't give him the sort of flannel that we're inclined to give in this trade. Contrary to what people think, you can try and advise him. You can't give him any bull, though. He'll listen, but if he says at the end of the day he wants this done, you do it. Then he sticks by his decision, and I like it that way; I love it that way.'

Extraordinary endeavour is likewise accorded to foreign royalty. When King Olaf's naval uniform was found to be inappropriate for a recent state visit, a Gieves's seamstress was rushed to Norway to stitch in the appropriate piece of braid, just hours before the royal embarkation – and Poole once responded with such expedition to a frantic phone call from Buckingham Palace at ten in the morning that it managed to measure and make a set of tails for King Boris of Bulgaria by dinner time. Savile Row favourites like the Sultan of Oman (Dege) and King Hussain of Jordan (Gieves) receive very special treatment indeed.

Britain's diplomatic envoys also merit particular attention, and the twilight of empire has seen some valiant efforts by a dwindling band of specialists to keep in glitter-order the dwindling band of Her Majesty's representatives abroad. 'We still make for all our governor-generals,' Malcolm Johnstone boasts, while acknowledging that it hardly amounts to much business any more: 'only the Falklands and Hong Kong, and then there's St Helena – he always wears the proper full dress, but the ones in the West Indies, they just wear the white uniform. . . .' The ambassador trade is likewise reduced, but the uniforms turned out by Colin McNaughton deep in the bowels of 8a Sackville Street are still calculated to dazzle the natives of Belgium or Luxembourg. McNaughton is full of rollicking tales of ambassadors caught in foreign parts without cocked hat or some other essential piece of ceremonial garb, and of intrepid couriers reaching them just in time.

The craftsman network required to produce the ambassadorial outfit is stretched thin and difficulties with a single individual can cause a crisis, such as happened when the feather-curler became overloaded with orders. As main contractor, McNaughton cuts and styles the silk-lined tail-coat and trousers and brings together the work of such specialists as the Hands family (gold embroiderers in a Soho basement for two centuries), the Wilkinson Sword Company, a gold button-maker in Northampton and the feather-curler, Miss Rule. The small South London firm of Sidney Patey, another specialist, can make and trim a cocked hat in three days, but first it needs the requisite ostrich feathers to be curled into the proper plenipotential shape; this tricky task can take up to one hour per feather. The success of feather-heavy theatricals like La Cage aux Folles caused a run on Miss Rule and resulted in a four-month backlog in ambassadorial hats, so that several envoys were forced to set forth in ill-fitting borrowed plumes. It was worst for McNaughton, for regulations state that he cannot submit his bill until the full uniform is supplied. From the sword of Elizabethan design to the oak leaf pattern in spun gold at throat, cuff and leg, the assembly cost between £1,500 and £2,000 (at 1988 prices), so his problem was appreciable.

McNaughton is retiring and handing over to Alan Bennett, who discovered a talent for fancy dress when making clothes for Madame Tussauds. Napoleon, Mao, the Duke of Wellington and Jimmy Carter – their Tussauds likenesses have all been tailored by Bennett to a standard that would have done honour to the originals, for Tussauds is jealous of its reputation for authenticity. The big names like Huntsman and Gieves have also made for Tussauds, in some cases repeating for the waxwork reproduction an identical set of garments to those it supplied to the actual person.

Other institutions with a need to dress up have stayed less faithful to

Savile Row; the Church of England, for example, has mostly gone ready-to-wear. It is the old story of rising costs and improvements in the factory-made alternatives. At Adeney & Boutroy, Ron Pescod (who made the Queen's coronation robes for Tussauds) likes to leaf through the Archbishop of Canterbury's accounts for 1814, when the bill reached £1,499 12s, and this at a time when the very best breeches cost His Eminence no more than £2 8s. Adeney used a bishop's mitre as its emblem and made for numbers of high churchmen until quite recently. Pescod's way of making wrinkle-defiant gaiters was celebrated, as were his purple dress coats, but he has not made one in five years; he recalls how 'the last was for the previous Bishop of Leicester'. He has fond memories of Hewlett Johnson, the Red Dean of Canterbury, and of the time the Dean left one of his gaiters in a cinema that had been showing a naughty film. Pescod was sent to retrieve the gaiter and spare the Dean's blushes, but arrived to find that all the buttons had been removed, presumably by souvenir-seeking usherettes. 'Oh, he was a very nice man,' is his verdict on the Red Dean. 'Actually, they were all rather friendly. Whenever I arrived to do their fittings, there was always a sherry or a port waiting.'

Well within living memory, scores of Savile Row craftsmen were kept occupied creating and maintaining the paraphernalia of pomp and privilege collectively known as Court dress. It took a 200-page book issued annually under the authority of the Lord Chamberlain to keep track of all the incredibly complicated trappings. A specialist like Wilkinson & Son on Maddox Street could trace its history back 300 years and took about as long to list all of its duties as 'Tailors and Robe Makers to His Majesty and the Royal Family'. Wilkinson made the monarch's robes for most coronations from William IV to George VI, and the last Mr Wilkinson exercised sufficient power to shame Rab Butler into leaving a Privy Council meeting shortly before World War II because he was not wearing the correct morning coat. 'Unfortunately, he spent more time making sure they were dressed properly than looking after his business,' observes Michael Skinner, whose firm, Dege, bought Wilkinson in 1939. 'Nice as it was to have that sort of power, it wasn't very sensible when he could have been taking orders for more suits.' Such sentiments were generally felt in the austere aftermath of the war and George VI decreed a regimen of much greater simplicity; *Dress and Insignia Worn at Court* eventually ceased publication. Ede & Ravenscroft in Holborn is now the only specialist robe-maker left.

The military's retreat from sartorial splendour can also be dated to World War II and its aftermath, although purists could argue that the slide started with the invention of khaki a hundred years earlier. Acting upon Darwin's theory that 'beauty is sometimes more important than success in battle', monarchs like George IV gave as much attention to dressing up their troops as themselves, as old Meyer & Mortimer accounts show. They piled on the plumage to often ludicrous and sometimes fatal effect, as in the Crimea, when the smart unbending leather on patrol collars left men unable to sight their rifles properly. Khaki (at first a coarse cloth dipped in coffee) proved its worth on India's North-West Frontier, but it took another fifty years before the British army abandoned its target-like scarlet tunics; however, even then the Boer marksmen could sight on the dazzling white belts which were retained.

British military style was determined by individual whim, and there was a strong tendency to copy the latest novelty from the latest victorious European army; from Cossack trousers to German spiked helmet and jackboots, all found a place somewhere, sometime, in the British army. And not just the army, for naval commanders were

allowed even more latitude for eccentricity: the captain of HMS *Blazer* did more than he realized when he put his boat crews into blue and white striped jackets for a visit by Queen Victoria. Eureka, the blazer!

By the beginning of the 1930s, the number and complexity of authorized 'dresses' which a naval officer might be required to wear called for the invention of the Gieves Dress Indicator, a spinning disc which helped an officer track his way through the confusion of Ball Dress, Ceremonial Dress, Blue Dress, Blue Dress (Alternative), Undress, Working Dress, Mess Dress, Mess Undress, White Ceremonial Dress, Modified White Dress, Modified White Dress (Alternative), White Undress, Modified White Mess Dress, White Mess Undress, Tropical Mess Undress, Tropical Dress, Tropical Working Dress, Action Dress . . . to name but a few. And this was the navy, which never had the same enthusiasm for dressing up as the army, and which had no official uniform until 1857.

As servant to the samurai class, Savile Row depended greatly upon the custom of the gentleman soldier, with firms establishing regimental bonds and trusting to hold a customer from first uniform through a lifetime of later civilian wear. Sign up the colonel of a regiment and all the subalterns are yours as well – that was, and remains, a working maxim. But no firm today can survive simply on the slim pickings of the modern military, whose officer class has lost its sartorial sensibilities to the point where a young officer will buy second hand and pay for a cheap adjustment. Gieves & Hawkes's experience exemplifies the changed circumstances: in 1948, officers' uniforms accounted for 84 per cent of its turnover; by 1978, this was down to 20 per cent, and today all of its bespoke work, civil as well as military, does not amount to 20 per cent of its business, despite appointments to the Royal Navy, the Royal Air Force and thirty-eight regiments and corps, plus a branch strategically sited opposite the Sandhurst military academy. The firm played a direct role in the post-war amalgamation process that streamlined the military for its new role of defending a small island state. 'We had to translate dreams and ideals into realities,' says Robert Gieve. 'With a badge from one regiment, a colour from another, we had to satisfy a need that traditions did not die and yet see that they became unified entities. It was stressful, taxing. . . .' Gieves broke out the champagne to welcome back from the Falklands War

Left
The Queen side-saddles the Trooping
the Colour, care of Weatherill.

customers whose uniforms had gone down with their ship. In the case of customers who did not return, the firm did not press for payment of outstanding bills.

Welsh & Jeffries, Prince Charles's military tailor, had much the same experience on a more modest scale. It used to have a staff of twelve; now there are two. Though it claims to tailor for more generals than anyone else and has contingency plans to relocate in the Dorset-Wiltshire area, near many of its military clients, should it be driven out of Savile Row by galloping rents, its production of nine to ten suits a week now goes to a mainly civilian clientele.

Savile Row still can put on a brave show of scarlet, as witness the sight of the Honourable Company of Gentlemen-at-Arms when they gather at Gieves & Hawkes to put on their vivid uniforms before proceeding to some state function. A sample of the Gentlemen's raiment, or one of the gold-embroidered scarlet coats of the State Trumpeters, often brightens the Gieves's shop, just as similar exotica can often be chanced upon in more humble Savile Row premises.

Then there is hunting gear, a subject as close to the soul of Savile Row as the dictates of Brummell and nicely encapsulated by John Masefield:

> New pink, white cords and glossy tops,
> New gloves, the newest thing in crops,
> Worn with an air that well expressed
> His sense that no one else was dressed.

Weatherill, now a part of Kilgour, French & Stanbury, is the leading hunt specialist.

If demand for the grand is now much reduced, tailor and seamstress can still keep their hands in with liveries for less exalted purposes – the pink tail coats for Bank of England messengers are another concern of Gieves, while Anthony Hewitt does Guards-style uniforms for the charitable Knights of Malta. Dege was even pleased to be commissioned to make uniforms for the Trump Tower doormen on Manhattan's Fifth Avenue. Described as basically a footman's livery with some touches reminiscent of a Guard's uniform, it got a repeat order.

Above
Breeches specialist George Roden tries
his own saddle. Paper bags at rear
contain patterns of celebrity clients and
are a rare example of such ostentation
on the part of a Savile Row firm.
Stencilled names range from the Queen
to Robert Mitchum and rock guitarist
Eric Clapton.

Is this enough to sustain ancient skills? A test arose with the appointment of a Savile Row tailor, Bernard Weatherill, as Speaker of the House of Commons. There is a traditional Speaker's livery, a velvet Court dress with pigeon-breasted front, knee-breeches and wig bag, of a style already obsolete in Henry Poole's day. Only much handed-down remnants remained, and when the Speaker disclosed that he faced the prospect of wearing 'George Thomas's coat and Selwyn Lloyd's trousers' for a State Opening of Parliament, fellow luminaries of the Federation of Merchant Tailors felt the honour of the Row was at stake. Their decision to make a new outfit, correct to the last stitch and court button, was easier than the operation. 'We had to scour the earth to find black pure silk velvet and we had to gut something like five old ones to get the hand-cut steel court buttons,' recalls Robert Bright, who directed the search. Eventually cloth merchant Wain Shiell found the black silk velvet and Moss Bros assembled the buttons. Weatherill cutter George Roden, one of the last traditional breeches-makers, was delegated to take charge. Unusual as it was for a hunting house to make a George IV Court dress, the biggest problem proved to be the working of the pure silk velvet. 'It's murder,' Roden reported. 'You can hardly touch, and you certainly can't press it, because the pile stays down. You even have to steam the seams open.' Nevertheless the Speaker got his fine new livery.

Multiply the aforementioned a few thousand times and one has a sense of the supreme test that lies ahead. The last coronation was difficult enough to costume; the next might be impossible. From Savile Row's point of view, it can't come soon enough, for each year increases the odds against success.

Robert Bright's fear is that 'when the next one comes along, nobody will be available with any experience of the last one'. He remembers the scramble in 1953, 'when everybody was digging into books and all the old masters had their brains tested'. To Bright, 'There is no way the same quality work could be done now, for the simple reason that there hasn't been the training; even the materials, the beautiful pure silk velvets, just aren't being made.' But he concludes that given time to prepare – perhaps as much as nine months – a creditable job might yet be possible.

Below
King Boris of Bulgaria strolling with his Queen while awaiting his instant Poole dinner suit.

Below
The Dress Indicator. Naval uniform became so complicated that this spinning disc was invented to help officers cope.

16

In Search of the Golden Fleece

Left
The best first view of tailordom – from the portal of the Burlington Arcade.

'We do not sell clothes. We sell a concept.' The essence of the Savile Row mystique is a distillation of such aphorisms. This one came from Robert Bright, though the most adept at talking up the Row is Robert Gieve, who can mesmerize the listener with the earnest flow of his philosophic spiel. 'It's been diluted,' he grants, 'but those houses that remain aspire to one common cause – to preserve that craft skill that manifests itself on the backs of customers in a way that nowhere else in the world seems to be able to copy.'

From serving aristocracy and Empire, the Row has adapted with the times to serve 'those who aspire to be gentlemen', of whatever pedigree. Gieve proceeds: 'Now, a gentleman is rather like good taste; it is many things to many people. But the fundamental characteristic of a gentleman is an understanding of good manners, and in the pursuance and observance of good manners, in the protocols of life, dress plays an important part. . . .'

And so to the famous formula of sedate propriety, of the exquisitely prosaic, constructed around an image of perfect manhood that has stayed constant since tailoring began. There is a statue of the Black Prince (another Prince of Wales) from the 1370s, whose padded chest and wasp waist would seem to be the abiding answer to a maiden's prayer. Of roughly the same date, the following description from *Sir Gawain and the Green Knight* could serve equally to describe the cut of a Bobby Valentine tea-dance special: 'For his back and his brest all his body was broad, but his middle and his waist were worthily small.'

It is in Savile Row's regulation of the ideal that attempts at exact analysis tend to come unstuck. Even Brummell's law of conspicuous inconspicuousness contains a trap, as Douglas Fairbanks Jnr found when the *Tailor and Cutter* ticked him off for commenting that 'the best-dressed man is the one who attracts least attention'. 'Nonsense,' it corrected. 'If good clothes were not noticeable it would mean that they were in no way exceptional. A well-dressed man will always attract attention. It is merely that he does it unconsciously and naturally.'

There is no lost golden age of tailoring; the technique of the eighteenth-century tailors was as crude as their clothes were rich and bright, being carved out of cloth so firm and thick that the edges could be left raw. To some, it is a supreme irony that technical perfection was achieved only when self-expression was curbed. 'The craft has become entirely divorced from the art, and Savile Row leads the tailoring of the Western world in expanding infinite trouble, skill and expense on the

The multiple faces of Savile Row. Peter Moore in his spotless sanctum: 'I try to enhance the male form by giving him a good shoulder line, a broad chest, a slim waist and slim hips, and to make his legs look as long as possible.' Next door on the first floor at 9-10 Savile Row, rhymester and homespun philosopher Maurice Sedwell reflects back on fifty years of making the ungainly look great. In tailoring as in boxing, 'it's the legs that go first', he finds. On Savile Row quality: 'Some are better than others, but charlatans don't last long. . . .It's all soul, this business.'

confection of a style of dress in which desiccation is deified,' critic Pearl Binder wrote in *The Peacock's Tail*. To such carping, the *Tailor and Cutter* would cite the wisdom of the ancient Persian philosopher, who sat all day long playing the same note over and over again. Asked why he did not occasionally attempt the cheerier business of a melody, the philosopher explained that the inconsistencies of scale were only for grasshopper minds. For himself, he had discovered the note that he liked and was satisfied to listen to it as often as possible.

So wherein lies the secret of the Row, Mr Gieve? 'It is in the interpretation of the client's individual needs, so that at the end of the day he shall be at one with the clothes that he has procured – at one in the sense that they are not so tight and stylish that they are uncomfortable, not so extreme in any aspect of fashion that the individual is conspicuous in a crowd; yet nevertheless he is an ambassador, for himself, and thereby for the street.'

Like a monk whirling a well-oiled prayer wheel, there is no stopping Robert Gieve:

> Sobriety is the essence, because there is never any sense of fashion anywhere in what we purists pursue. There is style, a wealth of style, but little fashion. The style is the totality of look; the style is the individual man, and I often go back to an observation of the subtle difference between being dressed well and being well dressed. I believe and hope that all those that have developed a relationship with us in Savile Row aspire to being well dressed, for that is the relaxed and natural way of presenting yourself. There are many others who aspire to being dressed well, who will spend a fortune on brand labels, believing that by the outlaying of expenditure in association and identification with names of renown they are going to be the bees' knees. They'll miss it by a mile, because they don't understand what this street has to offer; they don't understand that style is of the essence and not fashion. . . .

The situation thus clarified, the aspiring gentleman without a Savile Row connection is advised to scout around for a referral, if only to avoid one of the most confusing decisions that life has to offer. 'It's like a bit of crumpet,' says old sailor-cum-tailor Maurice Sedwell. 'The street pick-up is not like the girl you meet through introduction.' Certain persons of substance have even been known to solve the problem of choice by purchasing a firm of their own.

Those determined to window-shop might be advised to make their first approach to Savile Row through the Burlington Arcade, the passage of which should encourage an appropriate mood of timeless gentility, to say nothing of pricey exclusivity; besides, it is the only substantial bit of the past to survive largely unscathed. As you advance, try imagining the Earl of Burlington's neighbours throwing their oyster shells over the wall, or some nineteenth-century doxy smirking from one of the little upstairs windows.

Once through the Arcade, and with the bulk of Burlington House and the Museum of Mankind (once His Lordship's garden) at your back, you are in Burlington Gardens and the territory of the tailors lies before you: Cork Street dead ahead, Bond Street on your left, Old Burlington Street first on the right and then the thrust of Savile Row just beyond. It has grown a bit tacky over the years. There is no hint of eighteenth-century mischief in what has become of Queensberry House – it is a bank – and the gross encroachments of car park/office complex and police station bracket the Row in an ungainly manner, like two badly chosen book ends, so that hardly enough is left of the Palladian dream to give a sense of how it was. Yet there is grandeur in the manner in which Gieves & Hawkes at No. 1 anchors the top of the Row, like some self-important embassy for the enterprises beyond – Kilgour, Helman, Huntsman, Poole . . . and so on to Tommy Nutter. Wain Shiell and other cloth merchants are also here, having gone through much of the same period of tribulation as the tailors they serve with their myriad swatches of worsted, cashmere, vicuna, silk, mohair, tweed, cord and velvet.

Opposite, the car-park complex that replaced the original Henry Poole's provides unsentimental sanctuary to a string of mostly smaller enterprises, among them the original Nutters and the new Sexton; then comes Anderson & Sheppard, taking up the staid and solid corner block.

It is enough to terrorize the tyro, not least because prices (never displayed) can vary alarmingly, even while the product may be remarkably similar. Savile Row tailors charge what they can get, and novice customers are advised to buy at the level which brings them most satisfaction, for the exercise which this affords the ego is an important element in the therapeutic value of wearing Savile Row.

The cost of a Savile Row suit relates to no particular quality scale – other than in the choice of cloth – and is often a function of the overheads of the individual tailoring house. Thus, a small operator with humble premises and using only outworkers can afford to ask half of that charged by a bigger firm which nevertheless may be relying, at least in part, on the very same outworkers. Huntsman, most expensive of all Savile Row firms and rare in employing no outwork, has the burden of maintaining a large permanent workforce for its 'sectionalized' system of quality-controlled manufacture; this is much more costly than the traditional method of recourse to independently contracted coat-maker, trouser-maker and so on. Conversely, Anderson & Sheppard, for all its uppity attitude, is comparatively inexpensive.

If price is an uncertain guide, the look of the premises (sometimes seedy) and of the tailors themselves are even less of a reflection on the quality of the product. There is no danger of the average Savile Row tailor, in his stock-in-trade dark three-piece, committing the social gaffe of standing out in a crowd. Colin Hammick of Huntsman is an exception, in as much as his slight body and clothes-hanger shoulders make him a perfect model for his firm's inimitably neat, flared look. Hammick once found himself on Britain's best-dressed list, and he still smarts at the memory. 'It took me years to live that down,' he says. Tommy Nutter persists as a living model of his maverick wide styles, but for the rest, Edward Sexton's sharp appearance, pert as his pocket handkerchief, and Andrew Ramroop's spicy colour combinations, mark the limits of proprietorial display.

Ancient or modern, most of the shops still retain the gentleman's club atmosphere of leather armchair, mellow-chiming clock and *Country Life*-style magazines, with at least the suggestion of a workshop in the nether regions. Computer terminals may nestle among the brown paper patterns in some of the bigger shops, but customer relations are everywhere kept intensely personal. The family doctor is an analogy that Savile Row tailors like to dwell upon, and they make a big thing about never discussing a living client, even as they boast about the dead ones. Maddening to the tailors, this pact of silence is sometimes taken up by customers who, far from providing referrals, become jealous of others sharing their chosen suit-maker and are liable to recommend someone else when hailed with a 'Who's your tailor?' Sir Malcolm Sargent, a stickler about clothes, was a fine advert for Kilgour, yet he would never share that precious secret with his friends.

The number of variations on the 'clubby' theme is remarkable. As examples of the extremes, contrast Peter Moore, located above Helman in Savile Row, with Jones, Chalk & Dawson (a.k.a. Meyer & Mortimer) on Sackville Street. Moore has a substantial Swiss clientele and has converted part of Bobby Valentine's old premises into a suave salon with the cool ambiance – vast black leather couch, etc. – of an up-market psychiatrist's consulting room. Jones, Chalk is a poem in clutter. Ancient warrants, mementoes of Baden-Powell, Captain Oates, William IV, the King of Thailand and regimental regalia burden the walls; the cutting board is buried under plastic bags, coffee cups and bits of former or future garments. A large portrait of the Duke of Edinburgh, looking rather doleful in Highland dress, guards the way to further mysteries upstairs. Someone is looking for his trousers and someone wants to know who has taken his tape measure; a stray American youth is loose upon the scene, a little lost, but delighted just to be there.

The perfect suit is like the perfect wine – it does not exist, except in terms of individual taste. Savile Row house styles can be as similar and varied as fine Bordeaux, and equally confusing for the novice gentleman. In the past, an expert could distinguish the work of any of the top tailors at a glance. This is no longer true; a comfortable compromise between the square-shouldered, sharply waisted Continental look and the relaxed, but shapeless American sack suit has established itself as a standard Savile Row product for both sides of the Atlantic; it combines easy elegance with a royal patrimony, being an evolution of the Duke of Windsor cut. Yet an individual personality, sometimes born of a very long history, is stitched into each garment. According to Robert Bright, 'There is a distinct handwriting on all our products.' His evidence in this regard once sent a drug smuggler to jail as he demonstrated how the heroin-stuffed shoulder pads in a pair of jackets were made by the same tailor, while the jackets had been the work of two different tailors. Bright sees clear character traits reflected in the work of cutters like Edward Sexton – 'Ted is a sharp, live businessman and so you expect to see sharp lines and a clean touch to his clothing.'

Anderson & Sheppard's soft look and the structured contours of a Huntsman delineate the limits of the classic range, though Anderson is now alone in its refusal to accommodate a customer of independent desires. Military tailors like Welsh & Jeffries tend towards slightly tighter fittings, while Helman is distinctively high on craftsmanship, fairly soft in construction, yet well moulded and with a firmer shoulder line than Anderson's. With Sexton, the shoulder line becomes very firm, though not as monumental as former partner Tommy Nutter's King Kong creations. Poole prides itself in denying the existence of a Poole look and of simply counselling moderation. 'We'd give a man six-inch lapels if he wanted them, but we'd first try to persuade him how horrible it would be,' Angus Cundey has said, and on this everybody except Anderson would nowadays agree.

For all the abhorrence of fashion extremes, trends cannot be ignored and proprietor-cutters like Keith Fallan keep a close eye on the style magazines. At Wells, which also wholesales shirting material, Bright urges staff to 'get around the stores, see what are next season's colours and what's happening with ladies' clothes, and what they are saying about formal clothes. It's going to be an ingredient in what we do.' He believes that clients need to be encouraged to experiment, just a little, even if they don't want to. 'The easiest thing is to fall into the trap of giving him exactly the same thing as last time, and he'll say thank you – until his wife says, "Why don't you try another tailor, dear? They make you look so old."'

Veteran Bobby Valentine equates what has happened over his long lifetime with the changes wrought upon the motor vehicle – 'Once upon a time, Rolls-Royce and Daimler made motor cars with dignity; tall windows, comfortable seats and beautiful body work. They couldn't sell them today. Well, all we can do in Savile Row is maintain a measure of that dignity, even if it has to be in our hidden ways.'

Nothing is more hidden than the ways of making a Savile Row suit, which is far from the immutable creation of popular imagination. There is no agreed method of construction, and in some instances there is strong disagreement over what is permissible in crafting these golden fleeces of menswear.

The ritual as properly performed calls for the cooperative efforts of a cutter, trimmer, coat-maker, trouser-maker, waistcoat-hand, finisher and presser. The measurements taken, the cutter (who may have an assistant known as a striker) drafts a pattern on stout manila paper and uses this to cut out the cloth. The parts for the jacket (properly called the coat) and the trousers are bundled separately and passed with precise instructions to the specialist tailor of each garment, while the trimmer assumes responsibility for the linings, buttons and paddings.

Below
Dorothy Donaldson-Hudson, Savile Row's only lady guv'nor, with Groovy. As she tells it, her husband bought his family tailors in a romantic moment, then died after instructing: 'Now look, darling, you must hang on to J.B. Johnstone. I promised old man Johnstone.' That was more than forty years ago, and Dorothy has endured to become a Savile Row institution and militant warrior for the preservation of its traditions – even though these have mitigated against much female intrusion beyond the sewing bench. It was not until 1981 that women were even admitted to Savile Row's big annual charity dinner. Surveying the scene then, guest Peter Ustinov expressed surprise that they were not sitting side-saddle.

Within a few days, the suit is basted (the basic components are crudely patched together with temporary stitching in white cotton) ready for the first fitting, when the cutter lets fly with his chalk. Once approved, the baste is ripped apart and reworked for the more accurate 'forward' fitting, from which it may be sent back to the tailors for completion.

The bespoke tailor is a sculptor in the way he fashions a hollow shell to accommodate and flatter a particular body with all its oddities, and one of his special skills is in moulding the cloth into the contours by continual damping and shaping with a hot iron. The suit is given shape, bounce and further individuality through umpteen unseen stitches worked into its innards, and it is that which is least noticed which takes most time – particularly the construction of the 'canvas', which is the linen, felt, cotton or horsehair interlining that forms the jacket's scaffolding. The interlinings are covered with hundreds of containing stitches, then sewn into the jacket in layers. As jacket and linings are stitched together, the tailor gently rolls the layers of fabric in his hand so that the finish will have 'life' and not appear too smooth and perfect. Similarly, thousands of hidden stitches impart resilience and personality into collar and lapels. While some seams are machine-sewn for greater strength, hand-stitching is again used in such stress areas as trouser seats to allow more give. When all the tearing apart and re-stitching of the fitting process is included, the labour involved is formidable.

A classic test of Savile Row's artistry is to hold a lapel between finger and thumb and to feel the springiness: firm and yet soft enough to blow in the wind, as Cary Grant's did. Other signature elements recognizable to the cognoscenti include hand-sewn buttonholes that are fully functional even on the sleeves, and the hand-sewn loop behind the lapel buttonhole to hold a blossom in place. Oscar Wilde and Tom Wolfe alike described the hand-made buttonhole as the true badge of the gentleman.

Last comes the pressing of the finished garment, the task of another specialist who gives the suit its final shaping. If cutter and client are then satisfied, the suit may go public; if not, it is back to the workroom. Total work time: around forty hours. Normal delivery time: six to eight weeks.

In practice, there are almost as many variations from the norm as there are suits made. In a real sense, each Savile Row suit is a unique creation. Those who uphold the one-tailor-one-garment system speak of personal pride and of the client appreciating this sense of individual work, but there are pitfalls, particularly when fine craftsmen are in short supply. Former *Tailor and Cutter* editor John Taylor has used the same tailor for thirty years, yet he still grumbles about the occasional disaster. To true believers, that is part of the adventure, but Huntsman has achieved its celebrity through a system of quality control that denies individualism and consequently evens out the bumps. Huntsman's production-line system operates like a factory without machines, with craft teams assembling the garments to an exacting standard that can be maintained, if necessary, by restricting orders.

Huntsman claims to put the same amount of handwork into its suits as it did sixty years ago and it charges accordingly, but no two Savile Row craftsmen will agree precisely on what to do and how to do it. 'I like a certain look about the shoulders and lapel and so on, but I don't tell a good tailor how to construct it, because that's where you get problems,' says royal suit-maker John Kent. 'I've got one tailor who uses flax canvas and horsehair and I've got another who uses haircloth and real canvas; now, I'm not going to dictate how I want all my coats made, because if I do that I'm going to end up with rubbish. So long as the shapes are my shapes and provided it's done by hand, I don't care how he makes the inside.'

There are as many tricks to the trade as there are short cuts, and curious characters. A celebrated trouser-maker known as Rosey was reckoned to be able to turn out a remarkable ten pairs a day, scorning even to leave the workroom to relieve himself, but rather using old milk bottles for the purpose. Then there was the coat-maker who found a peculiar satisfaction, or egalitarian thrill, in wearing his work to the toilet, in cases where it was destined for some celebrity or a person of title.

There is also such a thing as too good tailoring. Some customers complain when stitching is so fine that it does not show, particularly around the edge of the lapel, because that to them is the signature of bespoke, as are horn buttons. Again, a brilliant coat-maker can put so much work into a jacket that it becomes heavy and unwieldy, and the piece-rate perfectionist also suffers in the wallet for his excessive commitment. Tom Leggatt at Kilgour was probably the most celebrated of modern perfectionists. Paddy Rice, who trained Keith Fallan, is another who surely made less by making well. One of Savile Row's best coat-makers is now a croupier in Las Vegas – he could not afford to stay at his craft.

Nothing stirs emotions more than fusing, which is a press-and-glue alternative to stitched-in padding. Fusing affords greater structural control, since the tensions and quality of hand-stitching varies from craftsman to craftsman; it is particularly effective with hard-to-tailor lightweights and in executing export orders where few fittings are possible, but purists detect a loss of character in the firmer, less resilient result. Wells and James & James are champions of fusing, and Wells is equally enthusiastic over other equipment adapted from the ready-to-wear industry. 'Advancements are going on all the time. I don't think anybody would disagree that the machinery upstairs will do a better job in a fraction of the time,' says Brian Lishak, who came to Wells from Huntsman, a stronghold of ancient ways. Wells's latest pressing iron comes with an array of shaping devices and a hospital-style drip feed for moisture control.

'Some people feel that craftsmen are dying out and that if you can't get it done well by hand, it's better to do it by fusing, because at least you know what you're getting,' says Keith Fallan, who was a fusing convert until he suffered an embarrassing failure: 'I thought it was the answer, but how can you justify the one that comes undone? You can't

Below
Cyril Castle did Roger Moore, while his friend, neighbour and rival Tony Sinclair, did 'the other fella, the Scots boy' (Sean Connery). Castle's early memories are of his father making suits for Rudolph Valentino, and he in turn has spent his life making for succeeding generations of showbusiness personalities. Sinatra ('a wonderful fella') came on a recommendation from Moore and looked, Cyril says, 'a bit of a mess' until sheared into conservative worsteds that did wonders for a figure with a tendency to bulge.

say to the bloke, "I'm sorry, it's come unstuck."' Fallan pauses to apply a shaping iron to a piece of grey pinstripe. 'You can do something on a machine in two minutes and by hand it will take you twenty minutes, but what's an hour on a coat, when it's sewn by hand with real silk which stretches here and gives a little bit of character there?'

Says Huntsman: 'There are now fantastic machines that can do very good padding in three to four minutes. For us, it takes a girl three to four hours. Why do we use girls? Because we believe machines are good, but not as good as a girl's hands.'

To be squeezed between the steady advance of mechanical processes and the steady decline – and escalating cost – of skilled craftsmanship: this is Savile Row's dilemma.

The duties of the customer are likewise in flux. There has been, as Robert Bright puts it, 'an adjustment to the pace of life'. He explains: 'In the old days, there might be twelve fittings, which meant twelve shots at getting it right, and out of a dozen suits, maybe five were fine and the rest went to the gardener. . . .' With few customers in possession of a gardener these days, and with no time for multiple fittings, the idea now is to get it right the first time.

Below
Arthur Catchpole, cutter at Hogg Sons & J. B. Johnstone, with old stock book containing hundreds of cloth snippets and complicated instructions for regimental, hunt and private livery orders.

Above Right
A customer darts into Sackville Street to check a cloth in daylight. Why some tailor shops let in so little light has exercised the curious for generations. A writer in 1806 suggested it was 'to prevent keen eyes from discovering coarse threads'.

This does not imply scrapping the ever-so-confidential relationship of client and cutter. 'These fitting rooms are like confessionals. There are things told to us in here that never go anywhere else' – Bright's voice is lowered – 'The relationship becomes so close that when we are buying the cloth, we can often picture our customer inside it. "Ah, that's Mr So-and-so . . . Sir Charles will be happy in that one. . . ." '

A tour of these places where great and rich men strip to their underpants reveals generally spartan accommodation, often only a cloth-draped cubby hole, with no concessions to modern notions of mood management. Again, do not be deceived by appearances: the alchemy of the fitting room lies in its levelling intimacy, for as Maurice Sedwell puts it, 'When you meet a man with his trousers off, it is different.'

Confidences tend to be exchanged. Sedwell once had a customer ask whether he knew of a quick cure for syphillis, and the great cutter J. K. Wilson had to defend the honour of his fitting room from an ardent Latin American millionaire, who arrived with a heavily made-up lady and an assurance that they would not be requiring it for long.

The first meeting of General Pershing and Lord Allenby in World War I took place at the fitting-room door, and more recently US Treasury Secretary William Simon used one of Wells's sedate Victorian sanctuaries to negotiate a crucial IMF loan for Britain. Simon set up the secret rendezvous with a phone call to Richard McSweaney, his cutter at Wells. 'He didn't have to ask for confidentiality; it was taken for granted,' Wells is quick to observe. The story came out only because Simon chose to write about it in his memoirs. McSweaney was one of those who made it a rule to call a customer 'Sir' in the shop, even when they were on first-name terms in the fitting room.

From the customer's point of view, the process is basically the same everywhere. For the first visit, he should allow one hour to meet his salesman and cutter (often the same person), select a fabric and style and be measured. Thereafter, he needs to allow time for at least two fittings, though these may not take more than fifteen minutes each, and tailors try hard to accommodate busy schedules. Subsequent orders are easier. All tailors keep their patterns, the bigger ones having many thousands of these brown manila templates in store. A phone call would be enough to set shears to cloth, though leafing through the swatch-books and chatting style with one's cutter is generally regarded as a pleasure not to be sacrificed. The patterns have an extra use, as a handy place to jot down the social details, likes and dislikes, even favourite joke, of the client, so that instant rapport can be achieved, no matter how long delayed is the next meeting. In these brown manila folds lie the ultimate secrets of Savile Row.

Image has always been the tailors' bugbear. There is an obscure saying that it 'takes nine tailors to make a man' and it has seemed to tailors that writers have conspired with folklore (Lady Godiva's Peeping Tom just had to be a tailor) to perpetuate this ancient slur. Portrayed as stupid in Arab literature and mocked as spineless weaklings by Western writers from Shakespeare to Shaw, tailors can be excused some of their complexes. It is small compensation to know that Samuel Pepys's father was a tailor, or that the FBI once had a director who was a tailor, or that the Marx brothers had an uncle who was the fastest pants presser in New York City; no, it is hardly enough that a tailor is Speaker of the House of Commons – for tailoring could do with a Hero. Perhaps this is why the legendary beastliness of Scholte to his customers so entrances the average tailor; it may not be true that he abused them so, but it is nice to imagine that he did.

It follows that the first-time Savile Row customer would do best to act with good-humoured humility and to place his trust in the person he has elected to build his suit. 'The customer is always right . . . on the surface,' J. K. Wilson instructed in his *Art of Cutting and Fitting*. 'At the same time, you have your job to do, and he must not be allowed to interfere with your working efficiency. Never let him teach you your business. In the fitting room always be courteous, but firm.' Writing in 1950, J.K. felt 'the reason why the Britisher is the best-dressed man in the world is that he doesn't fuss – he is content to go to a first-class tailor and trust him to see the job through. Your foreigner, on the other hand, usually regards the whole world with a distrustful eye.'

'Psychology is the key to the whole thing,' according to Brian Lishak, who has sold Savile Row to all sorts from all over the world. 'Within thirty to thirty-five seconds of a customer walking in the door, we will have made our own judgment – the type of person he is, what's going to suit him and so on. We will then talk to him and within the next two minutes, if that, we will have concluded what we want him to buy. If he comes in, as customers often do, knowing what he wants and it's wrong for him, then we have to very carefully try and steer him away

Above
Angus Cundey with cloth swatches. Leafing through the swatch books and chatting style is a pleasure not to be sacrificed.

from it.' When it comes to picking out a cloth from the thousands of choices in the swatch-books cast about every showroom, 'it is important to direct, otherwise people get bemused,' Lishak reasons.

The *Tailor and Cutter* in 1947 published an exquisitely wicked profile of the Mayfair Man, as the classic client type of the time. Its advice on how to tackle him is still pertinent reading:

> Call him 'milord' and charge him extra. Show him only your soberest patterns but let the material be of the best – that is his main interest. Be deferential (you may even rub your hands) and always escort him to the door. Give him every consideration. Because he is very rich you will have great difficulty in getting your money from him (or perhaps it is because you have such difficulty in getting your money that he is so very rich). He will complain at *all* fittings as a matter of form. Be prepared for this. If he points out a mythical fault, agree with him and make a technical looking chalk mark. When he has gone, brush off the mark and hang up the garment until the next fitting. He'll take it.*

Maurice Sedwell puts a modern slant on the matter. 'If a man feels comfortable with you, you have your way with him. It is the confident one who bullies you who is the least secure' – and the least likely to secure satisfaction.

Savile Row inevitably draws more than its share of cranks, from compulsive purchasers and those with bizarre requests to disturbed individuals who reject everything that they order. There is no black list operating (though the Tailors' Federation has an export advisory arm that tries to keep track of foreign malefactors), so impossible customers can plague one tailor after another through many years. The confidence trickster is also drawn to the Row, and most tailors fancy their talents at spotting a villain.

But it is the muddle-headed who cause most distress. 'It's not the sound things that drive you mad, it's the dozey things they come out with, like "When I bend over why do these trousers crease up?" or "When I sit down, what is this poking out of the front of my trousers?"' says John Kent, who describes himself as '43, going on 143 . . . "You've lengthened the trousers too much," they'll say, and then you put them back exactly where they were in the first place and they're satisfied. A time and motion man would laugh his head off at the things we do.' In retirement, Bobby Valentine is philosophic: 'It is those lunatic fusspot customers who teach you that you must strive for perfection, even when people do not ask for it. The other 99 per cent of your clients get the benefit.'

J.K. in his *Art of Cutting* . . . put names to seven categories of awkward customer – Mr Nobby Knowall, the Hon. Cecil Sidetrack, Mr Philip Fidget, Sir Pall Wearybore, poor Henry Henpeck, Mr Ivor Grouse and Colonel Peevish Crabbe. J.K. had the old Savile Row tailor's profound suspicion of women. 'Most female critics of men's clothing can be vastly irritating,' he wrote. 'Rarely is her criticism helpful: frequently it is ridiculous. *Never, on any account, allow her in until the fitting is completed.*' J.K. offered the cautionary tale of how he once lost a good customer by allowing his wife into the fitting room: 'She complained that the fly of her husband's trousers, instead of disappearing amidships at the bottom, took a cant to the right. I pointed out that there was a physical reason for the phenomenon, which I could not explain in her presence. The husband expressed himself as satisfied with my explanation, but I never saw him again. I wonder, did he die a martyr to his wife's aesthetic tastes?'

All tailors have trouser jokes, most of them schoolboyish, and all have personal anecdotes connected with *that* measurement. Marybeth

* One milord, the 13th Baron of Dudley, took it so personally that he demanded a published apology!

Kerrigan, an American writer who J.K. was fortunate never to meet, records how she made Angus Cundey blush deeply when she persisted in her researches into why Poole's cutters preferred their customers to wear boxer shorts rather than briefs. 'You know about dressing right and dressing left,' Cundey managed to reply. 'Well, if you wear briefs, you don't really do either.'

Reuben Synter, in his seminal *Art of Fitting Gentlemen's Garments*, set the matter straight for all time:

> A man's anatomical formation will not permit him to wear trousers in the centre of the body, as a woman can. Because of this he has to wear them either to the right or left of the centre of his body – usually it is to the right. If a man wears his trousers to the right of the centre of the body, this means that he 'dresses' on the left, and provision should be made for this anatomical formation, or 'person', as it is called, when trousers are being cut. When the trousers are worn to the left of the centre of the body, this means that the wearer 'dresses right', and provision for 'person' should be made on the right half . . . another matter which must not be overlooked is rupture.

Synter proceeded, with the help of a lugubrious model, to instruct on the taking of an inside-leg measurement:

> With the tape in his right hand, gently place the tape into the fork as high up as can be comfortably felt by the customer, then place the blank (or uppermost) side of the tape gently against the right leg, holding it there with the right hand. . . . The remainder of the tape now hangs freely down the inside leg. Bring the left hand around the back of the right leg to the fork section of the inside leg; and hold the tape with the left hand, gently pressing the brass end into the fork and against the right leg; free the right hand. . . .

Charles Emms, cigar-chomping, bowler-hatted extrovert of the 1940s, taught his apprentices 'never to have any qualms about feeling all along the tape, no matter how exhalted the customer may be,' and, all the while, to 'engage the client in conversation in order to ensure a natural posture'. 'There was no hesitation and above all no embarrassment,' the *Tailor and Cutter* wrote of Emms in action. 'Every little detail appeared to be noticed by his fingers.'

Savile Row pride precludes failure, whatever the circumstances. Dennis Ryan of Joce recalls with appreciation the customer with polio 'who had to put his trousers on lying down on the floor . . . when we were finished, I felt very satisfied; it really was a difficult fit.' Manning takes special pleasure in recounting how he solved the problem of an American eccentric who wanted something comfortable, yet distinguished, for wood-chopping in the morning: he made him a mink-lined dressing-gown from out of the pages of P.G. Wodehouse. Then again, Dennis Wilkinson knows all about making a suit for a monkey – 'fitting the hole for the tail is the trickiest part'.

In the 1950s, someone in Leeds invented a method of fitting with a spray-can. His idea was to put a jacket of celanese material on the subject and then spray on an acetate solution that shrank and set to give an exact impression of the figure. The spray was said to have a faint pear-drop odour. Even if otherwise acceptable, the method could not have suited Savile Row, where the main aim is to 'improve on the perfect fit', as Huntsman's Colin Hammick puts it. In too many cases, the perfect fit would be a perfect disaster, bearing in mind the lumpy, lopsided geometry of most males, especially the mature ones who make up the bulk of Savile Row's trade. Applauded for his apparently fine figure at the age of eighty, Huntsman *patrone* Robert Packer used to respond with a 'Would you like me to take off my jacket, sir?'

To facilitate the adroit cutting and stuffing of cultured camouflage, at least two dozen measurements are taken, some of them common to all tailors, others according to individual technique. Codes commonly used to summarize the client's condition sound alarming, but are merely the average man's lot and Savile Row's burden. DRS stands for Dropped Right Shoulder, and BL 1, 2 and 3 are Bow Legs to the First, Second and Third degree. Then there is the delectably euphemistic FS, which stands for Forward Stomach.

At Gieves, the first-time customer is ushered up to the 'Adam Room' for what Robert Gieve calls 'a conversational activity', from which habits and activities are ascertained and consequent cloth types and style points recommended. Then the cutter takes the measurements and establishes a rapport with the client, who will be his through a relationship that could last many years. 'It's not just the creation of a suit; it's a one-to-one personal friendship that develops and from that stems confidence and trust,' according to Gieve. If the premises are not everywhere so grand or the ritual so formalized, the

Below
The successful Savile Row tailor usually aspires to the gentrified life: a little golf and a retreat in the stockbroker belt. Cecil Tobias, who sold out to a businessman who was also a customer, here takes a retirement stroll down the Row with Mrs Tobias.

Above Right
Wells's pattern room – Savile Row's ultimate secrets strung out like so many kippers in a smoke house.

approach is much the same throughout Savile Row.

But what of Anderson & Sheppard, secretive and fuddy-duddy to a fault, and thriving upon it? An interview was at first declined on principle, then granted, though limited to those generalities that could be conveyed while stationed by the bolt of cloth nearest the door. However, an intrepid journalist named Simon Winchester managed early in 1988 to penetrate Anderson's security by the simple expedient of becoming a customer.

Lulling suspicions by arriving in a bespoke suit from the venerable Oxford firm of Hall Brothers, Winchester was greeted at the door by five rather serious looking men, among them manager Dennis Hallbery, who used a matador's flourish to present and drape upon the visitor a sample of the wispy light Anderson jacket. '"There, sir," breathed Mr Hallbery. "You have just experienced the philosophy of an Anderson & Sheppard coat."' Winchester was in.

He wrote in Condé Nast's *Traveller*:

> I was taken to a fitting room as large as most small houses and with mirrors that might have graced the main staircase of a Palladian mansion. The five men deployed themselves to battle stations – two

coming in behind the curtains. One sat with a large notepad and an enormous fountain pen. Another – he introduced himself as the trouser-maker – knelt before me with a tape measure. The other three waited their turns. The Kneeling Man began, with the great speed of a master surgeon, to measure and check the size and tone of muscles I had long forgotten I even possessed. There was a brief pause for the obligatory music-hall joke – 'Sir dresses to the left, I see?' – before more yards of tape were wound around more circumferences, and then the Kneeling Man stood, pronounced himself done, and allowed Mr Hallbery into the sanctum.

Mr Hallbery twirled around me, measuring, barking numbers at the Sitting Man, demanding that my jacket – or coat, I keep forgetting, even now – be on, then off, then with its pockets filled, next with them unfilled. 'Some folks swear by our coats. Others swear at them. It's an old joke. But it's quite true. You'll see. You'll want double-breasted, of course. No pocket flaps. Four-button cuffs. Perfectly normal, perfectly classic.' And soon he was finished, and the Cloth Man was ushered in, and he led me through a jungle of bales and bolts and swatches of pinstripes, finally persuading me to choose a strange little number in grey and white that had a diagonal sublimation to it that I was assured would suit me nicely.

And finally, the Money Man. He had a beard and was quite silent. There was a slim, rather battered leather book. He opened it to a page of numbers and, while looking discreetly towards the sky, pointed to one line, at the end of which was the number 675. Six hundred and seventy-five pounds. 'Would that be satisfactory, sir?' he breathed, and when I said it would, he mumbled about the 'unfortunate necessity' for a 'small deposit' of, let us say, 'about a third', and he continued to look away while I wrote a cheque, breathing only the phrase, 'Sheppard has two letters p, if you please, sir.' It was all done within the hour.

Above
Continental customers perusing Poole's. 'The accommodation provided [at Poole] equals that at the best appointed railway stations,' the *Tailor and Cutter* enthused in 1870.

The Anderson Money Man's awkward demeanour highlights that most sensitive element in the procurement of a Savile Row suit, the paying for it. It is only in recent years, and still not universally, that Savile Row has ventured to seek something in advance.

'Tailors, like woodcocks, live by suction with their long bills,' Francis Wilson wrote in an early nineteenth-century polemic against 'the evils of the wretched system of the West End', which he portrayed as a vicious circle. 'They are obliged to give long credit; their losses by bad debts are consequently enormous and the result is that for the accommodation they afford and the losses they suffer, they are compelled to charge exceeding high prices. Thus they make the good customer pay through the nose, as it is termed, for the defalcations of the bad one.'

It used to be said that Savile Row was expected to exist on nothing, gentlemen not wishing to embarrass their tailors by paying their bills. In olden times, the only pressure on customers to settle was a 5 per cent interest charge on accounts outstanding for more than a year. And not so olden times. Maurice Sedwell chuckles when he recounts how it was prudent to check the obituaries in *The Times* and *Daily Telegraph* and then to get the ledgers out – 'It was the only time you had a chance to get paid.' He also says that 'the best spender is the man who doesn't pay you'.

This may help explain the Savile Row fascination with bills. Often splendidly ornate, they are frequently among a firm's most treasured historical possessions. J. B. Johnstone, for example, has a bill for £24 6s that was seized by the Boers and then recaptured and returned by the British forces. Dege's earliest possession is a bill of 1827, with a bottom line that reads, 'to cash lent £1'. It belonged to John Jones, who set up shop in 1827 and became very rich (he left a porcelain collection valued in 1962 at £13 million), but maintained a strong sentimental

The average man is not symmetrical, but lopsided, and as individual in detail as a sack of potatoes. This, above all else, has been Savile Row's salvation in the age of the computer and laser. The perfect fit is not necessarily the object. 'We improve on the perfect fit,' stresses Colin Hammick at Huntsman. 'A suit that fitted perfectly might not satisfy us, where there are faults to hide or correct.' J. P. Thornton, a nineteenth-century professor of the tape measure, delineated the defects of man and how to accommodate them. These illustrations, all guaranteed to be 'drawn from life', are from his monumental *International System of Garment Cutting*. Each was accompanied by a lengthy treatise on how 'to alter the general appearance of the customer until the peculiarities of form are as far as possible concealed'.

The Fore-and-Aft Humps
'Difficulties that call for very careful consideration. . . .'

Prominent Hips
'If a tailor were called to cut a coat for a skeleton, he would at once realize the difficulty of providing for the abrupt projection of pelvic bones.'

The Pigeon-breasted Figure
'One of the most unsightly deformities
that poor humanity is inflicted by. . .and
very difficult to drape.'

The Man with the Crutch
'Students then progressed to The Man
with Two Crutches. . . .'

The Corpulent Figure
'May be defined as one whose waist
measure exceeds his breast measure.'

attachment to that early bill; or perhaps he was just hoping to get his pound back.

Today's customer, inured to the steep price rises of recent years, might find it sensible to take the same course and to cherish their bill (or better still their receipt) as part of the Savile Row experience. In doing so, they could reflect on the good fortune of Lieutenant Thomas Dyneley of the Royal Horse Artillery, upon being captured during the Peninsula War while in possession of a Hawkes's request for £16 12s 4d. The French were so impressed with the appearance of the bill that they mistook the subaltern for a Lord and treated him accordingly.

The customer might also find solace in this submission, prepared by a cloth merchant in the midst of the hectic price rises of the late 1970s:

> Before you can walk out of my shop with a beautiful wool worsted tailored suit, a few things will have to happen. The Australian sheep farmer has to tend and feed his merino sheep for a year. He must shear off the wool and freight it to the wool sales, from where it has to be shipped all the way to Britain. Over here it has to be sorted into the different grades, and then it must be washed and scoured. Next it must be carded and combed, and then dyed into all the necessary colours. Then it has to be drawn and spun and twisted before the warper can wind all the thread round his beam, whilst the weft threads are prepared on to the bobbins for the shuttles. Now the warp can be fed into the loom, with every thread painstakingly fed through the reeds in the loom, and weaving starts. Out of the loom the cloth has to be washed and scoured again, and then all the knots and blemishes have to be mended by hand before the cloth can be finished by shrinking and pressing. The finished pieces of cloth go to the woollen merchant, who cuts off and sends me the exact length I need to make your suit. The suit then has to be cut exactly to your measurements and requirements, and all the linings, interlinings, threads, pocketings, waistbandings, shoulder pads, buttons etc. have to be purchased and matched to the colour of the cloth. It is not then put into a magic machine, but the craftsmen have to sit and sew for days, paying attention to every detail and working and shaping your suit with needle and iron, making adjustments after fittings, until finally it is ready. Not really expensive, is it?

Below
Very raw recruits: a pair of tourists check coordinates as they stumble upon Savile Row.

Appendix:
The Complete Savile Row

The Savile Row Directory

The definitive is impossible, since there is constant movement in a trade still charged with some of the old itinerant spirit. Also, it is a calling of singularly secretive individualists, so that reliable statistics are as rare as moth holes in a bolt of Lumbs Huddersfield Golden Bale.

Savile Row's entire production is minute when compared with that of any popular ready-to-wear brand, and the longest name can hide the smallest undertaking, for just like Russian dolls stacked one inside the other, one firm will find sanctuary within another. Rather, the dynamic of Savile Row is in the one-to-one relationship of cutter/fitter and client, so that the size of an enterprise can be as irrelevant as

price, which here is keyed to the quoted base rate for a two-piece suit. £ to ££££ very roughly segments a scale that ranged from around £500 to more than £1,000 at 1988 prices. The symbol of a single pair of shears indicates a solo cutter-proprietor operation, with or without in-house workers. Two shears usually imply a two-cutter partnership, with a small team of tailors exclusively or largely working for them. Three shears signify the larger houses. The gradation is based on bespoke production only and does not necessarily relate to the size of the undertaking as a whole. This, then, is Savile Row in the late summer of 1988.

Adeney & Boutroy
8a Sackville Street. Tel. 734 2289
Dates from 1744 (Boutroy) and 1774 (Adeney). Incumbent Ron Pescod has been suiting an eclectic clientele of high churchmen and film stars (Tony Curtis, Rod Taylor, Trevor Howard, Ian Carmichael) since 1935.
Size ✄
Price £

Alan Bennett
36 Savile Row. Tel. 437 7986
Though with more than two decades in Savile Row, among the youngest of its cutter-proprietors. Wears blazers rather than the usual three-piece and has an easy manner to match. Describes his work as classically conservative and his clientele as 'businessmen, stockbrokers, a few lords, earls . . . nobody famous'. Likes a challenge and found it in making for Madame Tussauds and dress uniforms for Her Majesty's ambassadors.
Size ✄
Price ££

Alan Maitland & Riches
12 Cork Street. Tel. 734 5558
Ron Riches had eighteen years with Hawkes before starting on his own in the mid-1970s. Doctors, businessmen, some MPs are among his clients. Calls life 'a battle against peculiar human figures and peculiar human minds', but adds: 'Most of

my customers are my friends – you've got to stick with them even when they try you.'
Size ✄
Price £

Anderson & Sheppard
30 Savile Row. Tel. 734 2289
Currently Savile Row's most successful firm, thanks in main to cult following among Americans. Single-minded exponent of 'the Anderson experience', which is a roomy garment, almost cardigan-like in its softness, and never, ever supposed to look new. 'Basically, we drape bodies. We don't build them,' director Colin Harvey has explained. Prince Charles wears A&S double-breasteds.
Size ✄✄✄✄
Price ££

Billings & Edmonds
24 Dering Street. Tel. 629 1266
Hanging flower baskets and stacks of schoolboy uniforms bedeck this family firm in which bespoke was a natural development from outfitting many of the country's top schools and some of its princelings. Lately making twice-yearly trips to New York.
Size ✄
Price £

James Bone
32 Old Burlington Street. Tel. 437 2874
One-time Davies cutter who now shares premises with his old firm after industrious years elsewhere in the West End.
Size ✄
Price £

Bricker & Mellowe
27 Cork Street. Tel. 734 3087
Run jointly with Hilliers, the lone ladies' bespoke specialist, both firms having been acquired by ex-Poole cutter Jack Cavendish. No condescension to femininity on male side, where mood and cut are traditional/conservative. Travels to France.
Size ✄
Price £

Tom Brown
25 Prince's Street. Tel. 629 5025
Founded at Eton in 1784 and serving Old Etonians (and friends of friends of Old Etonians) ever since, it is run in a benevolently schoolmasterly manner by a seventh-generation Brown, who has personally ministered to four generations of some families. Stresses good value in an enduring garment; believes devoutly in such old values as braces and waistcoats; dubious of the trend towards lighter

cloths. A cousin runs the ancient Eton branch.
Size ✂
Price £

Burstow Logsdail
8a Sackville Street. Tel. 437 1750
Much of trade American – bankers, stockbrokers, some diplomats, politicians. Royal designer David Hicks called partner Lennie Logsdail 'the best tailor in the world'. Small in-house team with number of outworkers. Incorporates **Denman & Goddard** (tel. 734 6371), with century-old Eton connection; also **Carr, Son & Woor** (tel. 734 1926), which in turn incorporates **Hicks & Son**, established 1797.
Size ✂✂
Price ££

Cyril Castle
42 Conduit Street. Tel. 734 5005
Ravaged by rent hikes and the decline of an ageing clientele, Sinatra's tailor talks of hard times as he is reduced to turning out a few suits a week for his regulars. A favourite with generations of show-business personalities, his signature is the cuffed style of jacket he first made for Stewart Granger when that actor was unknown.
Size ✂
Price £££

N.H. Chapman
37a Savile Row. Tel. 437 4575
John Chapman, a fourth-generation tailor with classic credentials (Huntsman, Hawes & Curtis, Kilgour, etc.), prefers to build 'a traditional suit, fairly well-fitted, nothing too extreme'.
Size ✂
Price ££

Roy Chittleborough and Joseph Morgan
(formerly **Nutters of Savile Row**)
35a Savile Row. Tel. 437 6850
The creation of the 1960s that left neighbours 'slightly perplexed and even dismayed' is now the quite sedate domain of Morgan and Chittleborough, survivors of the original Nutters and creating stylishly on their own account. The original second-hand antique door also survives.
Size ✂✂
Price £££

R.P. Corley
26 Princes Street. Tel. 493 1991
Ron Corley is a classic example of the itinerant independent. Now at Tom Brown, he previously had a sitting at Blades and other locations around the Row.
Size ✂
Price ££

Davies & Son
32 Old Burlington Street. Tel. 629 2420
Creaky floorboards and furnishings from its splendid past provide a fitting ambiance for gentlemanly service in the old manner. Reduced circumstances oblige it to share premises with others, but these are of the same breed. Incorporates **Bostridge & Curties** (tel. 437 1603) and **Watson, Fagerstrom & Hughes** (tel. 434 2807).
Size ✂✂
Price ££

J. Dege & Sons
16 Clifford Street. Tel. 734 2248
Rhymes with 'prestige'. Energetically run coagulation of fine old names, most retaining identity for customer purposes. They include ancient (1662) Court tailors **Wilkinson & Son**, **Rogers & Co.** (1774), **John Jones** (1827), **J. Daniels, Winter & Tracy, T.W. Reakes, Alexander Cameron, C.H. Pedlar, Pulford & Co., Foster & Co., Eade, Peckover** (tel. 734 0733) and **Pope & Bradley** (tel. 734 0733). Strong equestrian/military background evident in tendancy towards shaped, skirted jacket style. Customers include Britain's richest man, the Duke of Westminster.
Size ✂✂✂
Price ££££

Errington & Whyte
8a Sackville Street. Tel. 734 1897
Soho-born Harry Errington trained under legendary Frederick Scholte. Harry was the only fireman to win the George Cross in World War II; he is also an international basketball referee. Opened own business in 1946, with many journalists, publicists and theatrical types among his customers.
Size ✂
Price £

Fallan & Harvey
7 Sackville Street. Tel. 437 8573
Good example of American-orientated house: 90 per cent of trade is foreign, mostly US, which Keith Fallan prowls coast-to-coast for fourteen weeks per year. Founded in 1975; stresses in-house production for quality control. Slim-fitting jacket and pleated trousers designed to promulgate an elegantly English look.
Size ✂✂
Price ££

Lewis Ferszt
2 Savile Row. Tel. 437 8463
Heir to **Robert Valentine** (tel. 734 1336), though after forty years in the trade he is no reincarnation of the flamboyant Bobby. Makes a soft suit ('not as soft as Anderson's') and regards innovation as hazardous, since 'man is a creature of habit'.
Size ✂
Price ££

Gieves & Hawkes
1 Savile Row. Tel. 434 2001
Glitzy shades of Nelson and Wellington: 200 years of officers and gentlemen in the headquarters of nineteenth-century exploration make this arguably the classiest gents' outfitters in the world. Bespoke now minor part of business, but important for image and conducted in heady environment of scarlet and polished brass.
Size ✂✂✂
Price ££££

T.G. Hammond
8 Stafford Street. Tel. 629 4969
Keenly priced 'standard conservative West End suit' from this one-time Hawes & Curtis staffer, with customer range extending from usual business types to some Arab potentates.
Size ✂
Price £

Douglas Hayward
95 Mount Street. Tel. 499 5574
A Hollywood soap opera about Savile Row could do no better than cast gregarious Dougie Hayward as the central character. Aspiring film star and tycoon types of the 1960s made him their own and have kept him that way through their glory years. Located away from the rest of Savile Row, round the corner from Harry's Bar and the Connaught; purveys personal selection of shirts, ties, luggage, etc., along with highly personalized bespoke service.
Size ✂
Price £££

Helman
10 Savile Row. Tel. 629 2949
An endearing double act, brothers Harry and Burt Helman are doyens of the trade they have enlivened for sixty years. Born and bred Savile Row men, their craftsmanship is as distinguished as the gentry who come calling (Rothschilds, assorted English lords, Swedish royalty, Arab potentates, a few clothes-loving actors like Terence Stamp, even Muhammad Ali) – 'very eminent men from all over the world who want to look a little better,' is how Burt puts it.
Size ✂
Price N.A.

Anthony J. Hewitt
9 Savile Row. Tel. 734 1505
Started his career with another famous Savile Row tailors and discovered he had a natural flair. Commenced business in a third-floor room in Clifford Street and graduated to his present well-appointed Savile Row shop front. Hewitt's meritorious progress was spurred on by combining with an operation making uniforms for industry. Travels America and Europe. Includes **Vincents of Savile Row** (tel. 734 1505) and **Burlington Uniforms** (tel. 734 2128).
Size ✂✂
Price ££

Hogg, Sons & J.B. Johnstone
19 Clifford Street. Tel. 734 5780
Tailors to Empire – 'We had the whole Indian Army,' recollects Malcolm Johnstone, who is still operational at eighty-three – now reduced to doing the very occasional governor-general and servicing faithful following with 'decent, classical' clothes made in the old one-man-to-a-garment way. 'The one thing we won't have is high pressure salesmanship,' says Dorothy Donaldson-Hudson, a commanding figure who is Savile Row's only lady guv'nor. Incorporates **Tautz & Co.**
Size ✄
Price £££

H. Huntsman
11 Savile Row. Tel. 734 7441
Offers excellence and charges for it: these are Savile Row's top prices. Was an old-fashioned breeches-maker when acquired and transformed in late 1920s by Robert Packer, who sought to achieve consistency of quality by devising a 'sectionalized' construction system, with no outside contracting. Distinctive slim-shaped style evolved from hacking jacket. Close to 70 per cent of sales overseas, mostly North America. Has ready-to-wear range made by Chester Barrie. Owns venerable (1750) royal boot-maker Maxwell in basement.
Size ✄✄✄
Price ££££

James & James
11 Old Burlington Street. Tel. 734 1748
Scandinavian background and pioneering use of fusing technology are features of brothers Eric and John James's partnership, which dates back to the acquisition of the legendary Scholte's business (and the Duke of Windsor's custom with it).
Size ✄✄
Price ££

Jarvis & Hamilton
11 St George Street. Tel. 491 3500
John Reed's red carnation and diamond pin is worn with an almost theatrical swagger, but he cuts a strictly classic line for a following of nobility and City gents (and he advocates sacrificing trouser pockets for extra elegance). Still in mourning over a pair of corduroys that upset Sir Adrian Boult in the days of the late Jarvis, so conscientiousness is clearly a strong point.
Size ✄
Price ££

Joce & Co.
11 St George Street. Tel. 629 2264
Founding Joce was a West Country descendant of a Spanish castaway. Dennis Ryan's father tailored at rear of Vienna Opera House before acquiring business prior to World War II. Substantial Continental trade. Won Dandy tailoring

trophy five times. Incorporates **C.L. Ostling.**
Size ✄
Price ££

Johns & Pegg
11 St George Street. Tel. 734 1713
Military and mufti tailor to the Household Division since last century. Has served various royals. Discreet and publicity-shy. Present (fourth-generation) Johns suffered fate of many when forced into shared premises at expiry of long lease.
Size ✄
Price ££

Jones, Chalk & Dawson
6 Sackville Street. Tel. 734 0656
A late-nineteenth-century offshoot from Hawkes that includes eighteenth-century venerables **Meyer & Mortimer** (tel. 734 3135), whose Regency era royal warrants and links with Beau Brummell add pungency to the enterprise. Founding Mortimer was a Scot, and the firm is still favoured by Scottish aristocracy. Also includes **Ward & Kruger** (tel. 734 4358).
Size ✄✄✄
Price N.A.

Kilgour, French & Stanbury
8 Savile Row. Tel. 734 6905
Famous old Savile Row house given face-lift after acquisition by large clothing group (which also owns cloth merchant Holland & Sherry next door). Presidents, maharajahs and Fred Astaire passed this way. Franchise/licensing deals in US and Japan. Incorporates leading hunting/equestrian specialist **Bernard Weatherill** (tel. 734 6905), which has a clutch of royal warrants.
Size ✄✄✄
Price ££££

Leslie & Roberts
11 Old Burlington Street. Tel. 629 6924
Very big between the wars (client list ranged from Valentino to Von Ribbentrop), now reduced to the lone efforts of Dennis O'Brien, who has spent entire career with firm and strives to maintain timeless style. Considers diplomats 'the ideal customers'.
Size ✄
Price ££

Lord & Stewart
41 Conduit Street. Tel. 734 4236
Upstairs from the imposing street-front emporium where once he reigned, slight septuagenarian Sammy Stewart (there never was a Lord) smarts over straitened times as he perseveres with his 'classic modern international look' for a largely business clientele with a spicing of showbusiness.
Size ✄
Price £££

Bryan Manning Tailoring (ex-Manning, Morris & Stone)
58 Maddox Street. Tel. 734 9100
Last of a large tailoring family of Irish origin. Eschews personal style and takes pride in executing whatever customer wants, including odd or difficult tasks turned down by others. Work for Hollywood yielded Emmy award for Richard Chamberlain suit in 1930s' style. Makes four US trips per year.
Size ✄
Price ££

Peter Moore
10 Savile Row. Tel. 437 0260
Youthful looks belie more than thirty years of gradual client build-up, initially from Soho back-room, lately in personally designed salon. Travels to Europe, which is source of most business. Stresses personal touch and benefits of small in-house work team in maintaining quality.
Size ✄
Price ££

Norman of Savile Row
39 Savile Row. Tel. 734 4341
One of the small shops on the site of the original Poole's. Norman Glazier is a product of the old Tailor and Cutter Academy with varied cutting experience around the West End before launching his own venture in the early 1970s.
Size ✄
Price £££

Norton & Sons
16 Savile Row. Tel. 437 0829
Firm dates from 1821 and once took pride in tailoring for the Kaiser, but America is the key market since staff cutter John Granger purchased business in 1970. Promotes a soft line with slight flare and shape 'reminiscent of the English shires'. Makes five or six US trips per year.
Size ✄✄
Price £££

Tommy Nutter
19 Savile Row. Tel. 734 0831
Pied Piper turned Peter Pan of Swinging London. Mixing gentle charm with promotional savvy, he garbed a generation of trendsetters. Aims for a 'sort of witty' look that has been variously described as tradition with a twist and English tailoring with American loudness. Favourite customer has to be singer Elton John.
Size ✄
Price £££

Richard W. Paine
32 Old Burlington Street. Tel. 629 2420
Primarily exports (two US trips per year) with some local trade. Worked for Castle, Tobias, Blades and Anthony Sinclair, whose business he subsequently acquired.
Size ✄
Price ££

Malcolm Plews
33 Savile Row. Tel. 434 1290
Latest small venture on the Row. Plews is a Kilgour product, whose work is highly regarded by his peers. When he plies America, his wife takes charge of the shop.
Size ✂
Price ££

Henry Poole
15 Savile Row. Tel. 734 5985
The Old Firm has mellowed marvellously through good times and bad to enshrine that which the world has come to expect of Savile Row. Chock-a-block with history, it prides itself in having no house style other than 'a built-in elegance that shows'. Fourth-generation Angus Cundey presides with patrician grace.
Size ✂✂✂✂
Price £££

M. Rice
12 Cork Street. Tel. 734 3641
Septuagenarian workaholic Max Rice – 'I am a tailor, not just a cutter' – still makes a 6.30 a.m. start after sixty years in the trade and still travels twice a year to the US. Quality craftsman of the old school, he fled Berlin three days before World War II.
Size ✂
Price £

Rose & Kent
11 Old Burlington Street. Tel. 734 2687
Chirpy personal tailor to the Duke of Edinburgh, John Kent retained his royal custom despite déclassé Soho location. Now back in the approved zone, though in an unpretentious basement and charging unpretentious prices. Says 'a guy may look wealthy, but like everyone he's looking for a deal'.
Size ✂
Price £

Scherer & Nilsson
19 Clifford Street. Tel. 734 4857
Ron Scherer and Peter Nilsson are both products of the prodigious Kilgour stable and have been together since 1972, making in the classic Stanbury manner. They do not travel; they do it the old-fashioned way – Americans, etc., come to them.
Size ✂
Price £££

Maurice Sedwell
9 Savile Row. Tel. 734 0824
Trinidad-born Andrew Ramroop and Swiss Bruno Frei make this Savile Row's little United Nations, with sort-of-retired Maurice on hand with his poems and salty comment. Their 'well-bred suits, cut without ostentation' have won awards, and a following of actors, politicians and the occasional royal.
Size ✂
Price ££

Edward Sexton
36a Savile Row. Tel. 437 0741
Cocky technician behind the 1960s' Nutter revolution, now energetically pursuing a formula for slotting Savile Row into the twenty-first century. Slickly welcoming shop/workspace designed as stage-set for Sexton and his cutting table, from whence he roams the US fitting and fixing deals. Says he 'makes a garment that has a certain romance to it'. Values sanctity of the Row's bespoke image, but stresses need for marketing ingenuity to sustain it.
Size ✂✂✂
Price ££££

Stovel & Mason
32 Old Burlington Street. Tel. 734 4855
Ian Gregarson had gained a go-ahead reputation for this old (founded 1818) firm when polio struck in 1957, since when he has tailored from a wheelchair, even maintaining a twice-yearly US trip schedule. Anthony Eden was an S&M emblem, famous for his double-breasted suits with distinctive bold lapels. 'People today are not bold,' Gregarson laments.
Size ✂
Price ££

Strickland & Sons
15 Savile Row. Tel. 734 0597
Dates from 1780; moved into present address in March 1887, upon first purpose-built reconstruction of a Savile Row home to accommodate tailoring. Early this century became one of first to make regular visits to North America and maintains important Canadian connection. Has been a tenant of Poole since 1982.
Size ✂
Price ££

William S. Thompson
6 Sackville Street. Tel. 437 5426
Lutz Wagner has run this firm since 1970 as a primarily American-directed operation, with some European travel as well. A tenant of Jones, Chalk & Dawson, he is unusual in also representing that firm on his extensive North American trips.
Size ✂
Price ££

Tobias Bros
32 Savile Row. Tel. 734 2551
Firm had difficulties after retirement of Cecil Tobias; now Anderson-trained John Coggins and Kilgour-trained John Davis are bent on restoring fortunes with a brightened image and some diversification – into blazer badges for instance. Substantial American clientele includes pop star Elvis Costello.
Size ✂
Price ££

Maxwell Vine
7 Sackville Street. Tel. 734 4727
Born into Soho tailoring family and spent lifetime around Savile Row, with World

War II break fighting in Burma. Was Cyril Castle's head cutter before going it alone. Has made for all sorts, including the Duke of Edinburgh and Burt Lancaster.
Size ✂
Price £

Wells of Mayfair
47 Maddox Street. Tel. 629 5047
At the same address since 1829 launch by ex-partner of the first Poole, which is a record. Series of mergers, notably **Cooling Lawrence & Wells** with **J.C. Wells** and **Cordas & Bright** (tel. 629 3183), made it one of Savile Row's largest houses. Uses team assembly system and fusing technology. Promotes training for Savile Row's future. US about 45 per cent of business, for which it uniquely runs a dollar ledger.
Size ✂✂✂
Price £££

Welsh & Jeffries
35 Savile Row. Tel. 734 3062
Uniforms the officer class (Royal Greenjackets, Gurkhas, etc.), including numerous generals and one prince (Charles); nowadays most call comes from business moguls (Ivan Boesky was one) and lords of the Bordeaux wine trade, who are visited twice a year. 'We're 100 per cent traditional – you might say old fashioned – with perhaps a military touch,' says director Alan Cooper.
Size ✂
Price ££

L.G. Wilkinson
11 St George Street. Tel. 629 5835
Incorporates **Sadler, Fowle & Bradley** and **John Morgan**, and thus bears the mantle of J.K. Wilson, from whom genial Dennis Wilkinson inherited such onerous tasks as suiting Harold Macmillan for his final stirring speech in the House of Lords. Proprietor combines a love of music with dress coat wizardry to make for more symphonic conductors (present count around fifteen) than probably anyone in history; since he also loves driving, he attends to a large French and German trade by whizzing down the autobahn to a stereo serenade.
Size ✂
Price ££

THE LADIES' ROW

Hilliers Couture
27 Cork Street. Tel. 437 1421
Savile Row's lone surviving exclusively ladies' bespoke operates in tandem with **Bricker & Mellowe**, an orthodox male house. Staple trade is military, with contracts for the supply of officers' uniforms, mess dress, etc., to the women's services. Occasional City businesswoman and American visitors provide some custom, but not enough to offset loss of an older generation of committed suit wearers. Strictly not a fashion house, but

184

makes an occasional wedding dress or evening dress to order. Price varies too much to categorize.

Most Savile Row tailors will cut a lady's suit, but one who encourages such trade is **Edward Sexton**. Equestrian tailors take the horsewoman in their stride.

SEMI-SAVILE ROW

Though Savile Row is sacred to traditional bespoken handcraft, most of the big names now lend themselves to foreign franchise/licensing deals in which these principles are sometimes compromised. Within the purlieus of the Row are some factory-reliant operations doing made-to-measure, or semi-custom, as Americans call it, at appropriately reduced rates.

Blades of Savile Row
8 Burlington Gardens. Tel. 734 8911
Japanese-style 'easy-to-order' suits made-to-measure by computer and latest machine technology in Denmark; jackets can be hand-tailored on request.

Tom Gilbey
2 New Burlington Street. Tel. 734 4877
Designer/tailor of many enthusiasms used attractive young female representatives to ply his 'measure-to-fit' service for suits produced in Italy. Targeted business executives, but found professionals and the occasional aristocrat amenable. Will make true bespoke (£££) in-house upon request.

OFF-THE-ROW

Beware the 'cloth' and 'Savile Row surplus' shops that lurk about the neighbourhood, waiting for the tourist. The fabric could be end-of-length stock from the mills, unloaded at a high mark-up, or merchants' mistakes of the kind that used to be dumped on Latin America, while the suit on offer is most likely a so-called 'stock special' factory product – 'You think you're getting bespoke and it's not even made-to-measure; it's hoodwinking the public,' says Ron Riches of Cork Street, who regrets the failure of attempts to institute professional qualifications for tailoring cutters.

The fact is that anyone can buy a tape measure and set up shop in the environs of Savile Row, and in that sense there is nothing exclusive about it. Likewise, good tailoring is not all wedged between Piccadilly and Regent Street, even if the cachet of the sacred zone means that prices tend to decline the moment one steps out of the magic triangle. All sorts of options open for those who are adventurous and not exclusively concerned with the status of a location. The explorer may gain courage from the knowledge that the tailors themselves are not obsessed by glory through association and that many a Savile Row suit is wholly or partly put together in some obscure workroom by craftsmen who might make a suit on their own account at half the price. There is the obvious risk of variable quality, and yet Off-the-Row, like Off-Broadway, can at times match the best.

Firms not Savile Row in the strictest sense, only because they are located across Piccadilly in the luxury boutique and bespoke shirt zone around Jermyn Street, include:

Benson & Clegg
9 Piccadilly Arcade, SW1. Tel. 491 1454
Tailored for King George VI. It has a special expertise in buttons and badges.

John Lester
97 Jermyn Street, SW1. Tel. 930 2841
Formerly Poole's cutter, he was in Cork Street before moving in with leading bespoke shirt-maker Harvie & Hudson, where he runs a typical small Savile Row operation with a pair of in-house coat-makers; he shares a trouser-maker with some big names.

Across the snob's canyon of Regent Street, the warren of Soho is traditional home to Savile Row's workers.

Brian Staples
47 Carnaby Street. Tel. 734 5069
Up a rickety staircase in an old low-rent workman's tenement that has harboured tailors for ever (Burstow Logsdail left here for Sackville Street), the former assistant to Douglas Hayward can afford to make suits at half Hayward's prices and, so he claims, more true to a 'classic soft cut' than Hayward himself is these days. Clients said to include Lord Stephens, Max Hastings and assorted Hayward defectors. The adventurous may care to call, but Staples will visit office or hotel for fittings. The work is in-house and service prompt, but do not be too demanding. Staples observes a four-day week and restricts output to four suits a week, reasoning that 'anything more would go to the tax man'.

Morris Angel & Son
119 Shaftesbury Avenue, WC2. Tel. 836 5670
The famous old (1840) stage tailor, costumers to *Tarzan* and *Brideshead Revisited* alike, also does civvy suits.

Moss Bros, Bedford Street, WC2 (tel. 240 4567), with branches throughout the country, categorizes itself these days as 'the Complete Man's Store', but the name remains synonymous with dress hire and the firm boasts of having a unique knowledge of court and ceremonial garments. The Royal Ascot race meeting climaxes the hire year with its mass call for morning suits and top hats.

Out west, honorary Savile Row status is enjoyed by **Harrods** of Knightsbridge (tel. 730 1234), which has a bespoke, or 'personal tailoring', department in its mighty store.

In the western approaches, **Redwood & Feller**, 89 Rochester Row, SW1 (tel. 828 9519) has a royal warrant (state livery) and makes for mainly professional people and has long benefited from the lower rents of the Victoria area. Further out, into the domestic depths of Fulham, there is **Dimi Major** at 11 Royal Parade, Dawes Road, SW6 (tel. 385 1023), who is simply Dimi to a worldwide following (Sean Connery, Paul McCartney, the Duke of Norfolk among them) and to Douglas Hayward, his former partner. 'Tailor to the stars ' **Robbie Stanford**, 24 Donnington Road, NW10 (tel. 459 0637), was an early employer of Hayward and Major. He once fitted flautist James Galway for three dinner suits in the course of one recording session break and he made TV personality Bob Monkhouse a suit with a built-in microphone. **W.G. Child & Sons**, 106 Wandsworth High Street, SW18 (tel. 870 3895), is a stickler for traditional ways, despite the unfashionable address. The firm is now into its fifth generation.

To the east lies the domain of the City tailors, which is a subject unto itself. As far back as d'Orsay's day, tailor-author Francis Edwards was urging avoidance of 'the court-end of town' with its high prices. He backed his argument with figures: 'Cheapest west-end price for a frock coat £5.5s. City (cash) £3.10s.'

The City trade has remained distinct from the West End, and as recently as 1985, *Men's Wear* was maintaining that a tailor could spot the difference between a West End and City cut 'long before he can see the whites of a man's eyes', but the Big Bang of 1987 and the emergence of the rich young City whizz-kid is bringing into question the principle of City tailoring that conservatism and price dominate other considerations. Prominent City tailors include **Couch & Hoskins**, 21 Eastcheap, EC3 (tel. 626 3831), **J. G. Chappell**, 15 New London Street, EC3 (tel. 488 0363), **Herbert Chappell**, 50 Gresham Street, EC2 (tel. 606 7451), **P.A. Crowe**, 40 Copthall Avenue, EC2 (tel. 920 9396), which is older than most on Savile Row. **Gieves & Hawkes** has a City branch at 18 Lime Street, EC3 (tel. 283 4914), and so has Chittleborough & Morgan, whose City shop is **Castles**, 4-5 Castle Court, Birchin Lane, EC3 (tel. 623 5063).

Beyond the metropolis, pockets of bespoke tailoring still prosper, and some of those have Savile Row visiting rights afforded by the leading cloth merchants, who provide a fitting room for cutters coming up to the West End.

KILLS, PIGS, PORKS AND HAND-ME-DOWNS

Lighter cloths and smaller wardrobes mean fewer opportunities to enjoy Savile Row at second hand: clothes tend to be worn out, rather than consigned to the lesser orders as of yore. **Hackett Gentleman's Clothiers**, 65c New King's Road, SW6 (tel. 731 7129), was founded in 1984 and tapped such a demand for noble old husks (Thomas Carlyle's word) that it launched its own ready-made range with Savile Row touches (proper silk linings, button-through buttonholes) and a made-to-measure option. Partner Ashley Lloyd-Jennings, a latter-day Moses Moses, credits the second-hand department for the firm's success, since it 'enables us to see how clothes used to be made and how to make them'. This Savile Row pastiche has attracted some influential customers (Ralph Lauren among several designers) and had Viscount Linley model for it, so that now it sometimes gets confused with the Real Thing in American magazine reviews.

Moss Bros, Bedford Street, WC2 (tel. 240 4567), with branches throughout the country, categorizes itself these days as 'the Complete Man's Store', but the name remains synonymous with dress hire and the firm boasts of having a unique knowledge of court and ceremonial garments. The Royal Ascot race meeting climaxes the hire year with its mass call for morning suits and top hats. Hats suffer the most – some get filled with beer and others get stamped upon by sore losers.

Savile Row Jargon

The close community of the journeyman tailor was forged through generations of hardship, of long hours, miserable pay and discrimination of all kinds. Taking refuge among themselves, the tailors developed a private language almost incomprehensible to outsiders. Some of their expressions have entered the wider English language. Others survive in the daily dialogue of the tailor and his guv'nor.

Balloon . . . having a balloon — A week without work or pay.

Barring — A tailor's way of saying 'present company excepted', as in 'this shop is a load of bodgers, barring'. Very useful in the close company of the old workshops.

Basting up a snarl — Starting an argument.

Bodger — Crude worker. Common to other trades.

Boot — Loan until payday. **Can you spare the boot?** — Can you give me a loan? Dates from crossed-leg days, when a tailor recorded the loan by chalking it on the sole of his boot.

Bunce — A trade perk, like mungo and a crib (see below).

Bushelman — Journeyman who alters or repairs.

Cabbage — Left-over material. Properly refers to customer's own material. A submission that it was by custom a perquisite of the tailor was rejected in a 1954 court case, in which a tailor was fined £50.

Cat's face — A small shop opened by a cutter starting out on his own.

Chuck a dummy — To faint. Allusion is to a tailor's dummy tumbling over.

Clapham Junction — A draft with numerous alterations or additions.

Codger — Tailor who does up old suits.

Cork — The boss.

Crib — Large scrap of cloth left over from a job, usually enough to make a pair of trousers or a skirt.

Crushed beetles — Badly made buttonholes.

Cutting turf — Clumsy, unskilled working.

Dead . . . a dead horse — A job that has been paid for in advance.

Doctor — Alteration tailor.

Drag . . . in the drag — Working behind time.

Drummer — Trouser-maker.

Have you been on the board? — Are you experienced?

Hip stay — Old-time name for wife.

Jeff — A small master: one who cuts out his garments and also makes them up.

Kicking — Looking for another job.

Kicking your heels — No work to do.

Kill — A spoiled job that has to be thrown away.

Kipper — A tailoress. So called because they sought work in pairs to avoid unwelcome advances. Phrase originally a corruption of Kick (see above).
Log . . . on the log — Piecework: the traditional and complex system of paying outworkers.
Mungo — Cloth cuttings, which by custom the tailor can retain to sell to a rag merchant for a little extra income (may come from 'that mun go', in Yorkshire accent).
On the cod — Gone drinking.
Pig — An unclaimed garment.
Pigged — A lapel which turns up after some wear.
Pinked . . . pink a job — Making with extra care.
Pork — A misfit rejected by a customer, but which might be sold elsewhere.
P.T. . . . rubbing in a P.T. — Doing a private job in spare time, such as during the lunch break.
Schmutter . . . bit of old schmutter — Piece of poor cloth (Jewish expression).
Skiffle — A job needed in a hurry.
Skipping it — Making the stitches too big (**Duck shooting** is equivalent East End term).
Small seams — Warning call when someone being discussed enters workroom.
Soft sew — An easily worked cloth.
Tab — Fussy, difficult customer.
Trotter — Fetcher and carrier: messenger.
Tweed merchant — Tailor who does the easy work: a poor workman.
Umsies — Someone being talked about who the speaker does not want to identify directly, because he is present.
Whipping the cat — Travelling round and working in private houses: common practice in old days when tailor would be given board and lodging while he made clothes for a family and their servants.

TRADE TOOLS

Baby — Stuffed cloth pad on which the tailor works his cloth.
Banger — Piece of wood with handle, used to draw out steam and smooth cloth during ironing.
Board — Tailor's workbench.
Darky — Sleeve board.
Dolly — Roll of wet material used as a sponge to dampen cloth.
Goose iron — Hand iron heated on a naked flame.
Mangle — Sewing machine.

TECHNICAL TERMS

Balance — Adjustment of back and front lengths of a jacket to harmonize with the posture of a particular figure.
Baste — Garment roughly assembled for first fitting.
Basting — Tacking with long stitches to hold garment parts together.
Block pattern — Paper template of the basic pattern shape on which design features can be superimposed.
Bundle — Components of jacket or trousers.
Canvas — A cloth usually made from cotton, flax, hemp or jute and used for providing strength or firmness.
Coat — Jacket.
Cutting system — Method of pattern preparation using a particular process of measurement and figure evaluation. Scores have been devised since methods of working out the proportions of the figure were first explored in the late eighteenth century.
Draft — Sketch or measured plan of a garment.
Fusing — Use of chemicals and heat to weld the interlining to outer fabric, as distinct from stitching.
Gorge — Where the collar is attached.
Interlining — Material positioned between lining and outer fabric to provide bulk or warmth.
Made-to-measure — Garment made to a customer's individual requirements, but not necessarily by hand.
Pattern — A template model used for cutting garments.
Rock of eye — Rule of thumb: using instinct born of experience, rather than a scientific cutting system.
Scye — The armhole: from 'arm's eye'.
Skirt — Part of jacket that hangs below the waist.
Striker — Assistant to a cutter.

INGREDIENTS

Stealing cloth is no longer a hanging offence, but choice of cloth remains a capital consideration. Natural fibre, the clothing equivalent of wholemeal bread, is the material most proper to true craftsmanship, and a small group of specialist merchants have the task of matching the woollen mills' capabilities with Savile Row's esoteric needs.

The woollen merchants once dominated Golden Square (which began as Gelding Square, when Soho was farm and paddock land, and a weaving industry was set up by Huguenot refugees from France), but traumatic times have cauterized their trade as much as the tailors', so that now a few wily survivors have the crucial go-between role in defining style trends and then meting out the consequences by the piece (60 metres) and the individual (3 metre) suit-length. On Savile Row itself are **George Harrison**, **Holland & Sherry** and **Wain Shiell**, while other woollen houses like **Dormeuil, Hunt & Winterbotham** and **Lesser** are all located within easy walking distance. Though existing in the closest of symbiotic relationships, there is only one case of a tailor and merchant under joint ownership.

'We're in it together,' says Walter Otten of Wain Shiell. 'It's a nice business. It's not like the ladies' trade. The people we deal with on the whole are very straightforward and most honourable.' His seventy staff deal with about forty mills, three-quarters of them small, specialized operations.

The larger tailoring houses like Huntsman stock hundreds of different materials ready for use and can call out for samples of several thousand more at a moment's notice, as can their smallest rival. The big houses have some designs exclusive to themselves, and personal patterns – even materials – can be made to order (e.g. George VI had his merchant procure him a grey check double the normal thickness, so that he could appear in public during the winter without wearing an overcoat).

Cloth weights, measured in ounces per yard (now grams per metre), have fallen steadily since World War II, largely due to American influence. Commonly, the range used to be 12 ounces to 22 ounces; now cloths as light as 170 grams are available. A gold trophy is awarded to the Australian grower of the year's finest wool. The winning bale is spun in Huddersfield and the cloth usually ends up in Japan, where businessmen are prepared to pay more than £1,000 for a suit length of this 'Golden Bale'. Cloth lengths cost the Savile Row tailor from £21 to £180 a metre at 1988 prices, with the drift steadily upwards.

Wool — Much of the best comes from Australian merino sheep. The breed originated in Spain and was brought to England in the reign of George III, where it did not thrive, so a Captain McArthur shipped some to Queensland. First exports shipped from Botany Bay in 1810, hence the term 'botanies'.

Worsted — Smooth-handling wool fabric with clearly defined structure and colour. A favourite with Savile Row for its ease of working and pliant nature. Small proportion of non-wool fibres permissible for visual effects, as in pinstripes, etc. Name derives from a small town in Norfolk. Technical difference between woollen and worsted cloth production – one is scrubbed and the other combed.

Other materials include:

Alpaca — Long, lustrous fibre from fleece of South American goat-like animal.

Cashmere — Soft, very fine wool from beneath the outer hair of Himalayan goats, though often a misnomer.

Flannel — From Welsh *'gwlanen'*, meaning woollen, it was originally all-wool and now is usually a mixture; loosely woven, with a soft feel, its immense popularity dates from the 1920s.

Mohair — Soft, silk hair of the Angora goat, characterized by strength, lightness and lustre.

Silk — Fibre from the cocoons of silkworms.

Tweed — Hard-wearing wool fabric with rough surface; **Harris tweed** — Hand-woven, heather-hued tweeds from the Outer Hebrides.

Velvet — Broad term that includes various fabrics with a pile finish.

Vicuna — Costly South American goat wool.

STUFFING

While some of the tailors and merchants date back to the eighteenth century, none can match interlining manufacturer **William Clark** of Northern Ireland, which was 250 years old in 1986 – and still with a Clark in charge of its celebrated linen interlinings. Here again, the number of producers have shrunk, with a consequent loss of choice, though **E. Rubenstein** still offers a wide range of woven canvasses, in horsehair, wool, shoddy and other materials. Three trimmings houses remain, though the selection of items like buttons has shrunk drastically. Tailors grumble that even the quality of pattern paper isn't what it used to be.

Care, Maintenance and the Complete Gentleman

Savile Row makes its suits for the long haul and provides a wide range of follow-up services, from cleaning and pressing to girth adjustment, replacement of linings and repairs in general. Extra cloth is built in for expansions of up to three or even four inches in the gastronomic zone.

A thoroughbred suit needs to be exercised like a thoroughbred horse – plenty of sponging, brushing, hand-pressing and airing, but spare the dry cleaning. Dry cleaning has been around for 140 years, but Savile Row has still not reconciled itself to chemicals saturating its preciously shaped creations: only when absolutely essential, and then only by the best specialist available, is the usual advice.

The trick is not to wear the suit on such a sustained basis that the dirt becomes embedded in the fabric. Regular brushing and resting for at least a week after a maximum two days' consecutive wear will keep the fibres in fine fettle, so that sponging and the occasional spot clean with a dab of spirits should be sufficient. The brush should be of best natural bristle.

After wearing, empty the pockets, flip the flaps out and select a hanger that fully supports the shoulder line. Set the trouser creases before hanging up; if the trousers have turn-ups, brush them out. A trouser press is strongly recommended, so long as it is not used to such excess that the crease edges become stressed. Records exist of a six-press family, with a father and his five sons each possessing his own.

Some linens and ultra-lightweight fabrics crease with alarming ease. After a crushing, put the suit on a hanger in the bathroom, turn on the hot taps and shut the door; the recovery rate of a pure wool lightweight in such steamroom conditions is remarkable – the fibres relax and revert back to their original woven state.

Some very fine worsteds crease without reason when new, which is a reason some tailors request a new suit's return for re-pressing after its first few outings. Press, leave to hang a few days, then press again to effect a home cure. If a crease persists after pressing, then the finishing process was faulty and the suit needs to be returned for re-finishing.

Home pressing requires only a good steam iron and a proper attitude of reverence for the garment. Always iron through a damp cloth (a dish towel will do) to avoid scorching or leaving an unsightly 'bloom', or shiny patch. Use a smooth wooden plonker (the back of a hair brush will do) to run over the crease edges as the evaporating steam rises from the cloth. This settles the fibre.

The brush is also Savile Row's preferred weapon against **moths**. Moth-proofing is not favoured (alien chemicals again) and such treatments are normally reserved for very heavy overcoats, which are rarely worn and consequently present idyllic pasture. A moth lays 50-100 eggs, which hatch in about ten days and lurk about in the grub stage for months and sometimes years, so the solution is to remove regularly each suit from the wardrobe for a thorough brushing. Wardrobes should be spacious enough to allow plenty of air to circulate. Suits should never be crushed together, but hung free, so as to relax and ventilate the fibre.

The properly suited businessman needs a minimum of six suits to allow for the necessary rest and rotation. Life-style and personal proportions (double-breasted does not flatter every figure) should dictate the mix. And never forget the usefulness of a blazer.

Clumsy oafs, clutterers and smokers need to confess their weaknesses at the design stage: the cutter will build accordingly. A fuller front can be cut on the jacket to accommodate jackdaw habits. Pockets made to personal need and proportions eliminate unsightly bulges – e.g. the heavy-duty inside pocket for a man with a well-developed chest might best be located low down below the rib cage. Heavy smokers' suits need especially thorough ventilation to keep down the smokey smell. Cigarette burns call for the services of the cloth menders, ladies adept at unravelling woven fibres from a hidden part of the suit and working them into the hole. That's expensive.

The **valet** being these days a rare beast, the gentleman has to be his own gentleman's gentleman, which means getting to know himself in the way a valet would. Sartorialists like Robert Gieve encourage a Zen-like state at the start to the day, with proper contemplation before a suit is matched with its accessories. A slight tug on the buttons is a good fail-safe routine to detect anything coming loose. Cautious types have even been known to install a back-up trouser fly system, in the form of a series of tiny hooks and eyes.

Packing is a science in itself. A welcome innovation is the popular zip-around travel bag that retains a suit in its hanger and can be hung up during a flight, but it is possible to store suits in conventional luggage without creasing. One way is to start with the trousers, laying them flat on the bottom of the case, with the legs stretched outside. Tissue is laid on top, then another pair of trousers laid down with legs stretched in the opposite direction. The rest of the contents is placed on top, with tissue in shirts and the little gaps stuffed with socks, underwear, etc. Fold the suit jacket inside out and stuff handkerchiefs and similar small items into the sleeve heads to reduce the danger of distortion and crushing. Pack any shoes into the hinge (i.e. bottom) end to discourage their tendency to roam. Finally, the trouser legs are lined with tissue and folded over the top. Upon arrival, any minor creases will fall out after a few moments hanging in a warm bathroom. A suitcase kept ready-filled and freshened up every week forestalls panic packing for the unexpected journey.

The legend of the Savile Row suit that never wears out was born of the doomsday fabrics and vast wardrobes of long ago: the greater demands placed upon today's lighter weights make the modern suit more mortal, yet Savile Row is as proud and able as ever to **recycle** a garment for the following generation, whether re-facing a dinner jacket for a son's first formal occasion, or altering and overhauling a set of tweeds as his starter suit. Not so long ago, the Marquess of Bath had Huntsman adapt an old jacket to fit his favourite teddy bear.

The maintenance of the rest of the wardrobe, and of the gentleman it enshrines, is of equal importance, for The Look is a matter of the Whole Man and a bonus that comes with a Savile Row tailor is free expert advice on shirts and ties and such. The bespoke **shirt** business lives in close association with Savile Row, and in some cases shares accommodation. A shirt from Poole in cotton voile costs 10 per cent of the price of a Poole suit, though there are less expensive materials almost as good. Ever since Beau Brummell mixed champagne into his boot polish and Colonel Kelly of the Guards was burned to death trying to save his best pair from a fire, Savile Row has been closely identified with superior shoemanship, and no craftsman in history can have brought more bliss to more of the privileged than George Cleverly of Maxwell, who is the answer to what Churchill, Bogart, Gable, Olivier, Edward G. Robinson and the three Coopers (Gary, Gladys and Duff) had in common; regrettably, such an item in its bespoke state costs as much as a suit these days and takes months for delivery. Shoe trees should be inserted into **shoes**, bespoke or otherwise, when still warm; this is also the best time to clean them, since the leather is then best able to absorb the polish. Ideally, a gentleman does not wear the same shoes twice in one week.

Finally, those patiently awaiting invitations to the next coronation should know to keep their gilded uniforms in air-tight tin cases, having first remembered to place therein some Russian leather parings, powdered camphor, naphthaline, carbonized paper, or turpentine sprinkled on brown paper. They will doubtless also be aware that slightly tarnished gold lace responds to a mixture of cream of tartar and finely crumbed bread, applied in a dry state and brushed lightly with a clean soft brush . . .

The **Federation of Merchant Tailors**, 32 Savile Row (tel. 734 0171), is Savile Row's voice. A century-old descendant of the masters organizations that battled the journeymen's unions, it still negotiates wage rates as part of a wider mandate to sustain and promote bespoke tailoring throughout the country, and lately it has given special attention to youth training schemes. Gaining the co-operation of often fractious and fiercely independent member firms is not always easy. 'There is a tendency to think of the Federation in terms of an insurance policy,' says centenary-year president Robert Bright. 'They hope they don't have to use it.'

Acknowlegements

Photographs and Illustrations

BBC Hulton Picture Library, London 75, 78 top, 79, 143, 162 left; Bridgeman Art Library, London 9 right; G.N. Brown Esq 144 upper centre, 144 left centre, 144 bottom; Cyril A. Castle Esq 171 bottom; A.H. Cundey Esq 57 top right, 57 bottom right, 115 centre; J Dege & Sons 160; Devonshire Collection, Chatsworth, reproduced by permission of the Chatsworth Settlement Trustees 13 top; Charles Dickens **Sketches by Boz** (1890) 90 top; Harry Errington Esq 95; Mary Evans Picture Library, London 10 left, 18 right, 21 left, 21 right, 29, 39 top, 48, 55 bottom, 61 top left, 61 top right, 87, 89 left, 99, 100, 128; Mary Evans Picture Library/ Fawcett Library 83; Federation of Merchant Tailors 7, 122; Fine Art Photography, London 81 right; Gieves & Hawkes 60, 92 top, 111 top, 162 right; Tom Gilbey Ltd 171 top; John A. Granger Esq 132; Greater London Record Office 9 left, 22 left; Rupert Lycett Green Esq 116 left; Captain Gronov **Reminiscences and reflections** (1892 and 1900) 20, 28, 34, 55 top; Hammersmith & Fulham Archives 54; Wilmot Harrison **Memorable London Houses** (1889) 64, 144 top; Douglas Hayward Esq 124; H. Huntsman & Sons 127; **Illustrated London News** (1849) 63; JS Library International, London 153 top left, 153 top right, 161 top; Captain Jesse **The Life of Beau Brummell** (1844 and 1924) 26, Kobal Collection, London 31 bottom; L. Logsdail Esq 136 left; London Express News and Feature Services 169 left; P. Hope-Lumley Ltd 23 bottom, 107, 108 left, 108 right, 114; Kirsty McLaren, London 129 bottom, 140 top, 140 bottom, 141 right, 148 bottom, 149 top, 149 centre, 152 bottom, 176 left; Kirsty McLaren/ Multimedia Books 13 centre, 13 bottom, 16, 24, 27, 30, 37, 39 bottom, 44, 45, 49, 52, 56 top, 57 left, 67, 73, 74, 76 left, 76 right, 77, 80, 81 left, 84 top, 84 bottom left, 84 bottom right, 89 right, 92 bottom, 93 top left, 93 bottom left, 93 right, 96, 97 left, 97 right, 101 left, 101 right, 115 bottom, 117 top, 117 bottom right, 120, 121, 125, 133 left, 133 right, 137 left, 137 right, 141 left, 144 upper centre, 144 lower centre, 144 bottom, 145 left, 145 top right, 145 centre right, 145 bottom right, 148 top, 149 bottom, 153 bottom, 156, 157, 161 bottom, 163, 164, 165, 169 right, 172 left, 172 right, 173, 176 right, 177; Mansell Collection, London 10 right, 18 left, 19, 23 top, 31 top, 32, 36, 42, 51, 53, 56 bottom, 61 bottom, 69, 70, 85, 86; Moss Bros 90 bottom; National Gallery, London 72; National Portrait Gallery, London 8, 12, 14; Henry Poole & Co 59, 62, 65, 91, 98, 103, 105, 142; Paul Popper, London 82, 110, 111 bottom, 115 top, 130, 131 bottom, 147, 154, 155 top, 155 bottom, 168; Rex Features, London 94, 136 right, 138 top, 138 bottom; George Augustus Sala **Twice round the clock or the hours of the day and night in London** (1859) 46; Sir John Soane's Museum, London, reproduced by courtesy of the Trustees 40; Syndication International, London 112 left, 112 right, 113, 116 right, 117 bottom left, 118, 119 left, 119 right, 123, 129 top, 131 top, 131 centre; **The Tailor and Cutter** 43; J.P. Thornton **International system of garment cutting** (1935) 152 top, 178, 179; Wells of Mayfair 78 bottom; Westminster City Archives 22 right; Harriette Wilson **Memoirs** (1909) 35.

191